It's in There!

It's in There!

The Innovation, Dedication, and Determination Behind the Birth of Prego Spaghetti Sauce

WILLIAM MORTON HILDEBOLT
& BONNIE BAJOREK DANEKER

Published by:
Hildebolt Books
275 East Twelve Mile Road
Madison Heights, MI 48071

Designed by: Jerry Dorris, AuthorSupport.com

Project Managed by:
Write Advisors, LLC
Atlanta, GA 30308

978-0-9993166-0-3 (PB)
978-0-9993166-1-0 (HB)
978-0-9993166-2-7 (E-Book)

ABOUT THE COVER

The cover of this book features a rendition of an oil painting of Prego in a glass jar by artist M. Strader. It was a personal gift to the Hildebolts by close friends Dan and Jolene Dalzell of Haddonfield, New Jersey. Dan Dalzell was a manager of corporate planning at Campbell Soup Company. Though Dan did not work on Prego, he collaborated on many other projects with Bill Hildebolt. The image of this painting is included to showcase Prego as a work of art for the kitchen.

The cover also features a tomato resting on a cutting board. The cutting board, handcrafted by Bill Hildebolt, is comprised of cherry and spalted maple from native woods of Southwestern Ohio. Hildebolt's 3Vs Cutting Boards series (Vigor & Vitality = Victory©) was designed to impart vigor and vitality to the food that you eat each time you use one. It is included to reflect the energy and enthusiasm needed to create the world-famous sauce.

The tomato is the foundation of not only Prego but many of Campbell's Soup's juices, soups, and meals, and it is one of the most important crops to our diets today. This book is the story of how tomatoes became Prego.

This book is dedicated to:

Dr. Wilbur A. Gould

Mr. Ralph A. Miller

Mr. Charles R. Gaehring

And our many other heroes in the food industry

CONTENTS

Introduction

. . . .

"It's in there" is the tagline for Prego spaghetti sauce. The origin of this advertising copy is actually a quote from the chef that created the recipe for Prego, Werner Schilling. When the Leber Katz Partners (LKP) advertising account reps were developing the creative content for this new product launch, they visited the R&D labs to interview the product developers and especially Chef Schilling. In one particular meeting, the NYC-based agency personnel were quizzing Schilling on the ingredients in his creation. They would ask, "Are there diced tomatoes in the sauce?" Schilling, never one to use more words than necessary, responded, "It is in there." "How about the spices, are they just like a housewife would use?" was the next inquiry. "It is in there." Schilling repeated. "The mushrooms, are they fresh, like homemade?" questioned one bright-eyed account rep scribbling notes as fast as she could. "It is in there," replied Schilling, with a faint smile. When the artwork for advertising was sent to product development for review several months later, "It's in there" was the central theme of the introductory advertising campaign. Even thirty years later, "It's in there" can be heard on TV ads for Prego echoing the words of Executive Chef Werner Schilling.

"It's in there" is also the title of this story about Prego. When I first started with the outline of the book, this quote was included to communicate the uniqueness of the ingredients and technology that was used in the development of Prego. But once I started interviewing the twenty-plus key Campbell Soup Company (CSC) individuals who had contributed to every facet of Prego, it became apparent that the most important driver of innovation is the team who devoted their hearts and souls to the success of the enterprise.

My orientation for the book changed from focusing on the science and technology as primary drivers to that of all individuals who made Prego the ultimate success story. Their contributions—through the general chronology of how the sauce came to be—are the center of this book. You'll see Prego Professional Profiles that highlight many of them along the way.

In talking with these contributors, I learned a lot about innovation as well. Innovation can be compared to water as it meanders its way to the ocean. The river starts as a raindrop on high ground. As millions of raindrops combine, puddles form, then ribbons extend, and the water moves. When the flowing water encounters debris, sediment, and erosion from violent storms, the character of the waterway changes or is arrested in a circular eddy going nowhere. To make it all the way to the ocean, the waterway must overcome the obstacles and continue to flow, not getting caught up in eddies. The waterway must become a creek, joining other creeks to become a river, which eventually flows to its destination, the ocean.

What seems to be the end of the journey becomes the beginning, as energy from the sun evaporates the ocean water to form clouds.

That energy is released by the condensation of water vapor into rain, and the cycle continues.

Innovation is a cyclical process too, beginning with the concept, which must be analyzed and evaluated amid other ideas. Before it can be actualized into practice, the concept must be encouraged to continue by other talented people who champion it and help it to overcome obstacles. Innovation is not solely a downhill process. Setbacks occur. You make ten mistakes before one of your efforts advances the project; then you build on that breakthrough, and alter course when necessary. Our biggest learning was about what didn't work. That's why they call it "*re*-search": you search, then re-search or search again. When you succeed in reaching your destination or goal, you start again to continue the cycle.

And that's what happened when we developed what came to be known as Prego. Talented people joined forces and passionately fought together and sometimes fought with each other to successfully bring to market a revolutionary new product. Even though we had not interacted in years (in some cases thirty!), my colleagues were highly engaged when I interviewed them for this book. Within five minutes, it was as though we were back in our white lab jackets, covered in tomato pulp.

For many, working on Prego was the highlight of their professional lives; for others, it was a launching pad for advancement and even more successful careers. I was involved in every phase of the creation of Prego; however, I was unaware, until these interviews, of the details behind some of the steps and the importance of the individual contributions. Further, I learned some of the history of this longtime privately-held company where few archives are available. While there is some inconsistency between sources—print, digital, and verbal interviews—we did our best to validate each date, figure, and historical "fact" presented in the book against the most respected authority. Likewise, we did our best to include the key people who were involved. We apologize for any omissions or errors and take responsibility for them. There is a list of references at the end if you're interested in reading more.

Speaking of reading more, you'll notice in the book that we've included detailed information on some topics in sidebars. There are two ways to read this book. To read it exclusively as the creation story, skip the sidebars and Profiles. If you'd like a more inclusive experience with some of the technical information and interesting personal facts of the people involved, read those sections as well.

Everyone knows the names of Edison, Jobs, and Musk but very few people know the people who actually did the work to propel their innovations into practice. In these cases—and others across industries—creative genius was the inspiration, but the execution was done by a multitude of very dedicated and skilled scientists and technicians. Without them, the dream would still be in the lab or workshop, or in the head of the originator. It was the same for Prego.

The stimulus to begin the arduous task of writing the Prego story came from a source that I was not much aware of at the time. It was in the form of a Wikipedia page that was brought to my attention by my brother and son. In this particular case, there were postings in which people claimed that Prego was their idea or that CSC had stolen their family recipe. All those claims were ludicrous and false.

In contrast to the hyperventilation of my brother and the warnings by my son that if the record was not set straight, this information would become a permanent part of Prego's history through the "validation" of social media postings, none of this really bothered me. I was dismayed that other people would take credit for something that they had nothing to do with but I'd experienced this many times previously, and I did nothing about it at the time. That changed when, by happenstance, I viewed a TED Talk video by Malcolm Gladwell giving credit for the development of Prego to a friend of his, Howard Moscowitz. (In reality, Moscowitz was a consultant who worked with our Marketing Research department four years after the launch of Prego on flavor profiles in product extensions.) I literally jumped out of my chair. I was so upset that my wife and son came to calm me down.

That was it: the gauntlet was thrown down and now it was time to get serious about telling the true story. With over 6 million viewers, Malcolm Gladwell's presentation is one of the franchise's most viewed videos. To those who ask why write this book, here is the answer: to honor the people involved in Prego's creation, the real story needs to be told. And, profits from book sales will be donated to fund college scholarships to encourage the next generation of food technology innovators.

So, that's why I'm writing the story behind the creation of Prego, and here's why you should read it:

- revenge
- passion
- scx
- intrigue
- politics
- disappointment and self-doubt
- high drama
- happiness
- accomplishment

It's in there.

Prologue

· ·

A bottle of Chianti and my wife's special spaghetti was big eating for poor graduate students in the 1960s. Our group had gathered in our tiny apartment to celebrate another win of the Ohio State football team, and my wife Sandi had fixed her family's secret spaghetti sauce recipe.

Being a farm boy of German-Irish, "meat-and-potato" ancestry, I viewed spaghetti as pretty fancy and exotic fare. The sauce tasted very good but in my humble opinion it had a fatal flaw. In scientific terms, it suffered from "syneresis" or, in everyday language, it "weeped." Liquid separated from the tomato pulp and little red rivers ran and collected at the bottom and sides of the plate.

So, I left the table, went to the sink, and drained off the free liquid, trying not to dump the whole plate of pasta and sauce into the sink.

I garnered some razzing from my fellow graduate students, but it made for a thicker, less messy experience.

"I can't be the only one who wants to eat spaghetti without the excess fluid, right?" I remember thinking. "If I ever have a chance, I am going to fix this weeping problem."

Prego Timeline

. . . .

1947—The Sacramento, California, soup plant is built and begins production of tomato soup, tomato juice, V8, and tomato paste.

1960s—Campbell Soup Company (CSC) President John T. Dorrance moves his family to 165-acre farm in Cinnaminson, New Jersey. He works with breeders to work on tomato cultivars, developing the famous Rutgers tomato.

1968—William Hildebolt observes extracted tomato pulp separate into two phases in OSU food technology pilot plant.

1969—Hildebolt joins CSC as Jr. Food Technologist.

1977—CSC purchases a tomato paste processing facility located in Dixon, California, from T. H. Richards Canning Company. More tomatoes and more processing capacity mandates more tomato product innovation.

1978—CSC contracts with a Midwestern-based custom packer to produce ketchup to be sold under the Campbell's food-service label. The special tomato paste was used to produce this market test product and a spaghetti sauce to compete with Heinz. The spaghetti sauce version is based on a classic Italian marinara recipe.

Early Fall 1978—CSC begins to explore packaging its spaghetti sauce in glass jars, a first for the company.

Fall 1978—The pressure is on to produce sufficient product of super hot break (SHB) tomato paste to supply the production of ketchup for the test market.

Late Fall 1978—On the last day of the test production, the experimental tomatoes were successfully processed at the eleventh hour. The viscosity results were better than expected and CSC was able to produce sufficient paste for the ketchup market test and to continue the development work on new tomato products.

Winter 1979—Spaghetti sauce undergoes various market tests and multiple formulations. Hildebolt is instructed to halt work on spaghetti sauce and development goes underground, until permission to continue is given again.

Spring 1979—With principals Stanley Katz and Laurel Cutler, Leber Katz Partners beat out CSC's existing ad agency, Needham, Harper & Steers (NH&S), to market spaghetti sauce after NH&S proposes putting the sauce in a can and calling it "Campbell's Very Own Spaghetti Sauce."

1981—Prego is launched nationally, capturing 28% market share and $110Million in revenue in its first year.

Glossary of Abbreviations

. . . .

BBDO–Formerly Batten, Barton, Dustin & Osborn

BTU–British Thermal Unit

CEO–Chief Executive Officer

CIAR–Campbell Institute for Agricultural Research

CIR&T–Campbell Institute for Research and Technology

CSC–Campbell Soup Company

FMC–Food Machinery Company

FTC–Federal Trade Commission

GO–General Office, Camden, NJ

IE–Industrial Engineering

LKP–Leber Katz Partners

NH&S–Needham, Harper & Steers

OSU–The Ohio State University

P&G–Proctor & Gamble

PME–Pectin Methyl Esterase

R&D–Research and Development

SBU–Strategic Business Unit

SD–Standards Department

SHB–Super Hot Break

UC Davis–University of California at Davis

1

Ohio Farm Boy Beginnings

. . . .

As soon as I could touch a clutch on the red-belly Ford, I drove the family's tractor, and before becoming a teenager, I learned to manage the hired hands and take on the responsibilities of helping my father run Hildebolt Farms. The 160-acre farm, in my family for generations, was my way of life. Daily care of the animals and the crops could be grueling, but I enjoyed working in the open air and doing manual labor. Farm work was in my genes.

Welcome to America

My father and my grandfather (who was especially gifted as a master storyteller) wove yarns of wars, cowboys, and American Indians that we would listen to with rapture. They also told the story of our ancestors and how we came to own our farm. Like other pioneers from Wales, Ireland, and England in the mid-1700s, the Dooley family boarded a wooden sailboat headed for freedom and economic opportunities in America. Taking that harrowing journey over thousands of miles was worth escaping the religious persecution, corruption, and poverty rampant in those countries, and they settled in Virginia.[1]

A new patriot, Moses Dooley, took up arms in the Revolutionary War, fighting on the side of the young country that had become his home. The victory of the war energized the man who was to become my great-great-great grandfather Moses. He gave in to the streak of wanderlust after the war, traveling with his brother from Virginia in search of open land. Word spread that near the frontier forts in the newly-formed state of Ohio there was land that was declared free. This beckoned like a siren call to the Dooleys.

Taming Preble County

The pioneers headed west, then north, past the forts until reaching Preble County, Ohio, where they each staked claim to hundreds of wild acres as their own. Living off the land tested them time and time again as they prevailed over American Indians, poverty, weather, and disease, but they loved it and made it their own. Moses' son Silas Dooley formally surveyed their land, wrote up an application for 160 acres of ownership in Preble County, and sent it to the White House for review.[2]

The deed came through. The lambskin document delivered to the Silas Dooley homestead was signed by U.S. Secretary of State James Madison and President James Monroe in 1811, twenty-three years after he signed the Constitution. And that was it. If the President signed your deed, you owned your land, and Silas Dooley now owned his 160 acres.[3] First known as the Dooley Farm, this acreage would later ignite the love of agriculture and food technology in me.

While Lewis and Clark's expedition was underway, the Dooleys were exploring their own lands, hunting deer, bear, and other game in the woods. Flanked by Miami and Shawnee Indians on all sides, they were ever vigilant against possible skirmishes but aimed for a peaceful existence. The Miami taught them to draw sap from maple trees for syrup, and how to better employ the land to bring forth food. They planted corn, beans, squash, oats, and barley on their newly-cleared farmland. Silas hired himself out in the early years, helping other settlers clear their land of stumps and roots. The going rate to clear an acre of forest was $3.50 ($62.02 in today's dollars), a princely sum then but probably still a bargain given the strenuous labor involved.[4]

While this made for a hearty lifestyle, Silas managed to find time for love and family. In his twenties, Silas met and married a local Preble County woman within a couple of years after settling in Gasper Township in 1805. Their marriage license was the first one issued in the county, and a few years later they welcomed Silas Jr.[5] With a growing family, Silas Sr. built a sturdier log cabin to replace his dilapidated lean-to. In 1830, he built the house where I was raised that continues to stand on the property. Silas Jr. continued in the farming tradition, shaping and defining the land and crops. Years later, the farm passed by marriage from the Dooleys to the Mortons.[6]

Enter the Texas Rangers

Few Preble County residents pursued a formal education, but Charles Hildebolt and his brother Harry were among the fortunate in 1905. However, graduating college wasn't enough of an achievement to keep Grandfather Charles and Great Uncle Harry Hildebolt local. Always hungry for adventure, they left Miami University of Ohio (which was named after the Miami Indians who were cleared from the property) and headed south. Their destination: Texas.

There was work as rangers and there was excitement in traveling to the southern state that was already a legend in most people's minds. The two men were hired by ranchers there to manage renegade Mexican desperadoes stealing cattle. They were, in a sense, policemen of the Texan frontier. Grandfather often regaled me with stories of their Texan escapades. They were each given a saddle, horses, and a pistol for the dangerous and isolated work, and were not shy about using the pistols. Unfortunately, the pay to be a Texas Ranger was extremely low, often coming in the form of promissory land grants that never materialized. Eventually the excitement wore off, and they headed back north to Ohio for a safer life.

Grandfather Hildebolt romanced Isabel, daughter of William Morton as well as granddaughter of Silas Dooley Jr. With no other siblings and no other relatives (the Dooleys and Mortons had all passed away or moved away), Isabel was the sole heiress to the Morton Farm, and after their marriage, Grandfather Hildebolt took over its management. The land was re-christened the Hildebolt Farms, and it remains with the family three generations later.

His Texas-formed appreciation of livestock propelled Grandfather to bring dairy cattle, beef cattle, and hogs to the land, and he saw the financial potential in raising them for sale as well. He became a championship showman, winning the World Grand Champion Boar Award in the 1930s at the Chicago Livestock Expedition. The Hildebolts became premiere swine breeders in Ohio, also known for their Belgian show horses, mules, and Ayrshire cattle.[7]

Farmer to Food Technologist

Emulating my grandfather, the accomplished storyteller and livestock showman, I learned to raise cattle. At a young age, I became adept at farm chores and tractor driving in the fields, like most of my farm boy neighbors. Working with the cattle, however, was my favorite part. Every year, my dad gave me a calf (and the corn to feed it) in exchange for working on the farm. I trained them and showed them for purchase at a 4-H fair. People would pay a premium for 4-H livestock, and I sold many of them. Those steers paid for my first two years of college at The Ohio State University (OSU), and the hard work and discipline needed to raise them made a good training ground for endeavors throughout my life.

Learning about hard work and discipline started early for me, well before my time as a student at OSU. In the late 1940s in rural southwestern Ohio, there was no such thing as preschool or kindergarten. Born in December, I started the first grade as one of the youngest in my class. I was immature and totally unprepared for classroom instructions. I hated every minute of being confined in the four walls of a nineteenth-century schoolroom. Bored and frustrated, I would escape in my mind by daydreaming about inventing a new helicopter design or mentally picturing the movement of a steam engine. Other times, I just daydreamed about being in some other place than class.

I would become almost paralyzed with fear when called on to spell a word or do simple arithmetic at the blackboard. It was so demoralizing, I was reduced to tears. No matter how hard I tried, nothing worked, not even special coaching from my teachers or my mother (who happened to be an elementary school teacher too). Rewards, punishment, and threats had no effect. I was so sick of hearing "sink or swim" from her when I failed to read a passage or add two numbers together correctly.

By the fourth grade, my teacher (Mrs. Herring, who was probably one of the best teachers in the whole county system, and who continued to teach into her eighties), suggested to my parents that I be held back a grade. This helped a little; however, repeating the fourth grade was an even bigger bore, and I spent most of the time planning my life as a cowboy. At least I was the same age as most of my classmates.

Things continued much the same on my tortured journey through the fifth and sixth grades. Although I scored high on aptitude tests, my classroom performance was so bad my sixth grade teacher had a warning for my mother: her son Billy was never going to amount to much and she should prepare accordingly. I only wanted to be a cowboy anyway.

One of my first heroes, next to cowboys Roy Rogers and Gene Autry, was Thomas A. Edison, the most prolific inventor of the twentieth century. Born in Ohio, he was a scientific celebrity and there were plenty of biographical books available in the library on the life of the Wizard of Menlo Park. When I read that Edison's elementary teacher told his mother she should remove her son from school because he was too dumb to receive an education, he became my lifetime avatar. This gave me hope that there may be career opportunities for me beyond being a cowboy.

Later, when my mother was studying for her master's degree in education, she learned about dyslexia. She realized that not only her oldest son, but also her sister suffered from the same learning dysfunction. That was quite a revelation, but too late to help with my elementary school struggles since we were both doing our graduate work at the time.

By the time my voice started to change in the seventh grade, a metamorphosis occurred. My brain fog cleared, and I matured physically and emotionally, seemingly overnight—metaphorically, an ugly duckling transformation to a swan. Today, I still have trouble with reversing letters and numbers, clearly eliminating me as a candidate for an air traffic controller or commodities trader.

Thanks to my tendency toward hard work and determination, I studied hard at OSU, but also left some time for friendship. No college education would be complete without some frolic and fun, and my fraternity, Phi Kappa Psi, was the setting for that and more. Marty Ziegler, an Ohio native, friend, and fraternity brother, had introduced me to his roommates, Bill Spain and Fred Hegele, who were the reasons that I transferred into Food Technology from Pre-Dentistry during my sophomore year. They both majored in Food Technology, and when I expressed interest in their studies, they recommended I talk to Dr. Wilbur A. Gould, who was the head of the department. I was so fascinated by my conversation with Dr. Gould and his description of Food Technology that I changed my major. Luckily, all courses I had previously taken for my major transferred seamlessly and I approached my new studies with zeal. I didn't know what I was looking for until I found it—once I got into the food technology coursework I knew it was the right choice for me— thanks to Dr. Gould.

[**Note: These Prego Professional Profiles are included throughout the book for those wishing to learn a little more about the professionals behind the product.**]

Prego Professional Profile

DR. WILBUR A. GOULD

Like many who devoted their lives to agricultural sciences, Wilbur A. Gould grew up on a farm. Amid the beauty of northern New Hampshire, he saw a future in horticulture and plant breeding, earning his Bachelor of Science in those subjects at the nearby University of New Hampshire. Degree in hand, he returned to working on the farm, as was the custom of the time.

The son of a strict disciplinarian father, Gould would often be severely reprimanded for the slightest infraction. One day, Gould baled hay and stacked the bales onto a truck for transport, as he usually did. But this day, the truck he had stacked had an accident, and bales fell out and fell apart—unusable and unsellable, as well as a huge mess to clean. Father went after son in a rage, certain that the younger Gould had not tied the bales tightly enough or packed them securely enough to cause this damage. It was the last straw; Gould sustained enough injury to convince himself it was time to leave the farm and immediately did so. He headed for East Lansing, Michigan, and pursued horticulture graduate studies at Michigan State University, but enlisted for service in the U.S. Navy during World War II. After honorable discharge, he returned to school, this time at OSU, where completed his master's and PhD degrees.

Gould joined OSU's teaching faculty, working for nearly forty years and advancing to become professor of Food Processing and Technology. By school accounts, he had taught and advised more than 900 undergraduate, 131 master's, and seventy-six PhD students.[8]

Known for his exacting standards, he was loved and feared by students who vied for his attention and often formed career decisions on his recommendations. To the undergraduates, he was a charismatic teacher; to the graduate students, he was unrelenting and not one to suffer fools. Gould was a taskmaster and would not tolerate less than top-quality efforts. One graduate student remarked that with the way Gould looked—decked out in his white uniform and helmet—and the way he acted to all the students, he was just like General George Patton. "The only thing missing is the riding crop!" he said. Working for him, you felt abused and frustrated, but it was a proving ground for the contact sport known as Corporate America.

Gould's strict expectations infiltrated his research responsibilities as well, and he became one of the foremost tomato processing experts in the country. His opinion was highly regarded, and he used his knowledge and connections to further Ohio's food processing industry. Adept at meeting influential people and raising funds, he became chairman of the campaign for the Food Industries Center at The Ohio State University College of Food, Agricultural, and Environmental Sciences. The Wilbur A. Gould Food Industries Center was named for him.[9]

The head professor in Food Technology was a taskmaster who had the reputation of pushing his students hard, and we were no exception. In changing majors, I learned that Food Technology was a specialized degree, requiring additional educational hours to graduate. If I wanted to graduate with my class, I had to attend summer school between my junior and senior years. The decision was easy, but the course load and work were not, plus I was newly married. My wife Sandi worked full time nearby in the district office of Phillips 66 as I earned a Bachelor of Science in Food Technology.

During the winter quarter of my senior year, I was in the lab working under the direction of Gould. He offered a teaching assistant position to me, where I would earn $125 a month and tuition abatement to manage the pilot plant and two labs, if I attended grad school at OSU to earn my master's degree. Though he was tough, I didn't hesitate.

Gould had my future path decided, including having my master's topic in mind: epidermal sloughing in the processing of green beans. I was to study what caused the outer layer of the beans to sometimes slough off and sometimes stay on in processing. It had something to do with the function of an enzyme called pectin methyl esterase, or PME for short. This was a concerning problem. The major food processors couldn't rely on the outer layers to be removed or be present in processing, which influenced the consistency of the final product. Thus, the research was begun. When I was not in class, writing, or teaching, I was managing the lab, researching and setting up experiments. I tested and ate so many green beans those years that I thought I would never want to see them again when my thesis was complete.

After earning my master's, Gould persuaded me to stay for a doctorate to continue studying this same powerful enzyme, PME, in green beans (proving his persuasiveness and ensuring my dislike for green beans for a long time to come), and promoted me to associate lab instructor. During my four years of graduate school, I was Gould's teaching associate responsible for the labs and pilot plant, becoming his right-hand man. Thus, I was exposed to and participated in numerous tomato research projects. I also worked two summers for tomato processors who packed whole tomato and ketchup products. Northwest Ohio had numerous small tomato processors, plus the giants Campbell Soup Company (CSC) and Heinz Foods.

Many of us questioned why we continued our studies here, especially when we worked the grueling marathon of tomato season in August and September. Sometimes the work went forty-eight hours nonstop. Only the most determined graduate students survived. More than one graduate student or staff would end up in the hospital of either mental or physical exhaustion after tomato season (like the student who managed the lab before me), and we all took the work very seriously.

Other graduate students would use the lab I managed to further their independent research. One day, I observed a five-gallon glass jug filled with crushed tomatoes as part of another research project. After a couple minutes, the tomato slurry had separated into two parts. On top was a red pulp consisting of skins, seeds, and flesh; the bottom half was a clear, amber colored liquid. The overall picture was reminiscent of what blood must look like when centrifuged: red cells on the top and serum at the base. Another student, whose family owned a large tomato processing company in northern Ohio, saw me staring at this and mentioned off-handedly that, "if the tomatoes were heated as they were being chopped, the tomato juice would not have separated." A reasonable response from a respected industry practitioner, I thought. This five-second observation was filed away in my mind and stayed with me to be used ten years later during the formulation of Prego.

The Midas Touch of a Gould Recommendation

Gould was a Patton-esque task master in the lab, but a smooth-talking salesman when promoting his students. Nothing shone brighter on his curriculum vitae than the list of successful graduates coming from his program to join the ranks at major food corporations like General Mills, Libby's, Nestle, Quaker Oats, and CSC.

From time to time, Gould brought in industry professionals to guest lecture and recruit. In my first year of graduate school, Ralph A. Miller from CSC's headquarters in Camden, New Jersey, toured the department. As vice president of Product Development, Canned Foods at Campbell Institute of Research and Technology (CIR&T), Miller held a keen interest in the pilot lab and the graduate students studying food technology. Unbeknownst to me, Gould had recommended me to Miller as a candidate for their research operations.

I was working in the lab when Miller walked in and introduced himself. On hearing about my field of research, Miller suggested a visit to Camden to interview. I reminded him that I was just finishing my master's degree, and that I really wanted to continue on to finish my PhD. "Ever been on an airplane, Bill? We'll reserve you a nice hotel room, give you a nice meal, and pay for your flight. Get to know us, and we'll get to know you."

As an undergraduate, I had toured CSC's operation in Napoleon, Ohio. The soup factory there, one of the biggest in the Campbell family, also was one of the largest in the nation, with hundreds of employees. To a naive undergraduate, this was very impressive. Several OSU graduates worked in the quality control and production areas. Now, I had a chance to visit the general offices (GO) in New Jersey. Once again, I didn't hesitate. I did take my first-ever plane ride, spend a night in a nice hotel with a nice meal, and spend a day interviewing at the R&D facility. Even more impressed after the visit, I stayed in touch with Miller.

During my final year of graduate school, Miller put on his full-court press. "We want to make you an offer to work for us. You'll work directly for me. We'll set you up in a lab. We'll give you a technician and a budget, and you can work on anything you want."

A heady offer for a newly-minted PhD, yet it competed with other offers. In the 1960s, food technologists were in very high demand in the food industry, and those trained in this highly-specialized field received offers from every direction, each more appealing than the last. Like the majority of my colleagues from the program, I considered positions outside and inside academia, looking at opportunities from the University of Hawaii and California Polytechnic State University—of particular interest because it was recruiting a tomato expert. Constantly at Gould's side, however, I witnessed some competitive behaviors in the upper ranks of academia. That swayed me towards options in private industry.

Quaker Oats promised me a future in pet food at a slightly higher salary than CSC offered. But I grew up on a farm; I had plenty of experience with animal food and was not particularly interested in gaining more. I had chosen to study human food for eight years, and I didn't want to have a career in animal or pet food.

As I considered the offer from CSC, I journeyed to my local grocery. This was a common practice for me, as I spent a lot of time buying supplies for my lab experiments. Standing in the checkout line by a cash register, I noticed that every cart had a Campbell Soup product. I was familiar with that company's product line and production capability but this was the first time I had really noticed its market presence. Between the efficiency of the company operations and its powerful market share, my future was clear. I wanted to be with this successful company.

I conferred with Sandi, who agreed. I accepted the company's $14,400 salary offer and we headed for Camden. Beyond the borders of Ohio, the world awaited. We were open to new experiences, but I had no idea that the next few months would land us face to face with Hell's Angels and New Jersey's Finest.

(Endnotes)

1   Dooley Family, *Dooley Family Archives*, History of Preble County (Cleveland: H.Z. Williams & Bro., 1881), Property of William M. Hildebolt. 157-77.

2   Dooley Family, *Dooley Family Archives*.

3   Ibid.

4   Ibid., "Value of $2,000,000 in 1920. Inflation Calculator for Today's Dollars," Saving.org, July 6, 2017, http://www.saving.org/inflation/inflation.php?amount=2,000,000&year=1920.

5   Dooley Family, *Dooley Family Archives*.

6   Ibid.

7   Ibid.

8   "The Wilbur A. Gould Food Industries Center," The Ohio State University, June 7, 2017, https://foodindustries.osu.edu/.

9   Ibid.

2

New Jersey and New Job

. . . .

The red-belly Ford of my boyhood was replaced by the fire-engine red Pontiac Tempest that transported us from the Buckeye State to the Garden State. In that time of our lives we were moving fast and not just on the road. My wife Sandi had stopped working a few months earlier to have our first child. We were learning how to be new parents as I prepared to defend my doctoral dissertation and continued working in the lab.

My $125-a-month salary did not go far to support the three of us and our finances were tight. We had bought the second-hand 1966 Pontiac Tempest from Sandi's boss, using nearly all our savings, anticipating the drive to Camden, New Jersey. My position as entry-level research technologist at CSC was contingent upon successfully defending my dissertation and had mandated a move to New Jersey with our young family. My defense was completed by the skin of my teeth (that's another story), then in the few weeks between my defense and my graduation, we planned and packed for our new lives across the country.

Graduation from OSU happened just a few weeks later, and the very next day we left for Camden. With money being scarce, we borrowed from Sandi's grandparents to make the upcoming trip. (CSC later reimbursed us for expenses and we repaid the loan.)

Leaving Ohio was a goodbye to everyone and everything we had ever known. With our Tempest filled with little more than the necessities, we drove nearly 500 miles over unfamiliar territory where we knew no one and no one knew us. I imagined it was like that for my exploring ancestors. Here we were, my young family and me, celebrating with friends and family one minute and driving cross-country by ourselves the next. We were growing up.

The Hell's Angels Welcome

The ten-hour drive was long and hot (without air conditioning in the car). This was before the advent of child car seats, and Sandi had been holding our baby boy the whole trip. By the time we reached Philadelphia, we were tired and ready for it to be over. We were not expecting any acknowledgement of our arrival into New Jersey, but we were in for a surprise. As we began to cross the bridge over the Delaware River, we were greeted with a heart-quickening "Welcome to the Home of the Jersey Boys" procession by a group of Hell's Angels. Our Tempest was surrounded—front, sides, and back—by large, loud Harley-Davidson motorcycles driven by sinister-looking gang members in full black leather gear, with their insignia flags flapping in the wind. Sandi and I looked at each other. I remember thinking, "What are they doing? What do they want? Are they going to hurt us?"

Not knowing what to do, I kept driving towards the safety of land. In the busy weekend traffic, we couldn't pull over, and there was no extra lane if we wanted to. If we shouted, no one would hear us over the roar of their engines. We were at their mercy, and we had no idea what would happen next.

This escort lasted the entire length—nearly two miles—of the Benjamin Franklin Bridge between Philadelphia and Camden. By the time we reached the sandy soil of New Jersey, the whole family was shaken. Sandi was in tears saying, "I want to go back home!" Then, just as quickly as they appeared, they broke formation and disappeared at the end of the bridge.

They didn't hurt us, but we had never experienced anything like that. We didn't even know who they were, but we were acutely aware that we weren't in Columbus anymore. There would be new threats, or at least curiosities, to deal with here. "Why were we doing this?" I wondered. "Am I putting my family at risk by moving here?"

But, I had committed to this job, and I was scheduled to start work that Monday. We knew we had to stick it out and finish the drive to our motel. CSC had arranged for us to stay at motel near my office for the short time until we decided on our more permanent residence. As soon as we located the motel, we checked in and unpacked, and I prepared for my first day at work.

Hey, Ohio, You're Going the Wrong Way!

In the early morning, I steered the Tempest through the burned-out and abandoned residential neighborhoods of south Camden, heading to the world headquarters of one of the biggest food processing companies in the nation. Again, I wondered what I was doing here. Distracted through the unfamiliar passages, I had gotten turned around when driving to my new job. Then, looking in my rearview mirror, I saw the blue flashing lights. I couldn't believe it. "I'm not even in the state for forty-eight hours," I was thinking, "and I'm already having a run-in with the law."

"Hey, Ohio, you're going the wrong way!" shouted the Camden,

New Jersey, police officer who pulled me over, as he sauntered out of his car towards me. "Don't you know that you are driving the wrong way on a one-way street?" Then he added, "Where are you trying to go?"

"Just point the way back to Columbus," I thought to myself, frustrated and anxious, but instead I responded sheepishly, "I am trying to find the Campbell's Soup factory."

The officer leaned down to my open window. In deference to my Midwestern naivety, he spoke slowly, very politely and deliberately, and gave me directions to the soup plant. The instructions were easy: just turn around and go the other way.

The home of the Product Development department, where my job as an entry-level research technologist waited, was just several blocks away in the opposite direction. The most embarrassing part was when the officer pointed toward the factory, I could easily see the iconic water towers on top of the building painted to resemble huge Campbell's tomato soup cans. I could also see steam coming out of several vents on top of the eight-story building, like beckoning geysers. Had I noticed either of these earlier, I could easily have found my way. I was glad for his assistance and made it safely the rest of the way.

The Neophyte's Initiation

We began to adapt our Midwestern upbringing to the Northeastern culture. Sandi managed the home front while I navigated the city and surroundings. On the first full day on the job, my boss Ralph Miller graciously took me on a tour of the Product Development and Basic Research facilities. Miller introduced me to the various managers, technologists, and scientists I would be working with. My expectations were exceeded with their impressive experience and the scientific and technical knowledge.

Within the research and development department, known as the CIR&T (Campbell's Institute for Research & Technology), there were occasional cliques and rivalries between the various departments and product groups, but overall it was a cooperative and positive environment. Part of the reason for the cooperation was that most research technologists had started in quality control at the various manufacturing plants spread throughout the United States, so naturally there was a diversification of geography and education, but consistency in Campbell's training. The other research technologists at Camden had worked their way up from the technician ranks there. The more junior technicians and helpers did not have degrees and were all locals, born and raised in the area.

I was an outlier. I was the first PhD-trained food technologist, one of the few outside hires, and I was reporting directly to the head of the department (as promised in the recruiting process). The other direct reports were managers who had worked ten to fifteen years for the company, and many were suspicious of this young neophyte who had direct access to "their" boss. This set me further apart from my co-workers. While they were generally friendly, I sensed there could be competition toward an outsider shown favoritism, as well as the potential for good-natured ribbing in an East Coast manner.

This showed itself later that first day. At lunch, Miller and I ate a bowl of soup with crackers in the company cafeteria. Miller introduced me to Don Maley, a research technician and my new assistant. "Don is going to show you around the soup plant. He has been with us many years, so he knows the inner workings of the factory as well as anyone," he explained.

I noticed Miller giving a wink and a slight nod of his head toward Maley as he left, saying, "Don, make sure you say hello to Mary for me." This should have been a warning, but I was still naïve to the world of the largest soup factory on the planet and its inhabitants. We left lunch to begin our tour, stopping first to dress for the journey. No loose jewelry or glass of any kind was permitted in the production area. Our eyeglasses were checked to ensure they had plastic lenses, and watches and rings were removed. We securely placed on lightweight, white plastic hard hats and white lab coats, and were ready to explore the interworking of the plant.

As we descended the steps, the sounds and smells of the factory came alive. A panoramic scene burst forth full of stainless steel kettles, carts, and white-garmented workers when we opened the door to the third-floor blending area. This was the heart of the factory, where all of the ingredients came together to be blended into the various soups.

We looked inside a large vat of vegetable soup that was being discharged to the filling line on the floor below. "Look at this. Nothing could be simpler than making vegetable soup, right?" he asked. "If you thought, 'yes,' then you were dead wrong."

"Each one of those vegetables in this mix has an exact three-dimensional dice size with no defects; each vegetable must be in the right proportion to the other vegetables when it's filled in the can. The vegetables have to be diced properly and added and blended in a precise sequence or there will not be the right distribution of corn to carrots, peas to beans, etc.; if over-blended, the whole mass turns to mush. All the vegetables and meat products are prepared on the above floors so that they can be gravity fed to the formulation area."

I learned that the upper floors housed the cleaning, peeling, and dicing equipment. All products were either visually or electronically inspected for foreign material and defects before being dropped to the lower floor where they were weighed and sent to the blending kettles.

"The soup from this series of kettles drops down to a dedicated line of equipment that fills empty cans with product at a rate of over 500 units per minute, and then a lid is placed on top of each can and sealed in place. The filled cans are heated to temperatures over 250 degrees Fahrenheit under high pressure, to sterilize the contents so the product will be shelf stable under room temperature conditions. This is interesting, but not as interesting as seeing how all the products are prepared for blending, so let's go upstairs," Maley guided me.

We retraced our steps and climbed an additional flight to the fourth floor. Little did I realize, I was about to go through a CSC rite of passage for all research technologists.

The ominous room we approached was sealed off from the rest of the processing area by large hinged doors and floor-to-ceiling walls. When Maley pulled one of the doors open, a stream of air gently pushed us explorers inside. Immediately, my eyes began to tear up and my vision became a blur. All I could see through the aromatic haze was the silhouette of women in white uniforms and hairnets hovering over conveyors loaded with whole onions on their way to dicing machines and then inspecting the diced onions on their way out of the machines. The odor and essence of onions was so thick, it could actually be seen in the air.

I felt like I had been sprayed with mace and then pushed into a maze. Tears were running down my face so fast I appeared to be sobbing. My immediate reaction was to rub my eyes with my hands, but Maley reached out and grabbed my arm saying, "Do not do that; you will only make it worse." He went on to say with a toothy grin, in a great understatement, "This is the onion dicing room!"

A few moments later, my vision went from blurry to nonexistent. Maley guided me by the arm—as someone would lead a blind person across a busy street—toward the direction of the ever-increasing hum of the dicing machines. En route, Maley told me he had spent a lot of time in this room as a technician running various trials on new varieties of onions.

"Yeah, the first couple of days in here damn near killed me!" he triumphantly explained and added, "After a while you get used to it. Your eyes somehow adjust." As we walked closer toward the whirl of the dicers, the level of the active ingredient in onions thought to make eyes water (1-propenyl sulfenic acid) exponentially increased, as did the sound, like a massive Waring blender. The centrifugal action of the spinning blades atomized this irritating chemical and spun it into the room like a raging tornado.

Prego Professional Profile

ONION MARY

Onion Mary was indeed a legend. She was the most widely recognized and respected laborer in the plant, more popular than the plant manager. Her fame went beyond just the Camden plant; Mary Comanda was talked about in admiring terms at the GO and held up as a role model by other plant managers from Ohio to California.

She was CSC's version of Wonder Woman. Dressed in white, a hair net and a paring knife in her hand, Mary could peel more onions than what was thought to be humanly possible. Dozens of industrial engineers and efficiency experts studied her every move. She could peel thirty to forty onions per minute all day long, better than any machine and twice what other mere mortals could achieve. She developed the technique whereby she would grab an onion and in one motion she cut off the top and removed all the peel in a flick of her wrist.

Workers in the onion room were paid a commission on every bulb they peeled, and, in the beginning, the accountants thought she was cheating by placing partially-peeled onions on the dicing conveyor. Yet, every study conducted concluded that she was properly peeling the onions. So Mary, being the most productive worker, was thus one of the highest-paid workers, man or woman, in the plant. After thirty years of peeling onions, "she earned over $200 a week, more than double the average for the job" —and more than four times my graduate student pay of $125 a month.[1]

By this time, I questioned the permanency of my blindness and my career choice. Undaunted, Maley led me deeper into this chamber of horrors, lingering as he greeted everyone he knew. Then he introduced me to "Onion Mary," one of the many professionals who influenced me on my road to developing successful products for CSC.

"Hey, Mary how are you doing? Ralph Miller says, 'hello.' This is our newest research technologist and I'm taking him for a tour of the plant," Maley shouted. Of course, everyone was in on the joke, including Mary, who I could barely see, so they played their role to perfection asking detailed questions on my background and how I liked the company so far. Finally, before my knees totally buckled beneath me forcing me to be carried out of the room, I was steered toward the exit. The door opened outwardly and a rush of fresh air swept over my face.

More of my sight gradually returned after a few minutes, and after dabbing my eyes with a clean paper towel that Maley handed me, I could see Maley was also clearing his eyes with a paper towel. Maley's eyes were not tearing up from an irritating chemical but rather from laughter, which suddenly erupted from him. "Sorry about all that in there. Everyone needs to experience the onion room at least once!" he said. That visit was my initiation into the exclusive fraternity of CSC product development geeks. As I later found out, this assault to my sight, smell, and overall sensibilities was a tradition, and how new hires reacted on their first tours would be discussed and retold many times with laughter among their peers for months to come.

Turning serious, Maley looked at me and said, "You know, all that work I did on testing those new onion varieties for flavor and texture went nowhere. The best processing onion was, and still is, the old standby yellow variety. They are huge and flavorful and cannot be beat for yield and final product quality. I cried a river to no avail!" He chuckled.

The glint of slyness returned to Maley's eyes when he proceeded to ask, "Do you want to see how pepper pot soup is made? It is a favorite of Philadelphia's elite."

Inside the Magic Kingdom

Before I could respond, Maley was off in rapid fashion headed to another enclosed room. This one held stainless steel tubs full of water to thaw large, rectangular gray-white blocks looking like some form of mystery meat. Maley reached his hand down into the cold water, lifted a rubbery strip out of the tank, and waved it in front of my face.

"Know what this is?"

I shook my head. "Ah, come on, you're an old farm boy, right? So you should know what this is." I shook my head again and replied, "It looks like a honeycomb of octopus suckers on one side and sharkskin on the other."

Taking the strip in my hand, I felt the spongy texture. When he brought the meat close to my nose, I involuntarily cried out, "This smells awful!" Maley almost exploded with laughter and said, "That is right; it is in fact 'offal.' It is beef stomach that has been treated with lye to remove all the gastric content!"

"Yuck!" I exclaimed, throwing the strip back into the tub and taking a few steps backwards. "You are telling me that people actually eat this stuff?" I asked in astonishment. "Yes, actually, it's quite good when you add tons of pepper and beef stock. You should try some," Maley responded, his smile as large as ever.

We left the tripe thawing room and continued on a tour of the marvels of CSC's engineering ingenuity. In another area, we paused to watch large pasta extruders depositing miniature Os directly into cans as they raced by. When covered with tomato sauce, these Os became Spaghetti-Os—one of the most popular kids' meals of the 1960s and '70s. My vision fully restored, I was mesmerized, watching them produced at a rate of many hundreds of units per minute.

Prego Professional Profile

DON MALEY

Our first weeks in New Jersey were a flurry of activity, getting acquainted at work and moving into our rented townhouse. My lifeline and guide was Don Maley. Maley was a skilled and veteran technician, as gregarious in his personality as he was skilled working with his hands. In the beginning, he joked to his colleagues that he was working for his "PhD" when he introduced his new boss to the other technicians and helpers in the department. These men and women were the ones who actually did the behind-the-scenes work. They set up the equipment, prepared all the ingredients, and cleaned up after the "professionals" (the chefs and technologists). Maley wanted to ensure that I knew the talent responsible for each department's efforts.

Maley was a local man who had grown up in the area and started working at CSC right out of high school. He and I were about the same age, and a natural kinship formed that matured into a Holmes-and-Watson-like partnership in the detective work of developing new products and processes. We became friends with an effective, if not symbiotic, working relationship. Working side by side with Maley helped me learn the people, the plant, and its history.

With my visits to each subsequent section of the plant, my appreciation for the engineering, processing, and technology of the CSC grew. I ended my first full day of employment, despite my brush with New Jersey's finest and my onion room experience, feeling validated that I had joined the best food team and company in the world.

Follow the Yellow Brick Road

Without Maley, I would have been as lost in the plant as an accidental tourist in the midst of New York City. Actually, the Camden soup plant was as big and self-contained as a small city. The factory was a massive eight-story structure of concrete and brick and, to the uninitiated, was a confusing labyrinth.

For all its twists and turns, the Camden plant was an example of intentional design. Each floor was carefully planned out for maximum efficiency as was known at the time, making best use of gravity, delivery logistics, and labor. The multi-use space was home to all executives at CSC, as well as the departments of product development, personnel, engineering, quality control, industrial engineering, purchasing and administration, with a fully-functioning pilot plant and soup production plant. The eighth-floor penthouse level held Campbell President Dr. Dorrance's offices and private residence, and supported the famously-painted water towers.

Throughout the building, concrete floors bore the tremendous weights of machines, equipment, raw materials, personnel, and finished products. Concrete walls separated divisions that were "shoe-horned" next to each other. There was no air conditioning, and workers opened windows or used fans in the summer for ventilation. It was a hot, humid, high-pressure environment.

The fifth floor, where I spent the majority of my time, housed labs and office space for the basic research and product development divisions. After a concept was developed, the technologist would be responsible for piloting the formulas in mass production and test marketing. The technologists who were working on existing and new products would spend most of their days working in the pilot plant and test kitchens with the chefs. Then, they would be responsible for shepherding the startup effort at the production factory.

The Path of the Cans

One of my first conversations with Maley, the one about the simplicity of making vegetable soup, stayed with me. He was absolutely right—making soup was NOT simple. Few people have been exposed to such precise complexity. These manufacturing areas were magical lands of high-volume, high-quality food production. At Camden, they occupied the ground level through the fourth floor.

I had ready access to all proprietary production operations and witnessed the interworking of a modern production facility with a mixture of awe and curiosity. I visited each area necessary to make a can of soup. Soup started with raw food preparation areas—most of these were much milder than the onion room—where a diversity of products were inspected, washed, peeled, diced, and inspected again.

In one of the areas, the smell announced the clams before I saw them—a pungent combination of fishy, salty, and earthy notes. Equally unnerving was the sight. In the most immense quantity I had seen in one place, whole clams hid within a knotted mixture of wet sand and broken shells, seaweed and branches, stones and dirt. Another person viewing this mountainous pile might call it "ugly," but after touring the rest of the plant I saw the conversion to something clean and refined, delicious and nutritious made from these raw seafood and vegetable materials. In this case, it was clam chowder.

Vegetable processing was just like preparing ingredients in a kitchen at home, but in much larger volume. After inspecting, washing, peeling, and dicing, the raw ingredients were loaded into carts with casters. These carts would be wheeled toward chutes and dropped down to kettles to be blended with water, seasoning spices, and other ingredients before being heated, then gravity-dropped again to filling machines below.

I admired the precision and efficiency of these high-speed machines, which filled up to several hundred cans a minute. After lids were added and the cans were closed and sealed, the cans were turned on their sides to be rolled to the heat sterilizer. Sterilization by heat was taken very seriously to avoid threats of possible contamination.

Regardless of the season outside, inside the plant was always hot and moist. Heat rose up in elevator shafts and stairwells, along with aromatic essence of whatever was being manufactured or processed that day. High humidity permeated the whole area; between the heat, hot soup being blended, and hosing the area to keep it clean, workers were bathed in sweat and needed to wear rubber boots.

Cleanliness throughout was of critical importance as well. Anything that touched food was made from stainless steel, and everything was thoroughly cleaned during the third shift to prepare for the first, second, and third shifts again the next day. Equipment and conduits such as pumps, piping, chutes, dicers, and filling machines were regularly taken apart, cleaned, inspected, and re-assembled.

After sterilization, the cans would come out of the retort (heater) then were cooled to reach ambient temperature. Next, the cans were rolled to a labeling machine, not to be touched by human hands again. They were packed into corrugated cardboard cases, transferred onto palettes, and finally lowered in multi-palette packs by elevator to the ground floor. In this packing and warehousing level, the product was ready for storing or shipping out in ready trucks, off to grocery stores, restaurants, or other customer sites.

Disorientation

The operations continued at a loud steady hum, and with so much activity you could easily lose your orientation when venturing into a new area. Many times, I was so confused as to where I was, I would have to reorient myself by walking to the nearest window to find a landmark. If I saw the Delaware River, I knew that direction was west. If I saw a dog looking into the horn of a record player, I knew that that was the "His Master's Voice" logo on the RCA building across the street, and thus north.

The first time I had to go to the "bone room" in the basement, this strategy was not possible. The basement had no windows and was a dungeon-like assemblage of storage cages and stacks of pallets of canned foods with forklifts buzzing up and down the ill-lit and musty-smelling aisles. The forklifts were yellow and black, and raced from the warehouse areas to the docked semi-trucks in an endless cycle of loading and unloading, reminding me of angry bumblebees. To walk along the aisles that the forklifts frequented was the shortest and surest way to navigate the confusing network of passages, but this was as hazardous as walking down the middle of Fifth Avenue in New York City during rush hour. If you happened to be there near the close of a shift and the daily quota of trucks had not been loaded, you would see the mad frenzy of activity to correct that problem. Any attempt to walk in this area was downright suicidal.

This was nearly my fate one day, caught with my container of beef stock, on the way to the "bone room" where the stock was made. I found myself on the wrong side of the forklift superhighway at the end of a shift. Frantically jumping out of the way, I resorted to back-tracking my way out. Dodging dock workers and negotiating numerous dead ends, I continued running until I found stairs that would take me back up to the relative safety of the fifth floor, my container of beef stock surprisingly intact. From then on, I made it my mission to know the cadence of the activity and the layout of the building so as to not get lost again. Part of that training included learning the backstory of the Camden factory and the history of the company.

(Endnote)

1   Daniel Sidorick, *Condensed Capitalism: Campbell Soup and the Pursuit of Cheap Produc-tion in the 20th Century* (Ithaca, NY: ILR Press, 2009), 57.

3

Birth of an Institution

. . . .

How, of all the cities in the United States, did Camden come to be the birthplace of the great CSC, Victor Talking Machines/RCA, R. M. Hollingshead Corporation, and New York Shipbuilding Corporation? My family and I pondered this question as we experienced Camden for the first time. Even today, many people visiting Camden would ask this question. The answer lies, as it does with most developments during the industrialization of America, with a major paradigm shift in transportation.

Camden, New Jersey, is ideally situated between New York and Philadelphia, and a natural transportation path between the cities emerged. Incorporated in 1828, Camden would likely have remained a bucolic suburb if not for a railroad chartered between it and South Amboy, New Jersey, just two years later.[1] This new conveyance made it relatively easy for people and goods to travel between New York

City and Philadelphia by ferry linkages to the train stations on either end, and therefore changed the business dynamics of the region. Fresh produce grown in the fertile fields in South Jersey, plus other manufactured goods, could now be shipped to and from New York City and beyond by overnight freight trains. This boom caused local farmers and manufacturers to embrace the downtown area of Camden. Soon they were building production facilities there, accessing well-developed rail lines in Philadelphia to ship all over the country.[2]

A Glimmer in Anderson's Eye

Seeing the potential in Camden commerce, Abraham Anderson, a tinsmith and an icebox manufacturer, traveled north from South Jersey and started a small canning company in Camden in 1860. A few years later, Joseph A. Campbell, a former Philadelphia produce merchant, partnered with him in Anderson and Campbell, selling canned fruits and vegetables.[3] After sixteen years together, Anderson left the partnership, and the company experienced one of several name changes. Newly-labeled Joseph Campbell & Company sold canned tomatoes, vegetables, soups, condiments, jellies, and minced meats. Its most well-known product was its canned New Jersey "beefsteak" tomatoes.[4] The flavorful and plentiful South Jersey beefsteak tomatoes were usually so large they fit only one to a standard-size tin can.[5] Smaller ones were boiled down and combined with sugar and vinegar to make ketchup. These products would remain standards for many years to come in CSC's product portfolio, contributing in large part to the growth of the thriving company.

Arthur Dorrance Takes the Reins

A new partnership sprung up in 1882, which included Joseph A. Campbell, his son-in-law Walter S. Spackman, Joseph Campbell's nephew Joseph S. Campbell, and Arthur C. Dorrance, Spack-man's personal friend. Their new venture was renamed to Joseph Campbell Preserving Company, then again to Joseph Campbell Preserve Company in 1891.[6] Campbell and Spackman provided the food manufacturing experience of this new enterprise; Dor-rance brought in much-needed funds which he had accumulated from his family's prosperous timber and flour trade in Pennsylvania. His well-developed business skills, honed while running his family's mills, were brought to the company as well. The company continued to thrive by selling salad dressing, pie fillers, ketchup, Worcester (sic) sauce, chili sauce, preserves, jams, and jellies.[7]

Arthur Dorrance had been with the company for ten years before he was appointed president in 1892. His business plan called for an immediate increase in sales and an expansion of product lines. By 1896, sales increased sufficiently in volume to justify a large factory to be built in downtown Camden, the foundation of which was the same building I explored decades later.[8] Like any building of its size, the massive structure demanded additional laborers for its expanded operations, an important priority for the growing company.

The Campbell Crew

The work ethic of the laborers at the turn of the twentieth century was deep-rooted and strong. These workers bore the weight of providing food and shelter for their families with pride in their heritage, community, nation, and employer. The original worker pool was a montage of Italians, Irish, Polish, and Germans. The Italians, Irish, and Polish tended to live in close-knit communities still speaking in their grandparents' native tongues, and preparing and eating the foods of their countrymen. The common link between the Italians, Irish, and Polish was the Catholic Church; this dominated their family lives and thus greatly influenced their proclivity to remain in close communities.[9] At Joseph Campbell Preserve Company the sons and daughters of immigrants were known to be hard workers, regardless of their backgrounds. According to Daniel Sidorick in *Condensed Capitalism,* "By the 1920s, most employees were immigrants or the children of immigrants ..." and most women worked in "food preparation, sorting and inspection" while men did the heavier labor and were allowed to be supervisors.[10]

The Doctor is In

In 1897, Arthur Dorrance hired his nephew, Dr. John T. Dorrance, a recent graduate from Massachusetts Institute of Technology (MIT) and Göttingen University in Germany. The company was in need of someone to run its laboratory and help manage the workforce, and Arthur saw in his brother's son a bright young man with a PhD in organic chemistry who would fit perfectly in his plans for the future. Dr. Dorrance was equally interested in working with his uncle, and agreed to supply all the scientific tools he needed to equip his soup laboratory—and to work there for the low salary of $7.50 per week.[11]

The company was struggling during Dr. Dorrance's first years; between construction of the large factory and decreased sales, the company was losing money.[12] Dorrance called on his advanced scientific training and inherent talents in creativity, innovation, and exploration. His breakthrough idea was to remove half the water in the soup formulation, and let the consumer add the rest. This water extraction technique was something that we would continue to look at with each innovation at CSC.

Condensing the product by Dr. Dorrance was a stroke of genius, the first effort in a very long line of innovations during his career in the food industry. Not only did this reformulation drop the weight of the can by almost 50 percent (because water is the heaviest ingredient), but the soup could be put in smaller cans and cases. Savings on freight and material costs enabled retailers to offer a can of condensed soup at ten cents, compared to the price of ready-made soups at thirty-five cents—an impressive comparison.[13] This extraordinary cost savings of twenty-five cents per can could also buy two and a half pounds of beef at that time; a homemaker could stretch her budget to add meat with the savings to feed her hungry family.

Still more amazing is the speed at which Dorrance brought this radical transformation to market. By recent standards, the gestation period for the development of a new food product from concept to the grocery shelf is greater than two years. Even with teams of food scientists, chemists, and chefs focused on speed within modern product development labs, it is very difficult to reduce this time frame. Dorrance accomplished this company-saving feat within his first year on the job.

His new line of condensed soups, including Tomato, Consommé, Vegetable, Chicken, and Oxtail, were introduced in 1898. This revolutionized the marketplace for canned soups, and the five new products were instant logistical successes, but not immediate sales successes.

Pounding the Pavement

Trying to sell a new food concept at the turn of the twentieth century to a skeptical public not familiar with processed foods presented some unique issues. First, no one had ever heard of condensed soup. Second, and more important, the United States was still an agrarian-based population that primarily ate main meals of locally-grown vegetables and meat. Third, Campbell's Soup was not a nationally-known brand, nor did it advertise aggressively. This was all about to change when Dorrance traded in his chef's hat for a salesman's fedora.

Dorrance realized that to sell condensed soup, he would need to convince the homemakers that using condensed soups would save them money and time, while helping them to provide delicious, wholesome foods for their family. He decided to bring the product to them, cooking samples for them to taste at in-store demonstrations, often carrying them in thermoses.[14] He became a road warrior, pitching and selling his newfangled convenience food. There was nothing comparable to condensed soups; the closest thing was condensed milk but the two had relatively little in common.

The chemist, product-developer, production-supervisor, and chef, now turned salesman, would describe in his memoirs a humbling experience. When he was stocking cans in the front window and doing an in-store demonstration in Cambridge, Massachusetts (the stomping ground of his MIT days), he was recognized by former colleagues and professors.[15] From their perception, a brilliant student was reduced to a stock hand in a grocery store. Yet Dorrance was willing to do any job to formulate, manufacture, and sell his brainchild, and his undaunted motivation was the driver for making Campbell's Soup one of America's favorite meals.

Dorrance was greatly encouraged that once a homemaker tried his soup, she was converted because of the convenience, low cost, and great taste. He was correct: By 1905, over 16 million cans of soup were sold annually.[16]

Fedora to Chef's Hat

When Dorrance first formulated his line of condensed soups, he undoubtedly referred to cookbooks of the day to refine his recipes. However, the exacting embryonic developer wanted to duplicate the delicate flavors of the soups that he had tasted during his university studies abroad.

To accomplish this goal, he started a pattern which would be the underpinning of his remarkable record of successes: he pursued on-the-job-training. He decided to become a chef—not a run-of-the-mill cook, but a chef trained in the culinary arts. For several months a year, Dorrance hired himself out as a chef's assistant working in some of the best restaurants of New York City and Paris. There, he trained under the demanding tutelage of classically-trained chefs who were considered some of the best of their art form. He studied every aspect of food preparation to make the best tasting dishes possible. It was difficult work. The priority was making the finest quality food possible and feeding hungry customers.

The chefs paid no regard that the apprentice from Camden, New Jersey, had a PhD and was part of the leadership of one of the largest canned food companies in the world. Executive chefs of the period were equal-opportunity abusers of every employee in their kitchens. If you did not carry your own weight in the kitchen, you might find yourself ushered out the back door into a dark, foul-smelling alley, and Dorrance himself received this treatment more than once, with the tale traveling down through the twentieth century until it reached me as part of the CSC mythology.

Dorrance learned his lessons well and incorporated this training into his exacting formulas and procedures for all Campbell's products. The experience of working in food service kitchens made Dorrance a true believer in the value of having a great chef as part of his staff; only an experienced chef understood good food and how to make it. Thus began the tradition of employing master-trained chefs (almost exclusively European) in Campbell Soup's product development kitchens. Chef Charles Louis De Lisle, a French-trained chef, was the company's first executive chef.[17]

Treasures in the Soil

Back in Camden, condensed tomato soup sales were wildly successful, largely due to its key ingredient, the beefsteak tomato. A staple in home gardens today, the beefsteak plant produces large, good-tasting fruit that ripens in stages and can be harvested multiple times over many weeks. These characteristics were attractive to the food industry in its infancy when the tomatoes were used primarily for canning, but viewed as a liability when a more mature industry and higher volumes demanded efficiency and faster harvesting. The delicate nature of the large tomatoes became a constricting factor for quality and yield with ever-increasing volumes of the tomatoes, which still had to be hand-picked and survive delivery to the manufacturing plant.

Dorrance was not satisfied that the beefsteak tomato was the best cultivar, or variety, for his new tomato soup and saw an opportunity to separate himself from other competitors by controlling the quality and cost of the raw materials.

He moved with his wife and two children to a 165-acre farm in Cinnaminson, New Jersey (just five acres larger than our Hildebolt Farm). He rented the farm from the company, and converted the front yard into experimental test plots for new strains of tomato cultivars. There, he clandestinely spent countless hours working alongside Harry Hall, a world-renowned tomato breeder and the first superintendent of Campbell's Soup Farms. Their work, in cooperation with the New Jersey agricultural department, developed multiple cultivars which became some of the dominant processing tomatoes through the 1960s.[18]

Literally, the first seeds of the company's policy of vertical integration were sown when they began providing their proprietary seed to their contract growers. The seeds were processed and packed at the Cinnaminson experimental farm. In 1918, R. Vincent Crine (who worked for Hall) suggested that tomato season could be extended if seeds were planted in southern climates and transplanted in New Jersey, Delaware, and Ohio, the plants could extend the normal shorter growing season and also deliver the high-quality CSC demanded for its tomato soup and tomato juice. They tried it, and it proved successful. Eventually, 40 to 50 million seedlings were grown each year and transplanted back to New Jersey and Ohio. Transplants continued until the 1970s when new technology developed by their agricultural experts permitted direct seeding of the fields with pre-germinated seeds in a gel.[19]

Some time later, he moved his expanding family of three daughters and a young son, named John T. Dorrance Jr., to the Main Line section of Philadelphia. The facility became the home of the Campbell Institute for Agriculture and Research (CIAR) and would earn the reputation as one of the leading plant breeding facilities in the world.

Roaring Campbell's

Almost two decades after hiring his extraordinarily prodigious nephew, Arthur Dorrance acted in a most avuncular manner by stepping aside as president. In 1914, Dr. Dorrance, the former lab technician, became the president and sole owner of a multi-million-dollar company. He had put in place a solid foundation for future growth and diversification that would benefit his descendants, customers, future stockholders, and employees well into the twenty-first century. The company changed its name again, adding "Soup," to reflect the importance of the product to the company operations and profits.[20]

Dorrance had a reputation as a stern disciplinarian who had high productivity expectations for his employees, but this discipline was matched by his dedication to their well-being. A sick or injured employee would receive the best medical attention possible, paid for by the company. If a person was injured on the job, that individual often got a job for life. Large donations of money were made to the local hospital to ensure good health care would be provided to his employees and the residents of Camden. His employees responded with loyalty and top performance.

In 1918, the company recorded a 24 percent increase in sales.[21] The Roaring Twenties were not only good for flappers and ragtime music, they were also good for manufacturers of convenience items like cars, vacuum cleaners, and condensed soup. CSC was at the forefront of this consumerism trend; this canned soup proved to be one of the first "fast foods" embraced by the American public. They loved the convenience, good taste, and nutrition, and best of all, its relatively low price. Dorrance's obsession with efficiencies and costs helped keep the price of a can of soup at ten cents, competitive with other meal choices.[22]

World-Famous Marketing

Dorrance realized that sending troops of salesmen canvassing all the stores on the East Coast would be a slow and expensive process. The company needed a much broader and effective method to communicate its message. The launch of these new condensed soups called for some marketing changes to catch the eye of the consumer in the grocery stores. Herberton Williams, a company executive, admired the red and white school colors of Cornell University and designed the new label in half-red and half-white, which remains the same coloring today; in fact, a shopper from that time period would recognize the current label because it has continued to carry these colors.[23] The gold medal seal on the front panel was added after prestigiously winning its category in the 1900 Paris Exposition. The seal, originally produced with French verbiage, was later translated into English, and appeared on the cans until the 2000s.

Dorrance also needed to catch the consumer's eye at home. His answer: advertising. He and his executive team became masterminds of promotion, and they budgeted a hefty 5 percent of sales for advertising. This was an unheard of sum for consumer products companies of the time, especially soup. Indeed, it became "the most highly advertised single food product in the United States."[24] The combination of a liberal advertising budget and brilliantly-conceived campaigns became an unbeatable combination.

CSC feature-focused advertising promoted Campbell's Soup as

being much more convenient than buying all the ingredients separately and making soup from scratch. The most well-known of these campaigns featured Grace Gebbie Drayton's illustrations of cute, chubby children, which became known as the Campbell Kids. The Kids were everywhere—on billboards, in newspaper advertisements, and in magazines. Magazines, especially women's magazines like *Ladies Home Journal*, were the primary means of promoting soup to the general public.[25] Dorrance insisted that all CSC ads be located on "the first right-hand page, facing a full page of text."[26] Even today, this location is known as "the Campbell's position." Dorrance also pushed the idea of using condensed soup as an ingredient in easy-to-make recipes. The first of many CSC cookbooks, *Helps for the Hostess*, was published in 1916.[27]

Dorrance's faith in the product and the advertising was rewarded by increasing sales each year. CSC became one of the first food companies to distribute its products coast to coast when it entered the California market in 1911. According to Douglas Collins in *America's Favorite Food*, "As sales increased, so did the amount of money spent on advertising. What had begun as a $10,000 allotment in 1899 rose steadily to $50,000 in 1901, $400,000 in 1911, and in 1920 to $1,000,000 (5% of the total sales [of $20 million])."[28] That investment in advertising would convert to $255 million in 2017 dollars.[29]

The Great Depression

The combined drivers of a shift to consumerism along with the delivery of high-quality, low-cost products propelled CSC from a regional specialty products canner to a major food processing company. In 1918, sales exceeded $50 million, netting an estimated $6 million in profit annually. The company incorporated in 1922 as the Campbell Soup Company (CSC). By 1927, CSC was producing approximately 1 billion cans per year.[30]

Up to this point the company's major competitors were the house-wives that made their own soup. Success breeds imitation, though, and a low-cost packer began manufacturing condensed soups that sold for five cents a can (half the price of the red-and-white-labeled condensed soups that were stacked next to them). Also, Heinz and Hormel were aggressively marketing their more expensive ready-to-serve soups. According to CSC lore, competition among other food processors became fierce as they eyed the fertile category of condensed soup; the major competition between Heinz and CSC had begun. Even though the company had a ketchup on the market since its Joseph Campbell & Company days, the rivalry likely wasn't recognized until Heinz entered the condensed soup market. Knowledge of the competition had been—and remains—an important part of the company's culture.

CSC, unlike the other large manufacturers in the region, stayed in reasonably good financial order by increasing efficiencies and productivity. Even though Dorrance was operating on razor-thin margins, he stubbornly resisted the siren call to reduce the quality and quantity of ingredients used in his recipes. CSC was privately owned by Dorrance, and he controlled all aspects of its operation. His quality standard was that of the classically-made soups he had eaten while studying in Europe. His colleagues in the food industry, however, did not share his vision and thus were likely poor comparisons in quality.

While the rest of the country was in a slow slide into economic recession, Camden was somewhat immune to the downward spiral. Its manufacturing base remained relatively strong along with the seemingly flush financial centers located in Philadelphia and New York City. Things were tight but the majority of people in Camden still had work.

The greatest economic expansion the United States had ever seen began in 1920; nine years later, the country experienced the greatest economic upheaval in its history, knocking down every sector from agriculture to transportation, manufacturing to retail. Worst of all, the banking and financial institutions were decimated, ushering in the decade-long Great Depression. The collapsed economy affected everyone, from rich to poor, and caused many children to be called into the workforce.

Gift of the Natives

Charlie Gaehring managed CSC's tomato processing operations for over twenty years. The first decade of these years was spent in the tomato processing building affectionately called the River Plant, because it was built on stilts over the Delaware River. The River Plant operated seasonally at summer's end, processing tomatoes at full ripeness to make tomato-based soups and other products.

Gaehring's boss, Dr. John T. Dorrance, being the innovative and shrewd businessman that he was, expressed concerns over the labeling and canning lines standing empty and the entire River Plant standing idle before and after tomato processing season. Dorrance had continually called on his own culinary training to devise a variation of the products that would be less costly to produce but maintain flavor and quality standards, and this time was no exception. What product could he create that would keep the facility operating all year, keep his workers employed, and provide additional enjoyment and nutrition for families?

Dorrance recalled an American Indian recipe of beans cooked in bear fat and maple syrup. A bean stew seemed the perfect solution: beans, stored dried, could be processed all year, and did not rot like tomatoes. Plus, a bean stew could be stopped for tomato season and restarted at the end of it. Dorrance expanded on the American Indian recipe by adding pork and spices, then tested it for consumer appeal. (When I heard this, I couldn't help thinking about my Dooley forefathers who learned about extracting tree sap from the Miami Indians, hundreds of miles away.) When the recipe passed

Prego Professional Profile

CHARLIE GAEHRING

One teenage boy whom Dr. Dorrance hired, Charlie Gaehring, would continue to work for Campbell Soup a total of fifty-four years, just two shy of Dorrance's fifty-six years of life. Gaehring's lifelong contribution to the company earned him an esteemed position among his peers and respect from the executives.

In 1918, Woodrow Wilson, the former governor of New Jersey and supporter of the agrarian economy, was in the White House. The Child Labor Act passed in 1916, but before that and even many years after it was enacted, children often started to work at a very young age. Putting food on the table was more important than going to school—a rather cold, hard economic fact of the times.[31] Gaehring dropped out of school to help support his struggling family. Just thirteen, he began his employment as a boy laborer at the Camden food processing facility.

Gaehring demonstrated to his superiors early on that he was a highly-motivated employee who had a bent for how systems worked. He was not formally educated, but his intuitive talent to make things work more efficiently and the experience he gained on the job paved the way to his ultimate advancement to the superintendent of Manufacturing for the entire soup plant. He contributed to the company's evolution from a regional food packer to one of the largest food processing companies in the world.

Charles R. Gaehring finally retired in 1972—three years after I joined the company. Gaehring showed his loyalty even after retiring by continuing his campaign to visit those in the Campbell's family experiencing death or loss. If one of his production team experienced a tragedy in his or her family, Gaehring

would visit them to offer condolences, assistance, and a listening ear. After retiring, he increased his reach by visiting his
fellow Campbell retirees, and even still others referred from his
church or other social agencies in Camden.[32]

taste tests, they canned it for distribution, allowing the production
facilities to be busy all year long. His new product, simply called
"Pork and Beans," was a "stop-gap" produced around tomato season
that became a lasting product in the company's portfolio.

The Legacy of Dr. Dorrance

CSC suffered an additional devastating blow a year later when
Dorrance died of heart disease at the age of fifty-six. The company
was not only facing unchartered waters in an economy that was
collapsing of its own weight, it had also lost its intellectual and
spiritual leader.

Dorrance was an extraordinarily talented visionary and businessman, ranking with some of his better-known contemporaries such
as Thomas Edison, August Busch Sr., Henry Ford, and Harvey
Firestone. While Edison was perfecting his phonograph, Busch was
brewing America's favored beverage, Ford was manufacturing hundreds of Model Ts a day, and Firestone was mass-producing rubber
tires for the nation's trucks and cars, Dorrance was busy developing
wholesome food products that gave time back to the overworked
homemakers and were affordable.

All these leaders had a major impact on the American way of life,
but Dorrance set an example for us by maintaining a sense of humility despite his many major achievements. Even decades later, when I
joined the Campbell's family, Dorrance's legacies were well-ingrained

in the culture and an expected part of the brand by the consumer base. Those legacies which remain in place today are:

- The invention of condensed soups—One of the biggest, if not *the* biggest innovations in food processing of the past century is condensed soups. The still-popular soup has remained mostly intact—in recipe and in marketing—for more than 115 years.
- The recruitment of the first executive-level chef for product development and the requirement of master-chef training—The CSC consumer promise is that no compromise will be made in the quality or quantity of ingredients in the company's products.
- The control of supply chain/vertical integration—CSC was one of the first commercial food companies to select and breed its own vegetables for processing, thus controlling the quality and cost of the raw materials.
- Consumer market trials—To encourage market acceptance, CSC brought its condensed soup product directly into grocery stores for taste testing by consumers.
- Dedicated workforce —Recruiting among the teeming labor pool, he hand-picked employees across the entire spectrum of experience and age. With each choice, Dorrance made life-altering decisions about the candidates chosen to join CSC, and they repaid him with unparalleled loyalty.

When the Streets Ran Red

Everyone associated with tomato season lived as if in a pressure cooker during that exciting time. Farmers had high anxiety about harvesting and delivery, processing people worried about rot and mold, plant management worried about anything that would contaminate or degrade their yield, executives feared not meeting demands for their largest commodity product (tomato soup), and everyone worried about keeping on deadline.

The tomatoes would start to arrive the third week of August on horse-drawn wagons, Model T Fords fitted with truck beds, and river barges full of tomatoes from South Jersey, which would be delivered directly to the processing line. During the next eight- to ten-week period, the plant would run twenty-four hours a day, seven days a week to manufacture all the tomato products that were anticipated to be sold the following year. In those years, all tomato-containing products had to be made in season. (Years later, an invention called evaporators would enable production of tomato concentrate products like tomato paste that could be stored frozen and used throughout the year). After the tomato season was over, no further tomato products could be produced; therefore, the tomato pack was an intense period of time.

When it was tomato season, everyone in Camden and the surrounding area knew it. Delivery traffic clogged the streets, and barges could be seen day and night bringing tomatoes up the river to the plant docks. Everything involved manual labor in those days, including off-loading fresh tomatoes in baskets from horse-drawn wagons or barges. CSC pioneered the practice of paying tomato farmers a financial incentive to deliver tomatoes of top quality.[33]

The tomatoes arriving at the plant had been planted sequentially in the fields. Given a consistent 100-day growth cycle from seed to maturity, they could be harvested in sequence based on when they were planted. Therefore, the deliveries continued daily for several weeks. Rotting and squashed tomatoes escaping from their vehicles often littered streets, alleys, and sidewalks, but the sweet smell of simmering ketchup permeated the air.

Farther south of Camden, residents knew it was tomato season because the Camden streets and the Delaware River "ran red" during these months of production. In an original—if not environmentally sound—form of recycling, the tomatoes came up the river and then the seeds and skins not used in processing were returned to the water and went back downstream. CSC was unknowingly ahead of the Environmental Protection Agency, as well as water and environmental concerns at this time.

Gaehring, well-seasoned himself after experiencing many tomato seasons, knew the factors he could manage and those he couldn't, the biggest of which was weather. Weather dictated the end of the tomato season, which normally occurred in the latter part of September, sometimes into October. The weather during this period on the East Coast can be unpredictable. A variety of scenarios could wipe out the tomato crop or negatively impact that year's production run, and if any of them happened, the company would have to wait twelve long months for another growing season.

Gaehring couldn't control the weather, but he could manage the hiring process and the training process for his employees. New temporary laborers were brought in each year who had to be taught every detail of the manufacturing process. Gaehring feared labor shortage during tomato season; he was especially vigilant during this period to ensure the correct number of laborers were hired according to projections, all his workers were well-trained, and all stayed busy to get the work done quickly and efficiently. Everything was fresh packed and needed to be processed within twenty-four hours to avoid mold growth and spoilage. If you do not process tomatoes within this period, you risk losing them. The pressure was constantly on to get as many tomato products stacked in the warehouse in wooden crates as was humanly possible.

A Short-Lived Retirement

Gaehring "retired" after forty-six years from his position as superintendent of production of the Camden plant, but his retirement was short-lived. When CSC pursued international sourcing of meat in the 1960s, the executives knew Gaehring was the one to

Deadly Lead

Spoiling tomatoes, unskilled temporary employees, and weather uncertainties were not the only problems that Gaehring was struggling to solve during production. His most pressing problem was to make sure that there were enough tin cans available in inventory for the projected pack. "It would be inexcusable and unforgivable to have product ready for canning then run short of tin cans during the pack," he must have thought, knowing the precision, care, and time it took to process the raw fruits.

The cans were handmade and soldered with lead one at a time. It was a most laborious and slow process that had to start well in advance of the season and continue nonstop through its end. Lead solder was also used to hand seal the lid to the top of the filled can, one can at a time. If the cans were poorly made or sealed, they would leak, and the product would spoil and make a great mess in the warehouse. Gaehring, always in the details, would constantly be checking on the quantity and quality of output on the can-making and sealing lines.[34]

The Pure Food and Drug Act of 1906 was passed to regulate the adulteration of foods and drugs sold in commerce. This was done in part due to the unscrupulous practices of meat processors, food packers, and mislabeled drugs sold as patient medicines. Public outrage in response to "muckraking" books like Upton Sinclair's *The Jungle* drew support from then President Theodore Roosevelt, whose administration passed the historic act to establish the Federal Drug Agency (FDA). Much later, Rachel Carson's *Silent Spring* continued to make the public aware of manufacturing effects on nature.

Even though this federal law regulated poisonous chemicals and hazardous practices, the dangers of heavy metal poisoning from lead solder used to seal tin cans (and, for that matter, lead pipes to convey city water), was not well understood at the time. Many unsuspecting people were made deathly sick by eating a constant diet of food from lead-containing products — which was what caused them to be sick eating tomatoes off pewter plates. Eventually, the solder in tin can manufacturing was converted to a tin alloy, and all of CSC operations became lead-free.

lead the processing operations. He had the expertise in processing equipment, personnel, and procedures, especially with heat processing and canning.

Corporate Engineering made Gaehring an offer he couldn't refuse to return to work, to assist in the startup of the Swift-Armor Meat processing plant in Argentina. He trained the staff there on how to cook beef and make bone stock. (Forty years later, this facility continues to supply the majority of CSC's beef and meat stock needs, as well as the beef needs for most of Europe, becoming an ever-more critical partner for the company following the mad cow disease scare in England and Europe in the 1990s.) The Gaehring tradition of working for the company continued with his grandson, Dave Gaehring, whom I would meet while working on one of the many top-secret, clandestine projects at CSC.

(Endnotes)

1   Christopher T. Baer, "A General Chronology of the Pennsylvania Railroad Company, Its Predecessors and Successors and Its Historical Context," *Penn Railroad Records*, July 6, 2017, http://www.prrths.com/newprr_files/Hagley/PRR1828.pdf; Collins, America's Favorite Food, 16.

2   "All Aboard! Railroads and New Jersey," Rutgers.edu, July 6, 2017, https://www.libraries.rutgers.edu/rul/exhibits/nj_railroads/.

3   Douglas Collins, *America's Favorite Food* (New York: Harry N. Abrams Inc., 1994), 13.

4   Sidorick, *Condensed Capitalism,* 15.

5   Aric Chen, *Campbell's Kids: A Souper Century* (New York: Harry J. Abrams, Inc., 2004), 13.

6   Collins, America's Favorite Food, 22.

7   Martha Esposito Shea and Mike Mathis, *Images of America Campbell Soup Company* (Charleston, SC: Arcadia Publishing, 2002), 71.

8   Ibid., 117.

9   Campbell Archives.

10   Dave Gaehring, *A History of Campbell's Soup* (Camden, NJ: Dave Gaehring, 2011)

11   Sidorick, *Condensed Capitalism*, 23.

12   Collins, *America's Favorite Food*, 30, 35.

13   Ibid., 30-32.

14   Mary Bellis, "Mmm Mmm Good [sic]: The History of Campbell's Soup. The Work of Joseph Campbell, John Dorrance, and Grace Wiederseim Drayton," *Thought Co.*, June 26, 2017, https://www.thoughtco.com/trademarks-and-history-of-campbells-soup-1991753. Collins, *America's Favorite Food*, 41.

15   Collins, *America's Favorite Food*, 38, 41.

16   Ibid., 41.

17   Ibid., 37-39.

18   Ibid., 69.

19   Ibid., 109-112.

20   Gaehring, *A History of Campbell's Soup*; Collins, *America's Favorite Food*, 109-113.

21   Shea and Mathis, *Images of America*, 72.

22   Campbell Archives.

23   Bellis, "Mmm Mmm Good [sic]," *Thoughtco.com*

24   "Campbell Soup Company," *Wikipedia*, June 26, 2017, https://en.wikipedia.org/wiki/Campbell_Soup_Company.

25   Sidorick, *Condensed Capitalism*, 18.

26   Collins, *America's Favorite Food*, 89.

27   "Campbell Soup Company," *Advertising Age*, May 22, 2017, http://adage.com/article/adage-encyclopedia/campbell-soup/98376.

28   Collins, *America's Favorite Food*, 90.

29   Ibid., 97.

30   "Value of $2,000,000 in 1920," *saving.org*.

31   Campbell Archives.

32   John Milton Cooper Jr., *Woodrow Wilson* (New York: Alfred A Knopf, 2009), 276.

33   "Campbell's Active Retiree," *Harvest*,(Camden, NJ: Campbell Soup Company) July/ Aug. 1965.

34   Gaehring, *A History of Campbell's Soup*.

35   Mary B. Sims, *The History of Commercial Canning and New Jersey* (Trenton, NJ: New Jersey Agricultural Society, 1951), 167.

4

Mission Impossible

. . . .

With my knowledge of the history of CSC and ideas for new products, I eagerly continued on my first few weeks of work. True to his word, CSC vice president of Product Development Ralph Miller allowed Don Maley and me to work on whatever projects we could conceive, if they had anything to do with food. This was a promise that had lured me to Camden and the CSC in the first place.

In the beginning, it was a dream come true. We were surrounded by world-class talent and equipment to create anything we could envision. This was easier said than done, and I spent many sleepless nights the first weeks trying to think up ideas for new foods to no avail. Maley and I struggled for weeks working on some of his ideas and then mine. However, after many attempts of trying to develop a new product, all we had a show for it were messy lab counters and full garbage bins. When we exhausted our product ideas, I resorted to asking anyone I knew, both inside and outside the company—including my mother-in-law—and nothing surfaced.

My dream scenario was rapidly filling with frustration and anxiety. The reality of the situation is that it is difficult to innovate new products even when you have experience, and it's nearly impossible when you have had no experience. My college education in food technology/science focused on understanding the fundamentals of biology, chemistry, microbiology, nutrition, food processing, and safety. There was no formal training in product or process development. I was well equipped to do directed food research and to solve engineering-type problems, but the creative elements of product and process development were beyond my capabilities. Ironically, for a food technologist but typical of men of that era, I didn't even know how to cook.

My boss remained pleasantly nonchalant concerning any lack of progress on our part, clearly a reflection of his own time as a researcher. This would later dramatically change as I advanced in my career; but for now, he was supportive and encouraged us to work on anything we thought had value. By the end of the month, I was becoming desperate and realized that working without a product portfolio was not going to build much of a resume.

Then a seasonal inspiration occurred. It was November, with Thanksgiving rapidly approaching, and pumpkins were plentiful in southern New Jersey. Having worked with a freeze dryer during my graduate studies, the concept of a dehydrated, instant pumpkin pie mix was born. We added the classic ingredients to the pumpkin purée for the filling, then freeze-dried them. The customer could just add water, place it in a pie shell, and bake.

The pie could be mixed in a matter of minutes, and after baking it, it was as good as if it were made entirely from scratch. This was a departure from the popular canned-filling approach to making a pie. When Maley and I showed the prototype to Miller, he complimented us on its novelty and good taste. A few days later, he informed us that he had scheduled a showing of our "instant pumpkin pie mix" to the famed Product Committee. In doing so, Miller was helping us to gain experience and be introduced to the executives comprising the committee. The president at the time was William Beverly "Bev" Murphy, a legend in the food industry who had taken CSC from a specialty canner to a broad-based food processing leader. His executive team was imposing, and I was appropriately anxious.

Instant Pumpkin Pie in the Shark Tank

Product showings to the executive staff were a life-and-death drama played out in a corporate conference room. Surrounded by white porcelain-tiled walls, we stood around a Formica-covered tabletop on a beige linoleum floor—no chairs were allowed in the Product Committee Room. The committee consisted of the CEO, president, CFO, and multiple VPs, as well as the presidents of the respective division responsible for the product being presented and shown, plus the manager/technologist presenting the product. This is where dreams came to fly or die. A product developer could work six months to a year on a new product concept, only to have a stake driven into its heart with thumbs down from the committee, all in a matter of minutes. All authorizations for product improvements, new product launches, and product-related capital expenditures were determined by the Product Committee. Careers were made or broken in this small, sterile conference room.

The product development manager or the product technologist would present the product or process request along with samples of the product for taste testing. The presenters would field questions and, if necessary, the marketing managers would provide market research data and the engineering costs. On most decisions, everyone followed the lead of the president. But on occasion the manufacturing and sales executives would take a stand on issues of concern.

Everyone had a vote, although some were weightier than others. The CEO, John T. Dorrance Jr., had a veto vote, but he normally remained in the background and did not impose his will unless it was a major policy decision. A formal protocol was followed and to the newly initiated, this was high drama.

The reality show called *Shark Tank* is designed to closely represent the interaction of venture capitalists and entrepreneurs, and it also captures the dynamics of a CSC Product Committee showing. The executives are the sharks and the product developers the entrepreneurs. The stage, however, is different. In the TV version, the investors are all sitting down in overstuffed, leather chairs on a hardwood floor covered with an Oriental rug, and at least three of the sharks are billionaires. In our Product Committee Room, everyone stood and only one of the participants was a billionaire, but the tension and the politicking among the investors traversed a very similar path. The investors ask pointed questions regarding the possible investment of their money and demand assurances from the entrepreneur that their investment will yield positive returns. The TV entrepreneurs and CSC product developers defend their brainchild and make implied promises in an identical manner. In both scenarios, those who best sell their vision usually win support and financial backing.

I was early for my presentation time. As a result, I was able to witness the prior presentation and very serious discussion on canned puddings. In the 1950s, CSC had pioneered canned puddings under their Bounty brand. The chocolate and vanilla flavored puddings were reasonably good and had established a dominant market share. Recently, several competitors had entered the market utilizing artificial ingredients such as colors, stabilizers, and flavorings. The competing products were superior in mouthfeel, color, and flavor; thus, their overall appeal was superior to the Bounty puddings (which were formulated under the CSC self-imposed restriction of not using any non-natural ingredients). The predictable results showed the former market leader was getting clobbered by the newcomers. Sales were falling faster than a soufflé in an earthquake.

The Bounty product developers easily matched the competitors' product using artificial ingredients, and it was not like CSC lacked the ability to react to this threat. The product developers presented the committee with three samples for tasting: 1) the existing all-natural Bounty product, 2) a sample from the competitive product, and 3) an artificially-formulated CSC prototype. The CSC artificial prototype was found to be equal or superior to the competitor.

Management had two choices: one was to reformulate the product using the best of modern food chemistry, the other to discontinue the line. After much discussion on the course of action, the son of the inventor of condensed soup and founding father of the CSC, John T. Dorrance Jr., spoke up. In his quiet voice and demeanor, the CEO stated that he would prefer to discontinue this business than to compromise his father's long-standing policy of using natural ingredients. Everyone nodded their heads in agreement. With one word from Dorrance, the well-established, revenue-generating Bounty pudding line was terminated, and then-president Bev Murphy signed its death sentence. This seared into me the concept of product integrity, and exponentially grew my respect for the company.

Energized and humbled at the same time, I approached the table to present. I was nervous and excited, and even more proud of working for the company, but had just seen the efforts of the other product technologists deflated instantly before me. I presented our idea, and showed them the before and after, even providing the cooked final product. Though they acknowledged this as a unique concept and tasty pie, they did not deem the project worthy of additional work. After all the discussion about the pudding, I felt my effort of instant, dehydrated pumpkin pie was anti-climactic; in a quarter of the time they spent on the pudding, my project was shelved. I had gotten off easy—my baptism in the shark tank was more like swimming with dolphins than sharks. That experience, like a lot of other things, would change in the near future.

Later, I realized that as good tasting and convenient as my product was, the product did not fit into any existing CSC product category line. It wouldn't have made sense for the company to go forward on a concept of this kind, but it was excellent learning for me. With the instant pumpkin pie's instant failure to launch, I went back to the kitchen, discouraged and out of ideas.

Lassie to the Rescue

Then Lassie the TV dog came to my rescue—not in his physical presence, but in the form of a dog food that Lassie ate. The company's new pet division, Champion Valley Farms, was developing a line of canned dog food under the Recipe label. Campbell's Soup had advertised for many years on *Lassie* and now wanted to leverage this relationship by manufacturing and marketing the dog food that was portrayed as Lassie's favorite meal.

The irony of this is that I had not planned on working on pet food, yet it launched my career. Just a few months earlier, I had turned down the job at Quaker Oats working in pet food which offered more money and was closer to home (plus, we had friends in Chicago). Now, I was pleased to have an assignment, but a little chagrined to be working on pet food.

As I began to attend planning meetings for the new project, I got to know some of the executives, and I learned the history of how CSC decided to start a pet food division. It started with the company's dedication to vertical integration and the importance the company placed on advertising to sell its products.

The CSC invested heavily during the 1930s in advertising, backing its new product introductions. The Campbell Kids were depicted in print advertising in all kind of activities like sporting events, at play, and gardening. Their voices could be heard on the radio, alongside FDR's "Fireside Chats," singing the famous "M'm! M'm! Good!" slogan. In the 1940s, the Campbell Kids were enlisted to help in the war effort by continuing to spread the message with patriotic slogans that nourishing soup was good food. In addition, the first advertising of the Campbell Kids appeared on television.[1]

In 1941, CSC's home economists group published full-length cookbooks under the pseudonym Ann Marshall (later replaced by Carolyn Campbell) entitled *Easy Ways to Good Meals*, which was quickly adopted in the home kitchen.[2] With more ways to use the products, home cooks were encouraged to use soup in other preparations, causing demand to increase dramatically. In 1942, soup product sales topped $100 million.[3]

The company also had notable commercial sponsorships. Among these was "The Campbell Playhouse," which had previously been Orson Wells' "Mercury Theatre on the Air."[4] CSC took over as sponsor of that radio the program in December 1938. After that successful endeavor, the company took on major sponsorship of *Lassie*. *Lassie* was a popular film and TV series about a young boy and his collie dog. Though it launched in the 1950s, it continued to be popularized through multiple movies and shows even fifty years later, and proved to be a wholesome, family-oriented partnership.[5]

The sponsorship of this program and the subsequent decision to manufacture and market Lassie's dog food broke with CSC's tradition of creating healthy convenience foods for humans. The company was sensitive to public perception and potential outcry that the same equipment, staff, and food would be used to make dog food as human food, so it created a separate division called Champion Valley Farms to introduce pet foods and treats. CSC leveraged its technology and process expertise honed in the production of Chunky soups in blending, filling, canning, and labeling for its first foray into pet food.

Lassie's Biscuit Challenge

Back inside the CSC R&D department in 1969, my reluctance to working with pet foods faded fast when my boss approached me to solve a unique problem. Lassie's dog food was to be a variety of meatball stews topped off by a chew biscuit in the can as a reward. This was a clever gimmick, conceived by the company's marketing arm and an outside ad agency, but it turned into a major challenge riddled with technical and production obstacles. In fact, the product development team at Champion Valley had already worked on the problem for over two years.

The problem was producing a dog bone-shaped biscuit that would retain its shape while the product was being heat sterilized. A traditional biscuit would simply turn to mush in the stew, and the pet food developers had come up with an oil-resin coating that prevented moisture from entering the biscuit.

Unfortunately, this approach doubled the processing time, and the coating's tacky surface meant that production workers, not machines, would have to hand-place the biscuit into the cans. All told, the biscuit idea was going to cost CSC millions of dollars more than anticipated to launch the Lassie dog food.

The development of the chew biscuit had stalled and was holding up the national launch of the dog food. The new Pet Food division was anxious to go into production but the projected cost was prohibitive and management was desperate for alternatives. The test market for the stew part was a success and Lassie and the product had already been on a photo shoot. The advertising was all set and the appearance of the product could not be changed, so eliminating the chew biscuit was out of the question.

Miller saw an opportunity for me, his new junior technologist, to provide a solution. I was eager to start a new project, and had no idea that this Lassie problem would position me as the one to tackle "mission impossible" projects.

The Dustup

My college education trained me for many things, but making heat-resistant chew biscuits for Lassie's dog food was not one of them. Don Maley, my technician, and I began working on various dough formulations for the biscuit. Thinking how nature would solve this problem, I analyzed real dog bones to learn they were composed of a complex matrix of minerals and protein. To mimic it, I formulated a blend of durum pasta flour fortified with various proteins plus calcium carbonate.

We started to make a series of experimental batches of dough in the commercial-size Hobart mixer. The mixer was housed in a special equipment room which was common to both the chefs and us, the technologists. I was to mix the ingredients to make the dough, and Maley, on a floor below, would roll the dough into sheets, hand-stamp it into biscuit shapes, and then bake them.

I had made one batch and I took a trip to deliver it downstairs. When I came back to the common room, ready to make another batch, I saw the dough hook from the mixer was missing, preventing further mixing of any kind. "What happened to the hook?" I demanded of one of the technologists working in the room, incredulous that this interrupted my calculated process.

Answering my inquiry, he shrugged his shoulders, and said that he thought he had seen Chef Werner Schilling working at the mixer earlier. I did not recognize the name. Learning that Schilling was a chef working in the Frozen Food Product Development division (a division separate from mine but just across the hall), I decided to search for the hook myself. As I entered the chef's kitchen, it was like alarm bells and flashing lights had been triggered, warning that a trespassing foreigner had just invaded the room.

Everyone in the kitchen stopped working and focused their eyes on Chef Werner Schilling and me. In his full chef's attire (his chef's hat adding another few inches to his height), Schilling cut an imposing figure. He clearly embodied the professionalism expected by Dr. John T. Dorrance when he inaugurated the use of European-trained chefs.

No greeting and no words were said. I finally spoke, meekly asking, "Has anyone seen the dough hook from the Hobart mixer across the hall? I was using it earlier, but it is gone." Again silence, then after a moment or two, Schilling answered with his Swiss accent, "The dough hook is mine. I have taken it back." He went on to say that they had been using the mixer earlier in the morning; now they had finished and he had taken the dough hook back for safekeeping.

I was so mad I was spitting proverbial nails as I said, "The mixer is in a common area to be used by everyone. We are making batches and I need the dough hook!" Schilling, more forcefully (and impressively without raising his voice), said that the attachments to the mixer were always getting lost by the technicians and technologists. He had purchased the dough hook for his own private use. It was his and he was keeping it. Despite my objections, he calmly suggested if I wanted to use the mixer in the future, I should get my boss to purchase a dough hook.

That was it. Only a few weeks on the job, and here I was having my first major confrontation. We were instant enemies. I was greatly outnumbered with all his staff in the kitchen, and a brawl probably would not have ended well. Fortunately, the manager of the Frozen Food Product Development division—and Schilling's boss—entered the kitchen and negotiated a compromise before any blows were struck or I embarrassed myself and said something I would regret later. I was allowed to use the dough hook to finish our work for the day, but I had to purchase a new one for my own use after that.

Schilling and I did not speak for some time, with our paths seldom crossing. Little did either of us know we would become the strongest of partners years later. That whole experience taught me a lesson that I have revisited regularly throughout my career: Don't burn your bridges. You may need to cross them someday.

Bounce

Back in the kitchen again, Maley and I were able to finish our test batches. We placed the cut-out biscuits into cans with water and sealed them before heating them to simulate the sterilization process. When the cans were cooled and opened, we were thrilled to see that the biscuit didn't turn into mush. We had solved the problem of the mushy biscuit!

Surprisingly though, the biscuits actually bounced when they were poured out onto the counter. They bounced like a super ball, which should have been an early warning sign that we had not quite arrived at the right formula, but did not think how the rubbery consistency would affect production. Plus, we were focused on other issues. This was to become another of our learnings; it's easy to have tunnel vision and focus on the constraints of one issue but lose track of the bigger picture in the process.

At the time, we did have a stable biscuit and we were ready to show our boss the results of our work. Miller was genuinely surprised and delighted in that we had been working on the project for less than two weeks. He did note that the color was slightly different from the target color in the ads. "Correct the appearance, and we'll take this to the Champion Valley executives," he complimented.

The problem was addressed very simply by adding beta carotene, and because beta carotene is a precursor to Vitamin A, the company had something else to promote on the label with Lassie. Miller brought me in for a formal product showing with the Champion Valley staff, and we were immediately instructed to prepare for a full-scale manufacturing test. We had fulfilled what marketing had pictured in its advertising; we had saved the company millions in manual production costs, and we got the market test back on track. The executives were ecstatic, smiling and clapping us on the back. For the time being we were heroes, and all we had to do was go into biscuit production.

Those smiles continued all around—with the exception of the Champion Valley product development team who were embarrassed about our quick progress in solving the same problem they had unsuccessfully toiled against for two years. In due time, they came around, and we were able to collaborate successfully. (We learned later that they were also relieved to have the tremendous pressure from their managers removed from their shoulders because the project was finally finished.)

Dough Jam

For a trial run in production, Maley and I borrowed some time on the Goldfish Cracker assembly line at a nearby Pepperidge Farms facility, acquired by CSC in 1961. Between two shifts, we confidently mixed up a large, production-scale amount of the dough. There again, we should have had another inkling that something was wrong—the amps on the mixing motor were maxing out, indicating that the dough was unusually stiff and elastic. We forged ahead, though, and placed the dough between rollers to form sheets. Within this rotary moulder machine, the sheet of dough would be cut into shapes.

This was the automated step that Maley and I had done by hand on a smaller scale in the test kitchen. In this factory that made goldfish-shaped crackers, the rollers were usually equipped with the specially-designed goldfish cutters. For this chew-biscuit test, the rollers were fit with the specially-designed biscuit-shape cutters.

The machine operators flipped the switch to start the rotary molder. Almost immediately, the normal hum of the machinery was interrupted by a huge bang, and bolts started to shear off the master roller. The viscous dough had jammed the rollers.

"Oh boy, are we in trouble now!" I thought. "Hero to zero in less time than it takes the moon to change phases!" Our first success immediately became our first failure.

The operators quickly turned off the machine. The twenty-four-hour production line was shut down, and the workers were irate at knowing they would not only miss another shift of regular production, but they would have to shovel out the remaining dough stuck in the rollers and clean the entire production line. Engineers would need to come in, repair the production line, and put on new bolts where the others were forced off.

I was almost banned from any future visits to a Pepperidge Farm bakery due to this formula malfunction. Maley and I knew there was no way we could let something like this happen again, but we didn't have a clue how to solve the problem. Back in the lab again, we determined that the problem stemmed from having too much protein in the biscuit formula. The gluten matrix had an elastic trait that caused the dough to actually "snap back" to its original shape. This snapping-back tendency was what caused the mixing and shaping problems in production, and it had caused the biscuits to bounce on the counter in our original test batches. After tinkering with the formula—taking out some protein here and some minerals there—we eventually came up with a chew biscuit that held its shape and didn't destroy the forming machinery. We finalized the formula that was to become the famous Lassie dog biscuit and handed the product over to the dog food division to launch.

We also learned a very important lesson in the process: It is a lot easier to work out production problems in the test kitchen and pilot plant before shutting down an entire Goldfish cracker factory. Going forward, we always tried to work out as many problems as possible prior to production, and though we strictly adhered to this policy, neither of us were popular among plant managers and production supervisors when we showed up at their facilities to run a "test batch."

Master Problem Solvers

Throughout our trials and hard-learned lessons, we were encouraged by my boss. Miller was very perceptive in recognizing talent and would assign positions and projects accordingly. In this manner, Maley and I were given increasingly challenging projects, including flavor, texture, and nutrition changes in existing products or requests for developing new products.

At CSC, I came to understand that there were no style points awarded for wearing the best clothes, driving the fanciest cars, or living in the most luxurious homes. It became obvious early on that I was there to solve problems and add value for a company that generated a slim three-percent margin on its food products. There just wasn't much room for error, and appearances were secondary.

If you can solve a problem better than your competitors, you have a definite advantage over them. Some individuals are fortunate enough to be intuitive problem-solvers, but most have to develop these skills. I was certainly in the latter category; as I've mentioned before, I had quite a bit of trouble learning starting in elementary school.

Despite all my early learning difficulties, I learned how to problem-solve effectively after a lot of trial and error. The recipe is a combination of discipline, focused technical ability, and persistence. There are no shortcuts or magic tricks to facilitate this process. True professionals realize this, and roll up their sleeves to attack the problem head-on. Solving problems and completing these special assignments with regularity taught me that our reward from the company was simple but profound: *being able to do it again.* When you delivered, you were depended on by the company and respected as a key contributor, meaning you were in a coveted position. Cooperating between projects would also help you get recognized, and it was important for your career to be connected to "star" projects.

This contribution culture was formed by the top executives from

Prego Professional Profile

RALPH MILLER

A true mentor, role model, and champion for product development, Ralph Miller was admired for possessing superior management skills and a photographic memory.

Ralph Miller grew up in Pennsylvania practicing the Moravian faith, which was the foundation for his high sense of personal integrity that would serve him throughout his academic, career, and personal pursuits. After earning a master's degree in chemistry from the University of Delaware, Miller joined CSC.

In one of his early roles, Miller continued to refine Dorrance's formulation on tomato soup (one of the five original condensed soups). He performed some primary work in tomato processing for soup and paste production, and was responsible for some of the major improvements and enhancements behind the famous tomato soup.

Miller was one of the best developers in the business. Because of his prowess in product development and personnel administration, he rocketed up the ranks to become the VP of R&D in the CIR&T. Campbell heart-and-soul, Miller was perfectly matched to this role.

His steel-trap mind remembered formulas and exact production procedures, which he respected and protected. His amiable personality brought him success in recruiting new employees and handling operational disputes. Plant managers would sometimes request exceptions on production rules from him, but Miller would never bend. There was no way you could intimidate him either, because he was on top of administrative details and knew what it took to consistently produce products correctly. This was a source of pride for him, and one he instilled in those that reported to him.

A constant supporter of our team of technologists, Miller nurtured our careers and our projects, his influence on par with many of our fathers and grandfathers. He understood the trials of research and he encouraged us to keep trying. He was the best executive leader I ever worked with, fostering loyalty with his every action.

In another part of his role, Miller was expected to participate in several taste tests and product inspections every day. Eating soups, juices, fried chicken, TV dinners, tomato products, and more (several times a day) resulted in Miller constantly watching his weight. He got to the point where he could accurately analyze a product with a very small taste. He became known as a "Top Tongue," readily able to tell distinctions in texture and flavor because of his vast understanding of product profiles, as well as his ability to articulate those distinctions.

Against other executives, Miller would fight for products he believed in. The point person for our group, he would stand his ground in battles over ingredients, costs, and timelines. Miller would never cut corners that could compromise quality. He was demanding—he had to be, because executive management expected results. Miller had high standards and delivered.

the early days of the company and continued through the time I worked there. The epitome of the executive leaders was William Beverly Murphy. He encouraged inter-company competition and an innovation spirit that allowed his colonels, like my boss, to manage their teams in a motivating, formative way. It was this culture of contribution which was one of the pillars of longevity of the company.

Prego Professional Profile

BEV MURPHY

William Beverly Murphy, better known as "Bev," held the company presidency when I joined CSC. Under his leadership, it became one of the largest food companies in the world. Murphy accepted the role in 1953 and one year later, he took the corporation public. His tenure was filled with acquisitions, line extensions, and product improvements. He expanded the company's brand portfolio with the acquisitions of Franco-American, Godiva, Pepperidge Farm, and Swanson, thereby adding gravies, pastas, chocolates, and broths to its product offerings.

The Camden headquarters was the command center for both domestic and foreign operations, and the corporate organizational structure Murphy orchestrated was a masterpiece of balancing power between the various departments, such as Quality Control versus Production. Similar in the ideology of the founding fathers when they established the Constitution, the purpose was that no one department could dominate and thus power was centralized in the office of the president.[6]

Murphy's background was not in production, as many of his predecessors' were, but instead in consumer research. Murphy was the voice of the customer with a creative spark that his team, including me, was inspired to follow. We became aggressive in supporting R&D, following in the company's quality tradition.

One of Murphy's early production hurdles followed the acquisition of V8. The product that was acquired from Standard Brands was plagued with product quality and consistency issues. He directed that the product should be brought up to CSC standards. At the time, V8 was made at multiple production locations, but he insisted that the product have consistent taste and quality regardless of where it was being produced. This was achieved shortly after the acquisition. Now, V8 is a mainstay of CSC's product lineup and it is the most popular vegetable juice in the marketplace.

An Early Total Recall

In the early 1970s, Murphy was called upon again to show this true character and his commitment to the Campbell philosophy for maintaining the quality and safety of its products. A spoilage problem was discovered in chicken vegetable soup produced at the Paris, Texas, manufacturing facility. The product was found to be randomly swelling and exploding in the warehouse.

The health risk was not with the bulging cans—no one was going to eat product from a bloated and stinking can. Those were easily identified and removed. The real concern was that there were cans potentially containing stealth killers, undetectable by any outward sign. In any canned product, there is a remote possibility of contamination with *Clostridium botulinum* bacteria, which produces botulism, one of the most deadly poisons known to mankind. The insidious thing about Clostridium botulinum is that it does not produce gas like most other microorganisms that swell the can, nor does it change the flavor of the product. If a consumer were unfortunate enough to eat a can of botulism-tainted food, he or she could die.

The actual cause of the spoilage was not easily discerned but was appearing in substantial enough numbers to raise major concerns. Everyone had a theory on what was causing the problem, but no one actually knew. The variables to create a spoilage occurrence like this are as numerous and complex as a Rubik's cube puzzle, which only intensified the tension and pressure to solve the problem. Fingers were being pointed everywhere. Product Development was challenged as to the efficacy of the process procedures (time and temperature of the retort process to sterilize the product), Quality Control records were scrutinized to make sure that the processing parameters were actually achieved, and Production was questioned on the operation of the hydrostatic sterilizer. Murphy and his team were scrambling for answers.

The media were drawing eerie parallels to another New Jersey soup company. Less than ten years earlier, a gentleman had died eating vichyssoise, a chilled potato soup produced by Bon Vivant. This tragic event spelled the demise of this specialty product maker. There were fears throughout the company that this same fate could descend on CSC if proper and immediate actions were not taken.

LIFE magazine even showed up at the GO to interview Murphy and the resulting cover picture on this iconic weekly magazine was a close-up of the president of the company eating a bowl of chicken vegetable soup. He intended to quell the public concern and prevent further loss of sales. The pressure to find an answer to the problem intensified daily, and I saw my boss Miller age ten years in the process.

Lacking any definitive information, Murphy made the courageous decision to recall every can of chicken vegetable soup that had been produced at the Paris plant. He directed Jim McNut, vice president of sales to mobilize his sales force to hand-remove every can from of every retail shelf. A large financial loss had already occurred and this request diverted the sales force from normal sales functions, but it was absolutely the right thing to do.

The first priority always had to be safety—for the employees and the consumers. This act of removing potentially dangerous cans demonstrated to everyone inside and outside of the company that regardless of the cost, Murphy would uphold the ethical principles of the company. The lines at the Paris plant were shut down and scrubbed. Newly-produced chicken vegetable soup was tested and retested before it was released to ensure that it was not contaminated.

These were strong and positive messages that were deeply instilled within the culture of the company and its customers. Years later, Johnson & Johnson would follow CSC's example in managing a recall of its compromised Tylenol product, and today recalls are an expected company response to potentially harmful products.

The Legacy of Bev Murphy

Murphy had been such a dominant force for so long he had ascended to regal status within the company and became a darling of the Dorrance family. While others may have noted that he was "impatient with people who don't think as fast as he does" and that he had "brusque charm," my experience was that his cult-like popularity was not only present with CSC employees and stock-holders, it was universally accepted by rivals in the industry and the media that Beverly Murphy was one of the premier food processing industry executives of his time.[7]

Murphy had perfected his style of leadership control to a fine art, but after nearly two decades, it had run its course. Murphy prepared its executives—like my boss, and later, me—for the current and threatening competition by surrounding ourselves with strong, capable employees whom he could rely on when other impossible missions arose. He created the culture of contribution and paved the way for his successor, Harold Shaub, and other major players like Dr. Allen Stevens, to strengthen CSC's place as a multi-national food provider.

(Endnotes)

1   Aric Chen, *Campbell's Kids: A Souper Century* (New York: Harry J. Abrams, Inc., 2004), 57.
2   Collins, *America's Favorite Food*, 139.
3   Ibid., 208.
4   "Campbell Soup Company," *Advertising Age*.
5   Ibid.
6   "Charles Secondat, Baron de Montesquieu" *America's Survival Guide*, July 6, 2017, www. americassurvivalguide.com/montesquieu.php.
7   Sidorick, *Condensed Capitalism*, 150-151.

5

The Passion of the Tomato

· ·

Commercial food production efforts were advancing worldwide in the 1960s and '70s, noticeably on the New Jersey agricultural landscape, and the Dorrance Farm and plant breeding facility were staffed with prestigious plant scientists. Under the direction of company president Bev Murphy, this setting of Dorrance's experimental tomato cultivar research became the Campbell Institute for Agriculture and Research (CIAR). CIAR would later house the pioneer lab of Dr. Allen Stevens, one of the world's premiere tomato geneticists. His research would shape tomato history, and I was about to get an in-depth education on his work.

Traveling Tomato

Tomatoes (also known as *Solanum lycopersicum*) originated in South America, most likely in the coastal areas of Peru, Ecuador, and Chile. The Aztcs ate the "tomatl" fruit (Nahuatl name) as early as 700 AD.[1] Traveling northward, tomatoes were harvested in Central America and then appear in salsas in Mexico where they were discovered by the Spanish.[2] The tomato made its way to Italy and France by Spanish conquistadors who were smitten by its taste. Pietro Andrea Gregorio Matthioli, an Italian doctor and botanist, is credited with classifying it as a nightshade and mandrake. He is also credited with naming the fruit (in about 1544) as "pomo d'oro" because it changed from green to yellow or green to orange-red. This name, which means "golden apple," morphed into "pomodoro."[3] Throughout Europe, the tomato was referred to as "fruit of passion" or "love apple" on the misconception that, as mandrakes, tomatoes had aphrodisiac powers. This myth seems to have been perpetuated by the French nickname for tomatoes, "pomme d'amour" (apples of love), which was probably derived from the Italian pomodoro.

North Americans Get Interested

While those on the European continent continued to eat *les tomates*, their counterparts in the Colonial North America were slow to adopt them. Early North Americans considered the tomato inedible, even poisonous. This false assumption was partly based on the tomato's membership in the *Solanaceae* (nightshade) family, whose members sometimes contain insignificant amounts of a toxic alkaloid. The botanical family *Solanum* includes tomatoes, potatoes, eggplant, peppers—and surprisingly, tobacco—which are significant to the diet and lifestyles of many cultures today.

Reportedly during the time of the American Revolution, a British supporter "made tomato ketchup in New Jersey prior to the time he moved to Nova Scotia in 1782," but it did not catch on in popularity.[4] Obviously, anything red, ripe, and luscious with "love" in its name and passion in its history did not play well to the Puritan heritage of most of our forefathers. However, in his journals, Thomas Jefferson reportedly fell for its beauty as an ornamental plant when he encountered tomatoes during his time as Minister to France. He brought back tomato seeds to plant in his magnificent gardens at Monticello and there are documented sources of the "recipes of his women" using tomatoes.[5]

Even the endorsement of a founding father and third president of the United States did not entirely convince the public that tomatoes were safe to eat. Some feared appendicitis or stomach cancer, as those eating tomatoes sometimes got sick with these and other afflictions.[6]

In truth, it was later discovered that eating tomatoes on tin or pewter plates could be deadly: the reaction between the acid and the metal blends would bring forth lead, causing lead poisoning. Wealthier planters in the southern states tended to use more china or ceramic tableware at the turn of the 19th century, and therefore were able to consume tomatoes more readily without lead poisoning. The connection of the reaction was not made until later when lead was found to be poisonous; tomatoes themselves were blamed as the culprit, though it was the lead in the dishes.[7]

A few decades later in 1820, Colonel Robert Johnson challenged the belief that tomatoes were poisonous. Johnson was a well-respected pioneer descendent, wealthy landowner, and farmer who brought tomatoes back to Salem, Massachusetts, from his travels. Johnson was also the president of the agricultural society and offered a prize each year for the largest tomato fruit grown, which was never eaten. Legend has it that he made a public spectacle of eating several tomatoes on the steps of the Salem courthouse to prove that tomatoes were not poisonous. He had some bloating but when he didn't die, the community saw that tomatoes were safe to eat.[8]

In other larger cities—specifically Philadelphia and New Orleans—many versions of tomato ketchup were being developed and consumed. Philadelphia physician and horticulturist James Mease wrote and released the first know recipe for tomato ketchup in 1812, reporting that, "'Love Apples' made 'a fine catsup.'"[9] Though there were many types of ketchups (among them walnut and mushroom varieties), tomato proved to be the most popular.

In terminology, tomato "sauce" was more readily used to describe a mixture with few ingredients and served immediately, while tomato "ketchup" was used to describe a sauce preserved for later use. It was the term "ketchup" that became more widely used.[10] By the mid-1800s, consumption of the tomato rapidly increased in North American households and the demand for processed tomatoes surged.

Early Hothouse Activity

Alexander W. Livingston of Reynoldsburg, Ohio, developed the first commercial tomato cultivar in the latter part of the nineteenth century. According to ohiohistorycentral.com, Livingston spent twenty years breeding a variety that was larger and sweeter than those locally grown.[11] He finally succeeded with his "Paragon" tomato, which he sold commercially through his Livingston Seed Company in 1870. Through the next twenty-eight years, Livingston developed more than thirty other varieties of tomatoes, continuing to sell seeds to Ohio farmers. Ohio became a leading contributor to tomato growing and processing in the nation at that time. (Each year, the city of Reynoldsburg ensures Livingston and his legacy are not to be forgotten by holding its famous Tomato Festival in August.)

In the 1920s, tomato plant breeding was primarily focused on developing disease resistance. Research at this time was conducted mostly at universities and by a few large food processing companies, such as CSC. Dorrance recognized this and partnered with the State

Tomato Anatomy and Taste

To more easily understand tomato genetics, it's helpful to have an understanding of tomato anatomy. Firmness, sugar-to-acid ratio, and volatile compound content are critical factors when breeding tomatoes for processing. The outer structure and internal walls are made up of skin and pericarp (flesh). The internal chambers, or locules, contain gel and seeds. The firmness of the fruit is determined by the wall thickness of the pericarp and the proportion of pericarp to locular tissue. Varieties with thick pericarps have a corresponding high amount of insoluble solids which produce thicker finished products. Conversely, cultivars with a larger ratio of locular tissue have better flavor.

The structural tissues of the fruit are complex polysaccharides consisting of cellulosic and pectin compounds. These volatile compounds give tomatoes their unique flavor. Other fruits and vegetables have the same sugars and acids as tomatoes. The preferred composition of the ripe fruit is equal portions of the sugars, glucose, and fructose and smaller quantities of the organic acids (citric and malic) that give tomatoes their tartness. The levels of sugars and acids in the fruit and the ratio of these components are crucial to whether the tomato has a desirable taste. A vine-ripened, fresh market tomato has a sweet taste with slightly-acidic background. If the ratio is reversed, the eating experience will be too acidic.

University of New Jersey at Rutgers to create a tomato variety called, appropriately, the Rutgers tomato. This was predominantly used as the standard tomato for mechanical harvesting until the development of other varieties.[12]

Major advances in tomato breeding have occurred after the 1960s with improvements in yield, disease resistance, and firmness.

The trend on where this research happens has been reversed; however, the majority of plant research is now done by food companies. Over the next thirty years, tomato products invaded grocery shelves by the hundreds, including whole, peeled, or diced tomatoes, purees and sauces, ketchup and salsa, pizza and prepared pasta dishes, and soups and juices. Demands began to grow for better-tasting tomatoes.

Machine v. Man v. Fruit

Until the 1960s, all harvesting had been done by hand to avoid bruising or "breaking" the fruit, but the yield volumes were lower than the demand. In addition, migrant labor issues had become a political flashpoint (along with many other social unrest disputes in the United States in the 1960s). Growers and food processors were moving as rapidly as possible to reduce manual field labor, and the best option available was the newly-invented mechanical tomato harvester.

Successful designs of this invention happened both on the West Coast and the Midwest. In California, an agricultural engineer named Coby Lorenzen at the University of California (UC) is credited with the early development of the machine, releasing the UC-Blackwelder model in 1949. Local machinist Ernest Blackwelder, with financiers and UC Cooperative Extension agents, helped to bring the concept to life.[13] However, use of the mechanical harvester did not spread widely until the 1960s, primarily because the crops harvested were not hearty enough—in plant or in fruit—to withstand the brunt of the lumbering machine.

Lorenzen worked in cooperation with Gordie C. "Jack" Hanna, a vegetable crops researcher at the University of California, Davis, to develop a plant hearty enough to withstand, or rebound, after harvest. The new harvester model was defined and distributed throughout the state, mechanizing California's tomato-growing business. "Partly because of this piece of equipment, California now produces 95 percent of the processing tomatoes grown in the United States."[14]

Meanwhile, Food Machinery Corporation (FMC) in the Midwest was developing a prototype of a similar mechanical harvester at various land grant universities such as OSU. Their needs were vastly different from the large farms in the sunny California climate. In the Midwest, growers tended to be smaller, and the expense of the harvester was borderline prohibitive. Plus, after a soaking rain, it would be impossible for any heavy equipment to enter the field without getting stuck. The fields would be rendered into tomato swamps of mud and standing water where no harvesting could happen mechanically. UC Davis and FMC played off each other's work, aiming to perfect the design of the mechanical harvester.

Red Top and the Square

Hanna's ideas regarding a breeding a tomato cultivar to withstand machine harvesting began to crystallize in 1947 and continued through the 1960s. His genetic research concentrated on three areas: 1) fruit maturity and ripening, 2) plant growth, and 3) fruit hardiness.[15]

To be able to economically harvest tomatoes mechanically, the majority of the fruit must mature at the same time. If the tomato plant continued to set fruit at multiple stages, there would be excessive yield losses due to uneven ripening. The red fruit has to be harvested before it spoils, and any green tomatoes harvested at that time would have to be discarded. The solution to this problem was the development of determinate varieties that, once the fruit sets, the plant stopped growing, thus forcing a majority of the tomatoes to ripen all at one time. A small determinate strain developed from Hanna's tomato breeding work between the classic cultivars Gem and San Marzano, which showed commercial potential, and was released as "Red Top."

The fruit and plant had to withstand the physical rigors of mechanical harvesting. As the heavy metal machine rolled through the fields with its long collecting arms and bulk containers, it would often crush, tear, or cut the plants and smash the fruit when harvesting. The research goal was to encourage the fruit to grow stronger skin and more solid walls to withstand this. Hanna discovered when the new Red Top was re-bred with San Marzano, a squarish-fruiting cultivar was developed and the resulting tomatoes would not bruise easily. When dropped, tomatoes from this newly-named "VF-145" cultivar would mostly bounce without splitting their skins.

Hanna also saw that this determinate strain met all three qualifications. They were taller, stronger plants with a very short fruit-set period to simultaneously produce a high percentage of ripe fruits, and the fruits they bore featured a greater firmness to protect them. Tested against the harvester, the VF-145 performed miraculously, with high yields showing little damage. It was released as "The Square" tomato in the early 1960s in California.

Almost immediately after the widespread adaptation of machine harvesters and planting of VF-145, this distinct competitive advantage shifted most of the tomato growing and processing westward. Thousands of rail cars began traversing the country on parallel ribbons of steel hauling tomato products out of California. With its desert-like sunshine, masterful irrigation systems, and large farms, California was the perfect setting to grow tomatoes used in processing.

Pioneering at CSC's Research Lab

Throughout the history of CSC, science was depended upon to produce its high-quality products. Scientists were located at all production facilities and at our research centers, especially at the CIAR. They were charged with the responsibility of evaluating the fresh vegetables that were being grown for our products. They also developed tomatoes, carrots, celery, potatoes, cucumbers, mushrooms, and many other vegetables. Eventually, we had our own vegetable varieties exclusively for use in particular products and for various growing areas of the United States and countries around the world.[16]

From the executive ranks to the plant manager level, demands were being made not only for fruit that could be successfully harvested by a machine but also for better-tasting tomatoes. Many of these varieties were needed, due to the very different growing conditions around the world (soils, rain, sunshine, temperature, and unpredictability of each). With the research advancing in other areas of the country, the executives at CSC were clamoring for cultivars achieving the company's flavor standards.

The company recruited a newly-graduated genetics PhD, Allen Stevens, to lead the charge. The lab was well-funded and had earned its excellent reputation as an agricultural research institution.

Dr. M. Allen Stevens started as a research scientist at the Agriculture Research Pioneer laboratory in the CIAR at the former Dorrance Farm. Interfacing later with him, I discovered a mutual respect and interest in plant breeding, similar academic training, and a shared distaste of academic politics. We were close in age, and both of us had brought our young families across states to work for CSC, Stevens arriving just two years before me. Our commonalities laid the foundation for a strong professional relationship.

When Stevens arrived at the tomato research facility, he found that he was in good company. His colleagues (some of whom had recruited him) were among the best plant scientists in the world. Among these were the prestigious Dr. Stuart Younkin, VP of the CIAR; Dr. Stanley Kazeniac, a Purdue chemistry graduate and his assistant; and Robert M. Hall. (Note: Kazeniac and Hall were actually in the Basic Research group in CIR&T.) They collaborated on the design of procedures that helped to promote and maintain these organic compounds in the formulating of finished products, as described in U.S. Patent No. 6,660,112 in 1969. Building on this knowledge base, Stevens began working to zero in on the gene and the physiology of the fruit that determined the creation of these highly-desirable flavor essences.

Campbell-146

The VF-145 cultivar, which had dominated processing tomato production in California for more than a decade, was displaced by an improved cultivar bred at the CIAR named "Campbell-146." The three scientists had identified two compounds. One was 2-isobutylthiazole, which is largely responsible for the unique flavor of certain varieties of tomatoes. The second was 2-alltylthiazole, which is an exceptionally strong flavor enhancer of the tomato or tomato food product and improves the mouthfeel properties. The scientists were able to breed a tomato with targeted levels of both in a new varietal, the 146.

Campbell-146 had excellent flavor and color characteristics for a commercially-grown tomato. CSC's food scientists and product developers had developed a proprietary process that enhanced the flavor of processed tomato products. No other food manufacturer had this capability and thus it was one of the main reasons for CSC's superior market position for tomato soup and tomato and V8 juices. Competitive products could not match their fresh-like tomato flavor. This became the gold standard, used for years to make tomato soup, tomato juice, V8, and other tomato containing products.

This advantage of growing its own tomatoes was featured prominently in the company's advertising during the 1960s and '70s. CSC

Prego Professional Profile

DR. M. ALLEN STEVENS

Few would predict that from a remote region of Utah known as "Little Hollywood"— where producers of Western movies came to shoot their films, a young agronomy student would make a major impact on the world's food supply. Yet Allen Stevens, who would become one of the leading tomato breeders in the world, grew up in Mount Carmel (with population of ninety in the 1940s) on a farm that can best be described as being just large enough to provide food for the Stevens family. Stevens would earn extra money during his vacation time wrangling livestock for the numerous companies filming cowboy movies. Employment opportunities in this sparsely populated region were mostly confined to tourism (Zion and Grand Canyon National Parks are nearby) and moviemaking, and it was obvious to the precocious high school student that his future career options would depend on being the first in his family to receive a college education.

Stevens headed off to the College of Southern Utah, now Southern Utah University, to begin his academic training, then transferred to Utah State University to finish his B.S. degree in agronomy. After a short stint in the military, he decided to return to Utah State University and pursue a Master of Science in soil science. Landing a job working for a food processor in Oregon, he moved north and later became an agriculture extension agent at Oregon State University. Soon, he was invited to apply for a horticultural fellowship funded by CSC. The catch: the fellowship was for a PhD in genetics and Stevens had never taken a genetics course in his life. This didn't stop Stevens. His ancestors, early settlers of southern Utah, were from hearty stock and used to meeting challenges. As their descendent, Allen Stevens was no exception.

Stevens readily accepted the fellowship and began his doctoral studies under the tutelage of Dr. Al Day, one of the premier flavor and food chemists in the world. Stevens was given the assignment to study the flavor profile of green bean cultivars that had been developed for commercial food processing. Compared with the gold standard of pole bean varieties such as Kentucky Wonders, the Bush-style grown snap beans lacked flavor. The goal of Stevens' research was to determine if the flavor difference was a genetic trait and, if so, if this serious deficiency could be improved through genetic modification.

Stevens completed his research work in an expeditious manner and successfully defended his dissertation. Although he did not crack the genetic code to improve the flavor of mechanically harvested snap beans, he helped to lay the foundation for future flavor improvement research work in green beans, sweet corn, and tomatoes.

Plant scientists from the CSC had followed his fellowship work and recruited him. His decision to join CSC was a win-win for both parties. Stevens joined one of the leading, if not the best, plant breeding research labs in the world; CSC attracted a protégé of Dr. Day, a recognized expert in flavor chemistry, and retained their investment in-house.

promoted that the quality of their tomato products was because of special tomato varieties that were developed by their plant breeders. The ever-popular Campbell Kids were illustrated as gardeners and truck farmers touting "You can't beat these!" tomatoes for fresh taste in CSC's products. Highly-successful campaigns featured pictures of plant breeders and tomatoes growing in the field were shown along with chefs inspecting a bowl of tomato soup.

The Square Rounds

Dr. Younkin's problem was that Campbell-146 tomatoes were so soft they could only be picked by hand. Newer cultivars, developed by crossing the Roma and Campbell-146, were called "Square Rounds." The name came from the shape of the tomato that had as its genetic base in the Roma cultivar, which had been used for years by Italian cooks to make sauces. Compared with both parents, the new, firmer Square Rounds had the taste and texture of red cotton, and this created major quality issues with Campbell Soup's flagship products. Right out of graduate school, Stevens was thrust head first into the crucible of the tomato breeding lab, greenhouse, and farm test plot. Similar to his work in Oregon, Stevens was to study chemical and genetic causes of the Square Rounds flavor.

Plant breeding is such a complex balancing act that if the genetics are modified to enhance some characteristics, a counterbalancing negative result can be induced. Breed a tomato to be firmer, and there is a corresponding flavor loss; tweak the DNA to produce a better-tasting product, and low yields with an increased susceptibility to disease occur. Referencing his graduate studies on snap beans, Stevens knew that the first order of business was to focus on the identification of the key compounds that represented fresh tomato flavor.

The young geneticist soon found himself walking a tight rope of complexity under unyielding pressure from management to attempt the seemingly unachievable. If increasing the volatile flavor components of the tomato were the only objective, the problem would have been a fairly straightforward process: identify the gene that controls the synthesis of aromatic compound formation and insert it in a new "Square Rounds" cultivar. In biology, nothing is simple and this is especially true when trying to improve plants that are being grown for their functional value, i.e., processed foods.

Multiple parameters have to be met before any cultivar could be released into commercial production. In the case of tomatoes, the new cultivar would have to demonstrate in multiple trials: high yields, high total solids content, desirable sugar-to-acid ratio, disease resistance, and adaptability to variable culture conditions. A negative score on any one of these determinant factors would render the cultivar as unacceptable.

Most experimental biological work is a reiterative process requiring many replications which results in slow progress. There are so many variables to juggle that rarely will one individual or lab achieve a breakthrough. It is a building block process and the more collaborators who are involved, the quicker the ultimate objective can be reached. While Stevens never solved the flavor problem, he laid the groundwork for the future C-38. Stevens' genetic discoveries were observed by Younkin, who encouraged Stevens to publish his research findings in biologic reproduction. Stevens' academic research experience, combined with CSC's excellent genetic material library permitted, in short order, the development of new hybrids that became important to the company for years to come. So successful was CSC's breeding program that a separate company was started to sell seeds on the open market. (Dr. Arnold "Bud" Denton, vice president for Research and Technology and president of the CIR&T, had a key role in the development of Campbell Seeds. Profits from the sale of seeds helped to pay for the entire vegetable research program.)

Return to Academia

After Dr. Stevens presented a paper at the American Society of Horticulture, he was approached by the UC Davis about the possibility of replacing Jack Hanna, the pioneering researcher in the development of tomato cultivars that could be machine harvested, who had retired. He took the job at UC Davis. However, Stevens was a researcher, not a politician, and didn't mesh well with inter-campus politics. He came back to CSC in 1979.

Plant Breeding Professionals

Providing the right varietal for the food concept was the puzzle these nine men—Livingston, Kazeniak, Hall, Day, Younkin, Lorenzen, Hanna, Stevens, and Crine—and dozens of others contributed countless hours of their lives to solve, understanding the modifications needed for growing and eating healthy and flavorful foods. Their scientific discoveries influenced generations of tomato offspring. Plant scientists and other agricultural professionals seem to be some of the most underappreciated professions in the world. Few people realize the significance of genetic research in food preparation and processing. The contribution they have made to the wellbeing of the billions of humans who populate the world should guarantee their positions as heroes. Yet, the fruits of their labor go primarily unrecognized, probably because they have been so universally successful that their advancements are taken as commonplace occurrences and the way things should be.

One hundred years ago, the nation's food supply was fraught with contamination, adulteration, and appalling spoilage losses. Just a few decades ago, millions of people were suffering from malnutrition and large numbers died of starvation every year. It is amazing how soon people forget when they are no longer starving. Norman Borlaug (1914-2009) was an American-trained plant pathologist who launched the "Green Revolution" that saved millions of people from starvation through the implementation of improved cultivars of rice, wheat, and corn (along with best agronomic practices) in Third World countries around the globe. For this effort he won the Nobel Peace Prize in 1970 and ranks as one the most important individuals of the twentieth century.[17] However, very few people in the United States would recognize the name "Borlaug." If one mentions the Green Revolution today, most people would think you are talking about windmills or paper recycling, but it was a major effort to save the world's population and plant life. Without his discoveries, the number of food products available globally would be noticeably fewer, possibly extinct, because of susceptibility to plant illnesses, natural predators, and food's own degenerative processes. Today, our food supply is the safest and most nutritious in the history of mankind.

Fortunately, there is a new awareness around the security of food availability. The image of agricultural professions has shifted from backwards, stupid, and dirty to exciting, high-tech, glamorous, and in-demand. Professionals working in these areas have been showcased on many cooking shows, restaurant competitions, home and garden magazines, blogs, and social media, as well as sustainability events. Agricultural programs are a vital part of many colleges' curricula, and jobs for graduates of these programs are abundant.

The two Campbell employees, Stevens and processing expert Steve Stewart, formed a very strong team who greatly advanced the company's tomato breeding and processing expertise. This team helped provide CSC with a distinct competitive advantage over other food processors and is one of the reasons CSC still processes the majority of its own tomatoes. (Most other formulated food manufacturers, like Heinz, now contract out all their tomato paste requirements and no longer operate tomato processing facilities.)

After that, Stevens was promoted to the vice president of Agriculture Research for the entire company, overseeing programs as diverse as improving the stability of okra in canned condensed soups to nutritional research on chicken feed formulations.

Agricultural professionals may not yet have the prestige of computer scientists or aerospace engineers, but the perception about them is changing. Many are starting to realize that the science and business of farming (and its associated enterprises) have had a greater impact on the quality of life in the United States and the world than any other endeavor (next to modern advances in medicine). Advances in agriculture to increase food supplies and nutritional value increase the standard of living worldwide, making all other advances possible.

And it is the plant scientists and other the agricultural professionals—like those who worked for CSC—who enable ground-breaking research such as this. The company continued its commitment to farming and breeding, fostering a competitive advantage it enjoyed for decades.

(Endnotes)

1   K. Annabelle Smith, "Why the Tomato was Feared in Europe for More than 200 Years," *Smithsonian*, May 24, 2017, http://www.smithsonianmag.com/arts-culture/why-the-tomato-was-feared-in-Europe-for-more-than-200-years-863735/.

2   Andrew T. Smith, *Pure Ketchup: A History of America's National Condiment* (Washington, DC: Smithsonian Institution, 2001), 18.

3   "Tomato," *Wikipedia*, June 26, 2017, https://en.wikipedia.org/wiki/Tomato.

4   Smith, *Pure Ketchup*, 18-19.

5   Lucia Stanton, "Tomato: An Article Courtesy of the Thomas Jefferson Encyclopedia," *Thomas Jefferson Foundation, Inc.*, May 31, 2011, www.monticello.org/site/house-and-gardens/tomato.

6   "Robert Gibbon Johnson History," *Tomato and Health*, May 22, 2017, http://www.tomatoandhealth.com/index.php/en/article/story/robert_gibbon_johnson.

7   Smith, "Why the Tomato was Feared."

8   "Robert Gibbon Johnson," *Wikipedia*, June 26, 2017, https://en.wikipedia.org/wiki/Robert_Gibbon_Johnson

9   Smith, *Pure Ketchup*, 19.

10   Ibid., 19.

11   "Ohio's State Beverage–Tomato Juice, *"Ohio History,* May 24, 2017, http://www.ohiohistorycentral.org/w/Ohio%27s_State_Beverage_-_Tomato_Juice.

12   Ibid.

13   Ann Filmer "How the Mechanical Harvester Prompted the Food Movement," *UC Davis*, June 8, 2017, https://news.plantsciences.ucdavis.edu/2015/07/24/how-the-mechanical-tomato-harvester-prompted-the-food-movement/.

14   Kathy Coatney, "The Machine that Revolutionized a Harvest," *Ag Alert,* May 17, 2017, www.agalert.com/story/?id=554.

15   Filmer, "How the Mechanical Harvester Prompted the Food Movement."

16   Gaehring, *A History of Campbell's Soup.*

17   "Norman Borlaug," *Wikipedia,* May 14, 2017, https://en.wikipedia.org/wiki/Norman_Borlaug.

6

Tomato Solids
Task Force

. . . .

"**S**haub reminds me of a plodding Dutch farmer," remarked one
Campbell executive, who obviously was not in Harold Shaub's
fan club, when walking out of a difficult planning meeting.
The statement of frustration was in reference to Shaub's rural Pennsylvania roots and his understated personality. It was also suggestive
that the recently-appointed president of the CSC was stubborn. For
me, this reference conjured up someone who was concerned about
stewardship relative to the company and its employees, dedicated,
hard-working, modest, and most importantly, honest. Yet I could
see the difference in the two interpretations and was bothered by
this statement. First, because I did not believe this was a true image
of the man; second, I wondered if the same individual referred to me
as a "plodding German farmer."

Prego Professional Profile

HAROLD SHAUB

Harold Shaub grew up near the Amish farms in Lancaster, Pennsylvania, and started his employment at the Camden soup factory after graduating from Drexel University in 1938. His training in mechanical engineering provided the foundation for rapid advancement through the production ranks to the Standards Department (SD), where he developed an expertise in and a thorough understanding of operations. He was a quick study and had a talent for numbers. He was transferred to the Chicago production facilities as part of the management team and then was promoted to head all of the Canadian operations. Shaub's extensive understanding of manufacturing gave him the tools to greatly improve the overall organizational structure of production. He was the guiding force in the construction and staffing of the new plant in Maxton, North Carolina, and he supported equipment upgrades leading to the improvement of efficiencies within the existing manufacturing operations.

Over time, and contrary to this early "plodding" assessment of the company's top leader's abilities, Shaub proved to be a shrewd operator with well-thought-out ideas when he replaced the retiring Bev Murphy as president in 1972. The decade of the '70s proved to be the most turbulent time in the American economy since the Great Depression. Shaub upgraded the financial controls function and recruited key executives in strategic planning and accounting. He shifted the primary focus from production productivity to a balance between productivity, strong financial positioning, and development of proprietary ingredients and technology. Together, these would enhance CSC's vertical integration strengths in raw materials processing and keep the company strong.

Leadership Transition

The three presidents of the canned foods, frozen foods, and international divisions were hard-working, highly-intelligent individuals who started their careers with CSC. They were superior logisticians and had survived a Darwinian-like selection process to advance to the top positions within their division. All three were corporate officers and heavily invested career-wise and financially in the company. Each was a unique force unto himself, but the trio had another similar trait—they were stuck in the same myopic rut of short-term vision. Their focus was on making their year-end production goals and covertly resisted making expenditures for capital improvements or marketing they were not certain would make a desirable return on investment within a relatively short time.

When the annual plans were submitted for each division, they were essentially duplicates of the previous year regarding budget and development plans. The percentages may have changed for each line item depending on special circumstances, but in reality, it was the same document, year after year. This was a Campbell legacy holdover from the 1930s and '40s and deeply engrained as the modus operandi of the senior management team. This is how they had been trained and thus how they operated. This incremental approach had served CSC well for the last three decades, but Harold Shaub instinctively knew the day he was selected to be president things had to change at every level. Going forward, excellence in logistics had to be matched with excellence in strategic planning if the Campbell Kids were to survive the Decade of Aquarius.

In the last quarter of the twentieth century, CSC was the world's top-five leader in the production of each of the following commodities: tomato products, poultry, fresh mushrooms, tin cans, and cooked beef. The company was vertically integrated in the growing and processing of almost every major commodity used in its finished products. This combined expertise gave CSC further competitive advantage in procuring and formulating its raw materials in high quality, value-added food products.

Where many in the company viewed these satellite operations as stepchildren to the soup and frozen food plants, Shaub saw a gold mine of opportunity. All that was needed was imagination and technology to turn these commodities into proprietary ingredients. Shaub had the vision and the commitment to provide the resources to fund the development of the technology. Throughout the tenure of Shaub's presidency, his initiatives to streamline the labor-intensive and time-consuming poultry processing, explore microwavable containers, and improve tomato paste production paid large dividends. "Plodding Dutch farmers" are very difficult to detour once they set their course, and regardless of his pace, Shaub's course was full of impactful, fulfilled initiatives.

It may be true Shaub was not one of the more charismatic executive leaders within the CSC organization, but he was smart and he could envision operational improvements where others were blind. He however did not suffer fools and he expected everyone within the management organization to understand in depth the details of their job and areas of their responsibility. Shaub also had a sensitive side, which most employees rarely saw, and he treated people fairly, giving opportunities to those in which he saw potential.

Forming the Task Force

It was Shaub's initiative to impanel a task force to explore and develop additional usage for tomato paste in new and existing CSC products—thus addressing a critical need of the company to utilize the increased capacity of tomato paste available after the purchase of the Dixon, California, plant in 1977. Campbell already owned two other paste plants to provide tomato solids for its line of tomato soup, tomato juice, V8, and other assorted soups and products—making the company the second largest tomato processor in the world. The addition of the Dixon processing facility, however, created a large surplus capacity which was a very ominous, unprecedented situation in the CSC culture. It was critical not to waste this surplus or the opportunity to launch new tomato products and strengthen the company's position in the market. After all, the competitors never slept. Representatives for the task force were chosen from Marketing, Production, Product Development, and an external advertising agency, and the team was ready for the challenge.

High-Viscosity Paste Pursuit

Drawing on my observations from a decade earlier in my graduate school pilot plant, I leveraged my green bean research on pectin methyl esterase (PME), as this enzyme is also present in tomatoes. I began to focus my attention on how to process the tomatoes so that the pulp and liquid phases would not separate, or "weep."

As part of the Tomato Solids Task Force, I had toured the Sacramento and Dixon tomato paste plants. On my return, I made a recommendation that even though it was late in the season we should try to make a high-viscosity tomato paste (that had arrested the PME reaction) so we would have product to run experimental tests on ketchup plus other tomato-based products. Harold Shaub gave the go-ahead and the Stockton tomato paste plant was chosen as the manufacturing site. I was on a plane two weeks later headed back to California.

Top Secret Test at the Stockton Plant

In late fall of 1977, we ran a "secret" test at CSC's Stockton tomato paste plant. With existing "cold-break" soup production lines, I raised the temperature as high as I could to process the tomatoes. Arguing with the engineer and plant manager, I was finally able to

PME

Most of us have heard of fruit pectin, which is often used in making jellies and jams. Pectin is the glue that holds the cell structure together, and the name of enzyme that causes a breakdown of the cell wall structure is "pectin methyl esterase" or PME.

When an apple falls from a tree and hits the ground, a reaction is triggered which starts the rotting process. As the fruit breaks down, it also provides nutrients for next year's germinating seeds. This reaction is known as an "auto-catalytic" reaction. When the flesh is bruised, an enzymatic reaction immediately takes place to begin the breakdown of the pectin. This process is nature's way of breaking down vegetation. Without this reaction, apples would pile up knee-high under a tree year after year, and next year's seedlings would potentially starve.

It's easy to see this spontaneous reaction by cutting an apple slice and then bruising the cut profile with your thumb. Soon the flesh will turn brown and start to lose its structural integrity. PME acts as an acid to break down the walls of the cells in this reaction in most vegetation. This same reaction occurs in tomatoes. With simple physical pressure to the skin of a tomato, a soft spot develops at the point of contact. After the tomato is bruised or cut, the surrounding tissue turns to mush.

Enzymes are nature's catalyst; without them life would not be as we know it. Enzymes allow biochemical reactions to occur at the lower temperatures of plant and animal life than otherwise would occur without their presence. Some enzymes help to form the complex building blocks of life and others break down these forms to their original constituents. In food processing and preservation, an understanding of enzyme reactions is critical to the final quality of the food product.

My graduate research study was on the impact processing variables had on PME in green bean quality related to firmness and epidermal sloughing. What I learned in my research on both tomatoes and green beans is temperature during processing is a most critical and important variable in determining firmness of the green bean pods and thickness of puréed tomatoes. To my surprise at the time, the results were counterintuitive. Lower preprocessing temperatures for green beans produce a firmer and more structurally-sound pod after heat sterilization than a higher temperature on processing. This would ultimately figure into the solution to weeping spaghetti sauce.

You can smell a tomato when you cut it because of complex biochemical reactions that create intense flavor notes and aromatics. Slicing or chopping fresh tomatoes activates these enzyme systems instantaneously at ambient temperatures; however, the enzyme is inactive at certain higher temperatures. If the tomato is heated to a critical temperature prior to chopping, the enzyme is denatured and the pectin is retained in its natural form—so the walls do not break down instantaneously and the product will not weep.

To achieve non-weeping paste, we would have to denature the enzyme. Though this sounds like a simple concept, it was very difficult to achieve. The PME reaction would need to be arrested before it happened. The challenge was to develop a process which could handle large volumes of tomatoes—tons of tomatoes per minute—being simultaneously heated and chopped without the environment dropping under that critical temperature. Even micro-seconds at a cooler temperature will allow the enzyme to break the down the wall, causing the mixture to lose the viscosity. We were in for a big challenge against PME.

jack up the temperature in the break tank enough to complete a hot break process. The plant people were nervous that the thicker tomato paste was maxing out the circulation motors plus there was concern the seals on the scrape surface chillers would be blown out. I knew this was a risk, but we needed a high-viscosity tomato paste to do our formulation work and this was the last chance of the season. It was a tense situation but I stood my ground knowing that I had full backing of the top executive back at the GO. I have to admit though I did have nightmarish-visions of shutting down the operation as I did the Goldfish line trying to make a heat stable chew biscuit, but thankfully nothing like that happened. The resulting paste was "good enough" to do experimental "kitchen runs" with tomato-based recipes in Camden. It was time to give the new tomato semi-hot break paste to Chef Werner Schilling. He and I would work on formulation while the engineers would continue to work on the experimental equipment design to be tested at the R&D pilot plant located at the GO in Camden, New Jersey on tomatoes flown in from Florida.

PME and the Heat Sink

The pilot plant equipment was designed in Camden on a small scale to replicate a large manufacturing plant hot break unit for Sacramento. There was one major departure in the design, based on my observations of the Stockton test pack (plus research as a student at OSU), and that was the tomatoes must be "broken" (crushed or chopped) while immersed in a liquid bath of tomato pulp at a temperature greater than the critical temperature, hence earning the name "super hot break" (SHB) process. Any deviation below that would immediately activate the PME enzyme and break down the pectin in the tomato tissue.

The Ketchup Wars

Through Murphy's and Shaub's terms, Heinz and CSC were involved in a major competitive battle. Heinz had been continually losing market share in the canned soup market through the 1960s, and in an effort to try to cover its manufacturing overhead expenses, that company resorted to "private labeling" soup products for the large retail chains. Private labeling is the production of generic products to utilize excess manufacturing capacity. They were generally not held to the same standards as the branded products. With less expensive products and no marketing expense, these private label brands could be sold for a lower cost. CSC had made a strategic decision never to do private label, because the lower pricing of these products did not cover the overhead to make them.

Heinz maintained its "Heinz" product line while producing private label, and their overall operating margins became less and less. Frustrated at its lack of ability to compete with CSC at the retail level, Heinz management struck out with whatever weapon they could—and the most well-known of these was lawsuits.

In two very famous legal battles, Heinz attempted to drag CSC's name through the mud. The first was via a major accusation of false advertising. In 1969, it had been revealed to the Federal Trade Commission (FTC) by an unknown source that in photography sessions for soup advertising campaigns, an over-eager account executive from the advertising firm had placed marbles in the bottom of a soup bowl so the garnish would be more visible. This was obviously an embellishment to enhance the appearance of the soup to make it appear to have more ingredients than it actually had. It was also illegal, and CSC received a summons from the FTC. Even though the marbles had been placed in the soup unbeknownst to anyone at CSC, the responsibility fell on the company.

The embarrassment turned into sheer anger when CSC was informed that the complaint of marbles in the soup was brought to the FTC by none other than H. J. Heinz Company—the marble incident had been shared with them at the advertising agency, who also had Heinz as an account.[1] From this point on, the tension between the two companies ratcheted up several degrees from a purely business rivalry to one with strong personal overtones—CSC's integrity was being challenged.

The FTC suit was settled amicably when it was revealed CSC had no knowledge of what the ad agency was doing during the advertising shoot and CSC agreed to change the procedures to ensure all future photographs would not be doctored. In addition, all photography sessions would be witnessed by a member of the product team who would be responsible for ethical images. However, the complaint was revisited a year later by FTC Chairman Paul Dixon, who began formal proceedings against CSC. With suits and countersuits between Heinz and CSC, the mudslinging complaint litigation lasted an additional two years through multiple petitions and appeals, and involved fourteen federal judges and cost multiple millions of dollars to defend.[2] Though the complaint was finally dismissed, the undercurrent of animosity between the two companies would continue to run strongly.

Heinz Lashes Out Again

In the mid-1970s, Heinz went for CSC's jugular. Though filing multiple complaints over the years, the granddaddy of them all claimed "Unfair Trade and Predatory Practices" at the retail level. Simply put, they claimed CSC was maintaining too much space in the grocery stores aisles between their many soup lines. The lawsuit would go down in the soup business as the biggest copy operation in CSC history to provide evidence for the trial. Files from executives and managers about known retail practices at many levels were subpoenaed for evidence. I saw when the defense required a separate building to be commandeered for defense activity and preparation, as this was the time before digital records and everything was done on paper. The suit interrupted operations in the sense that efforts were diverted from normal operations to this trial. In the end, the case was settled without prejudice.[3]

Heinz continued to intensify its well-known practice using its ketchup as an inducement to force restaurants and food service operators to purchase their other industrialized food products. If these customers wanted Heinz ketchup, then they had to purchase soup, sauces, and other products offered by Heinz's food service division. It was all or nothing. Customers could not purchase CSC's products if they were buying Heinz ketchup. When CSC's sales teams met resistance in trying to sell CSC's products, top management decided to go after Heinz where it hurt: in the ketchup franchise.

In effect, the complaints were saying CSC's top management were crooks and liars; this obviously did not go over well with the Philadelphia elites, who thought of themselves as above such behavior. John T. Dorrance Jr. and Harold Shaub each took these charges as personal insults. Shaub handed another directive down to the Tomato Solids Task Force: use some of the surplus tomato paste to develop a new ketchup that would compete with Heinz. Our mission was to develop a superior product, develop it fast, and beat them at their own ketchup game. Ketchup had been one of CSC's flagship products in its early days, but declining sales had mandated that the product be taken off the shelves. It was time for a rejuvenated effort.

As a director of special products within Product Development, I was asked to be the technical product development representative on this project. I was both thrilled to be appointed to a top-level task force reporting to the president and anxious about having to develop a product to go against Heinz ketchup, the gold standard in the industry.

Know Thy Enemy: Heinz Ketchup

In preparing for this ketchup battle, the Task Force members investigated every aspect of its competitor. Heinz ketchup was one of the most entrenched consumer food products in the mind of the American consumer, and our team had to find any weakness. Consumers of the ketchup were unshakably loyal, which CSC understood in relation to its own successful tomato soup.

The most loyal customers of a particular product seem to be those individuals who began consuming the product at an early age and acquired a taste for the product. In nationally-leading products, there is a unique factor, in either the formulation or the manufacturing process, which creates a flavor signature that distinguishes itself from other similar products, and the consumer palette expects that. Just like a key in a lock, the mouth registers a fit with the recognized product. If there is any difference to the taste, color, and/or mouthfeel there is a mismatch, and thus a rejection. Consumers don't like it, as was seen in the "New Coke" product rejection.

CSC conducted more market research to further decode the attraction to Heinz ketchup, hoping the studies would pinpoint something to replicate or replace in a Campbell's Soup product. The results on consumer preferences of Heinz ketchup were discouraging. When asked what they disliked about Heinz ketchup the answer was, "Nothing," and when they were asked what they would like to see done to improve their favorite condiment, they responded even more strongly, "Nothing. Why would you even try?"

They had a point. H. J. Heinz had first started making ketchup in mid-nineteenth century, which became part of their Anchor Brand product line.[4] Heinz ketchup was ubiquitous on grocery store shelves, holding the dominant position while Hunt's, Del Monte, and local producers fought for any remaining retail space. Further, the majority of restaurant tables had a bottle of Heinz ketchup sitting next to the salt and pepper shakers—so Heinz ruled both the home-use and commercial-use ketchup kingdoms. The Heinz neck label and the octagon-shaped bottle gave a very distinctive appearance, one which had originated in 1890, and was easily recognizable.[5]

Heinz had released several different brands and sizes of ketchup, with a unique flavor profile that many of its competitors—including our chefs—tried to deconstruct. We had another Mission Impossible.[6]

Breeding, Breeding, and More Breeding

Meanwhile, the research scientists at the company's three breeding facilities (pioneer labs in Cinnaminson, New Jersey; Napoleon, Ohio; and Davis, California) aggressively continued research on a multitude of cultivars for products in addition to ketchup. In particular, the Napoleon-based plant breeders had been focused on developing a more durable tomato for the variable Midwest summers that could produce high yields with high-solids characteristics and be mechanically harvested. After years of breeding and refinement these goals had been achieved in a new tomato cultivar known as C-38.

The often forgotten X-factor in Prego's success was the new high-solids, high-viscosity tomato cultivar developed by plant breeder Bill Taylor and the breeders at CSC's Napoleon agriculture research center. Its parents were the Italian sauce tomato Roma and the relatively-new Square cultivars that had been developed for its thick walls that would hold up to machine picking. These tomatoes formed the foundation for tomato paste and tomato products.

It had performed admirably under production conditions at the Napoleon plant's production of tomato soup, tomato juice, and V8. It was decided that this would be the cultivar to be planted under secrecy for the planned SHB paste test run at the Sacramento paste plant. It had the best characteristics likely to produce a superior SHB paste of any other Campbell cultivar available. Seeds of the C-38 cultivar were shipped from the Napoleon research labs and given to trusted growers who had long-term relationships with the company, and there was no security concern on this front.

Secret Weapon - Discipline

CSC was comprised of two divisions, one for canned foods (i.e., soups, Franco-American pasta products, pork and beans, and juices) and the other for frozen food (Swanson dinners and fried chicken). Each division had its separate organization structures with a director and product managers forming the leadership. A major reorganization promoted Ralph Miller to vice president within CIR&T, as the head of all product development activities for the company. In this role, he created the Product Technology group to explore and development new processing techniques.

As part of this group, the product technologists and development managers employed both luck and technical expertise, interwoven with a creative mindset and the ability to bridge the cultural divides of the various functional departments within the corporate structure. These ranged from Production to Marketing, Finance to Sales, Bench Research to Plant Breeding, and Engineering to Executive Row. The successful manager had to be able to communicate with these various disciplines, gain their respect, and sell his vision.

Fifty years ago, college curricula (especially within the food sciences) did not focus on teaching how to develop new products. The product development manager of this era was primarily self-taught, learning from the inputs of the current environment, reviewing what had happened in the past, and studying market research to forecast market needs.

Product development within the company could be re-iterative or linear. The food technologists innovated, improved, or extended product lines, considering input from market research and other sources. Ideas were conceived by any number of sources including the chefs, the food technologists, marketing, and consumers. Hundreds of ideas would be evaluated.

Formulation occurred when prototypes were developed in the kitchen or tested in the pilot plant. From there, good ideas were separated from bad (undoable, impractical, or too expensive). Dozens would be attempted with the chefs daily preparing prototypes for approvals to test. When an idea was deemed worth pursuing, the product would continue to undergo various stages of analysis including rigorous taste testing, reformulation, mass production adjustments, costing, and refined packaging. Where corrections were needed, they were made, and the cycle was repeated in that part of the process. Only a few ideas would make it to the end consumer. The product development gestation generally took twenty-four to thirty-six months on new products and eighteen months for line extensions. With the stress of constant market competition and potential tomato inventory building up, there was never time to waste.

The key to all this, I was to learn, was tenacity. After a particularly taxing project, Denton, vice president for Research and Technology and president of the CIR&T, said to me, "Bill, congratulations on finishing this project. Of course, you know why you and your team succeeded, don't you? Discipline was the key, and it's always the key to getting something done."

While listening to this impromptu lecture, I thought to myself, "Boy, are you nuts. Do you realize the technical hoops we jumped through to complete this job? Do you realize the long hours we put in and the number of reformulations we tried? Discipline had nothing to do with it. If he thinks this was how the job was done, he was badly misinformed."

Denton was in charge of all of R&D so ultimately he was responsible for Prego during its later stages. He and Bill Williams—Alexander M. "Bill" Williams, vice president and later president of the Canned Food Division—worked together like Generals Grant and Sherman, hard chargers who did not believe in "giving quarter." Each would be in their respective offices at 5 a.m. and would be the last to leave at around 7 p.m. Both were tops in their profession and there was no way anyone was going to outwork or outsmart them. In yet another reorganization of the R&D department in the CIR&T, I found I was reporting to Denton.

Denton always expected immediate results when we were working on any development (most likely because he was getting pressure

Prego Professional Profile

DAVE GAEHRING

"Who or what was that?" I asked my colleague, as a blur of white zoomed passed us in the hallway. At the time, I had only been on the job a couple of weeks and was still getting to know the product development staff. "Oh, that is Dave Gaehring. He is a technician working on V8 and other tomato products," was his response, quickly adding with an amused look, "We call him 'the Roadrunner!'"

They say first impressions are never wrong, and my intro-duction to my future partner on the SHB tomato paste process development team proved on target for our many years of working together. Dave is the grandson to Charlie Gaehring of plant management fame, and arrived at CSC in 1962. He was a veteran R&D professional in his own right, working in the Beverage Product Development group.

I came to realize Gaehring's pilot light was never off; a flick of the switch and his burners were at full throttle ready to take on any challenge. Head and back erect with arms swinging in synchronization with his legs, he moved with purpose and efficiency that some of the best-trained athletes in the world would envy.

As we worked together, I saw that he was one of the rare individuals not shaped externally by education or career path, but instead shaped by the internal forces of fortitude, faith, and a solid work ethic in his DNA. He wasn't shaped by peer pres-sure; he was confident in his own abilities. Like his grandfather, the younger Gaehring was equally passionate about his job, family, and religion. Any external influence only refined his per-sonality and can-do attitude. As one colleague later remarked, "Dave Gaehring is the best. He was a tomato guy backed by great basic research on tomato paste. Not a political bone in his body. He just wanted the best product from a consumer view."

Gaehring quickly was recognized for these contributions and promoted within the Product Technology group. As the V8 processing expert, he accompanied me to the various plants to conduct research in the winter, later taking over the responsibility of the entire project.

from Williams) and when I would try to explain what obstacles we were up against he would dismiss them with a gesture, which meant if you just worked harder with more discipline you could solve any problem.

Years later, I came to understand what he was saying as one of the watershed learning experiences of my life. With so much experience under his belt, Denton knew the only way to overcome obstacles and complete tough tasks was through rock hard discipline. Little did I realize that those hoops, long hours, and extra efforts we put in on different projects were exactly what Denton was defining as "discipline." With all the distractions of the world we live in today, without strong mental and physical discipline, it is very difficult—no, it is impossible—to stay on task, let alone complete those tasks, and that's where tenacity comes in. You need the willingness to submerge yourself in the details and keep at it until a solution is reached.

The great thing is that discipline, and focused technical ability, can be learned. Like a well-trained soccer team or military unit, a disjointed group of people can be trained to become champions. Precise training and repetition of results-oriented activity with positive reinforcement helped employees of the CSC, like me, understand their important roles within a larger unit, and how they could continue to assist in the achievement of company's desired results.

The A Team

By that time, I was heading up a Product Technologies team that included several product development technologists, two chefs, and two secretaries, as well as Bill Stinson, my fellow Buckeye, who we had recently hired as a manager. Together we were working on multiple exciting product concepts in addition to the tomato solids formulations. Delegating the work from the Task Force, I immediately identified Dave Gaehring as a top contributor. Since the day I met this research technologist, I was impressed with his energy and dedication.

Our Quest for the "Non-Weeping" Spaghetti Sauce

Without brand managers on our Product Technology team or the Task Force, it was up to us to surface product development initiatives. We had numerous projects we were exploring, always adding new ideas to the list of possibilities. I recalled my "weeping spaghetti sauce" saga from OSU (See the Prologue.). At that time, I said if I had the chance to develop a much more superior tomato sauce for the market, I would. And here it was, the chance to develop it. To top it off, I had just read an article about Ragu and Hunt's, competing in the market using large advertising budgets to market inferior products. It was time for a new opponent to launch in the market, one using fresh and natural ingredients. This became my focus.

My first step would be a trip to California to tour the Dixon and Stockton tomato paste plants and review their operations for capabilities and capacities.

(Endnotes)

1   Scott, Linda M. "Shooting Marbles: Another Look at the Landmark Campbell Soup Deceptive Advertising Case." *Advertising& Society Review 12, no. 4* (2012): page range. Accessed June 24, 2017. https://muse.jhu.edu/article/468053.

2   "Complaint in the matter of Campbel Coup Company, et al. [sic] *Federal Trade Commission,* June 2017, http://rms3647.typepad.com/files/campbelsoupftc.pdf

3   Ibid.

4   Collins, *America's Favorite Food*, 27.

5   Smith, *Pure Ketchup*, 43.

6   Ibid., 43.

7

Plant Works

· ·

D iving deep into the details was the modus operandi of CSC's management, especially in the Production division. Most corporate officers did not have many pictures on their stark walls, but Bill Williams, by now president of the Canned Food Division, had prominently displayed a framed plaque which said, "God is in the Details." When I first saw it, I thought instead, "The Devil is in the Details," but I was quickly instructed on his perspective.

Williams graduated top of his class at Princeton, and despite understanding both macro and micro thinking, he wanted the details. He would sit behind a mahogany desk in his leather chair, expecting anyone reporting to him to be into the details as well. Denton was also detail obsessed, and if you were so unfortunate as to be in front of either in Williams' office, you could expect a Spanish Inquisition-like firing of constant questions. To be fair, Denton and

Williams had the ultimate of trainers in this methodology, learning the culture from a long line of managers of the same ilk: Dr.
Dorrance Sr., Bev Murphy, and of course, CSC's sitting President
Harold Shaub, the ultimate detail man. And the tradition of reliance
on details was extended down to the plant operations to show their
control of their quickly-expanding business.

Every plant manager and his team of managers and supervisors
were expected to have encyclopedia-like memories for *every* detail
of plant operations and mental computing skills which would rival
Dustin Hoffman's role as a savant in the movie *Rain Man*. For some
individuals, this was a natural extension of their native intelligence or
the product of extensive training; for other plebeians, their mode of
survival was carrying small notebooks with crib notes (or in some cases
thick three-ring binders). Being able to recall return on investment
(ROI) percentages for functional and esoteric pieces of equipment, to
recite material yields and labor efficiencies, and to know the grade and
type of lubricants used on every piece of machinery was a given. The
plant manager was also expected to know the name of every worker in
his organization and, if the employee was in a supervisory position, he
was advised to know the names of the employee's spouse and children.

A State Affair

A visit by a senior executive from headquarters to any plant was
treated as a state affair. Plant management welcoming the visiting
dignitaries had an opportunity to showcase their facility, people,
and knowledge, but as their knowledge was tested, their pride and
their patience were tested as well.

My corporate education included witnessing the rituals taking
place before, during, and after these visits while working in the
Sacramento plant one tomato season. The plant would go on
high alert weeks before by cleaning, painting, repairing, and quizzing each other on every topic that could possibly be asked. There

Explosive Growth

In the 1970s, CSC's footprint spread wide across the United States, providing jobs by the thousands and developing new products by the dozens. The company built and acquired multiple locations to optimize the geographic strengths, seasons, and climates throughout the nation. Specialty operations for producing chicken, turkey meat, and broths were located regionally. The company's frozen food plants generated products in South Carolina, Maryland, Nebraska, and Arkansas. Biscuits, cookies, and other Pepperidge Farm delights originated from the main bakery in Connecticut. Canned food plants, manufacturing the famous condensed soups and other products, operated in New Jersey, North Carolina, Ohio, Illinois, Texas, and California.

Tomatoes were grown in the Midwest states of Ohio, Indiana, and Illinois, as well as the East Coast states of New Jersey, Delaware, and Maryland. In time, the central valley of California became the major tomato growing and processing production area in the country. Its endless sunshine—coupled with huge quantities of water available through government-financed dams and irrigation canals—made a perfect habitat for growing tomatoes. For CSC, tomato paste processing operations were located in Sacramento, Stockton, and Dixon, California (acquired in 1977). The River Plant in Camden, which had been a large part of CSC's tomato processing in the early part of the century, became obsolete, when in 1947, the Sacramento soup plant was built and began production of tomato soup, tomato juice, V8, and tomato paste. It remained in production for a few years as a specialty tomato processing plant, no longer using river barges to deliver tomatoes.

were planning meetings and rehearsals to present the compulsory numbers and projections. Tensions ran high, layering on top of what was already a highly-stressed atmosphere.

Then, the big day came when Shaub arrived, and everyone stood at attention on pins and needles. As with all dignitary events, the Sacramento leadership team greeted Shaub and Williams at the front entrance of the factory. As they entered the lobby area, Shaub paused and commented, "My, your lobby looks beautiful." Glancing at the floor and then looking straight at the plant manager, he asked, "What is the name of the wax you use to make the floors look so nice?" Stunned, the plant manager desperately searched the faces of his staff for a lifeline, but all eyes were on the highly-polished floor, so in a resigned voice he responded, "Let me get back to you on that question." Obviously, this head of a $1 billion-plus company could care less what kind of polish was used on the linoleum floor in the lobby of the Sacramento plant. This question had nothing to do with profit and loss or the quality of the products being produced, but it had everything to do with the mastery of the details of the operation. Questions such as these established hierarchal control with implied intimidation that you never could know all the answers, even if you thought you did.

Under a Magnifying Glass

Expectations of the plant manager were high. In addition to the preparation for executive visits, daily reports were sent to head-quarters and numerous questions from corporate staff were fielded. If the production numbers or relations with labor deteriorated, the plant manager's position was in jeopardy. In return for these lofty expectations, plant managers enjoyed a wide range of autonomy and most ran their operations as modern-day feudal warlords.

All plant managers had been trained, or rather had survived, in the Darwin-like process of eliminating those weak of heart, energy, and intellect. Only the toughest made it to the top of this proverbial food chain. All others were consumed by the system and delegated to important but lesser positions within the chain of command or

Prego Professional Profile

FRED TYLER

Fred Tyler, head of the Dixon Tomato Paste Plant, was the epitome of a plant manager. His plant, located just outside of Davis, California, is approximately seventy-five miles northeast of San Francisco and fifteen miles southwest of Sacramento. As part of his vertical integration initiatives, Shaub purchased the plant to augment the tomato solids needs for its various tomato-based products. The plant owners, the Richards, were selling their tomato paste on the open market and were only too happy to sell their operation to their largest customer. The facility was purchased "as is." Campbell made only minor equipment modifications in the filling of the fifty-five-gallon finished product containers, which, once full of tomato paste and frozen, would be shipped across the country for use in Campbell's Soup's various tomato-based products. Everything else was already according to the company's specifications. The existing management staff, including Tyler, was retained to ensure a smooth ownership transition and operation.

In the fall of 1979, I met Tyler as a member of the CSC's Tomato Solids Task Force. Tyler was a young John Wayne-type with a hint of Clint Eastwood, impossible to miss. He accented this aura with Western dress and high-heeled cowboy boots that added several inches to his already large six-foot-five-inch frame. He had the build of an NFL tight end, but his speech and vocabulary was that of a rodeo bull rider. His intimidating physique was only exceeded by his Texas-sized attitude about California. It didn't matter what the subject was—people, women, music, agriculture, tomato processing, or car manufacturing—anything from California was the best, in his opinion. Like most people who do not travel far from their birthplace, their beliefs become provincial facts in their minds and no argument will convince them otherwise.

Like many individuals who went to work for food companies in the 1960s, Fred Tyler had grown up on a farm. His father was a manager of a 500-acre tree farm in northern California. Life on the farm instilled a deep passion for agriculture and an interest in food production in young Fred. His mother was from a pioneering family which had come west from Boston, Massachusetts. Her parents were school and college teachers following the legacy of her grandfather, who in 1860 was the first schoolteacher in Marysville High School in California. Under his mother's tutelage, he developed an intellectual curiosity for learning.

When Tyler turned nineteen, he knew the time had come for him to look for a job. He had set his sights on becoming a field man for one of the local food processing companies. He was acquainted with the buyers who called on his father to purchase peaches and other fruits, so he asked for a job. He was hired and his first job was working in the Bercut-Richards Packing Company in-house gas station.

After a short time on the job, he worked up the nerve to approach the owner of the canning company, Tom H. Richards Jr., for a job as a field man. Richards, who would become Tyler's lifetime mentor, took an instant liking to the tall teenager; however, Richards had a different take on Tyler's future employment path. He told Tyler that all managerial personnel must first work inside the plant to learn the processing operation and systems. Following Richards' advice—as he would do throughout most of his career—Tyler took a job as a mechanic trainee, working approximately a year in this position before he was drafted into the army. Richards graciously welcomed Tyler back to his old job after service and asked him if he would like to go to school. Tyler readily accepted Richards' sponsorship and worked summers as a mechanic while studying food processing at Cal PolyTech. Tyler earned an associate's degree after two years of study, and then returned to work in his former position along with eleven other young men, all in their twenties. Richards was a seasoned and experienced businessman, gaining invaluable management and leadership skills as a commander of a quartermaster company landed at Omaha Beach, Normandy, on June 6, 1944. He led the company throughout the European campaign supplying the ever-demanding General George Patton's Third Army. He was also a keen observer of rising talent, and he saw himself in Fred Tyler.

During this time, the war in Vietnam was rapidly escalating, and so was demand for California's food products. At the start of the 1965 season, Richards held a company meeting with all the factory workers and when he introduced the twelve new hires, he asked all those gathered, "Anyone less than forty years of age please stand." Only twelve people rose from their seats. He next asked, "Everyone over fifty years of age please stand." When everyone in the room except the new employees stood to be recognized, it was obvious that the company was heavily weighted with long-tenured employees. The need was apparent: to learn to work together quickly, transferring knowledge from more experienced to the less experienced. And they did. As these older workers started to retire, the younger generation employees began a rapid succession up the ranks of supervisors and managers with Tyler leading the pack.

Nine years later, Richards named Fred Tyler the plant manager. Fred brought with him two of the original mechanic trainees he had started with, and when CSC purchased this tomato paste production facility five years later, Tyler and his colleagues remained in place. He was to hold that post for over twenty years.

outside the company. By the time an individual had reached the plant manager level, he was so steeped in CSC culture that, when cut, he would proverbially bleed the patented Campbell red.

Plant managers were held strictly accountable not only for every detail concerning the operation of their plant, but also the resulting finished product on the grocery shelf. I once observed the president of CSC admonishing a plant manager because a soup can, produced at that plant manager's location, had a torn label in the store. It did not matter that the label may have been torn by the stock boy putting the can on the shelf; it ultimately came back to be the responsibility of the plant manager. How does a plant manager control the appearance of his products on distant grocery shelves? He ensures that all products leaving his facility are in first class condition and communicates with the sales force in his distribution area to make certain that all goods on display are of top-quality appearance.

Despite these pressures, the plant manager role was a coveted leadership position in the CSC hierarchy. He was the "captain of his own ship," and, as in most navies, there were more aspirants than ships available. He was invested with a large responsibility over a complex facility that, in many cases, was the size of a small town. Operations were carried out with military-type precision in an organizational structure that emulated the U.S. Army in World War II. It was top-down, command-and-control, and the plant manager's word was law.

S.O.B.

The term "S.O.B." is an apt descriptor for the rarefied few who achieve the plant manager title. To the casual observer, plant managers could be arrogant, mean, driven, and myopically-focused individuals; however, the abbreviation S.O.B. stood for "Survival of the Best" at CSC. In the truest sense, the best did survive and flourish. So much was expected of the plant managers—especially during executive visits and tomato season—they passed this pressure down like a hydraulic press with exponential force to their staff and then on to the production floor. The lower you were in the organization, the greater the applied pressure per square inch you faced. Plant managers were always respected and sometimes feared by the factory workers. No one was safe from rebuke, even in the restroom. One day early in my career, I overheard two laborers talking while in the restroom, and one said to his colleague, "I was in here the other day and John Miller walked in, and I swear he is the only person I know who can make a person stop peeing midstream!" I had not yet met the Camden plant manager, but I resolved then and there to take all future bathroom breaks in the R&D area no matter where I was in the factory when the call of nature beckoned.

Behind the Scenes at the Paste Plant

Oversight of a manufacturing operation demanded a tremendous amount of focused energy and attention, and even with complex electronic controls, skilled supervisors, and regular plant walk-throughs, it was not an easy task. Plant equipment contained too many pumps and motors to be counted, with the multitude of conveyors to process hundreds of thousands of pounds of raw materials into finished product. The job is not for the faint of heart, which helps explain the ego and confidence associated with most plant managers.

All employees of the tomato processing plants shouldered pressure and pain during tomato season from mid-August through mid-October. During that time, the plant ran continuously, only shutting down for a major equipment failure. This seldom occurred. The experts, veteran plant engineers, spent the off-season maintaining the equipment, taking machines completely apart, and replacing any worn equipment or parts. They were responsible for everything mechanical to be cleaned, reassembled, and lubricated, much like servicing a car but exponentially more intricate. Lines were shut down sequentially at night and cleaned one by one, while tomatoes continued to be processed on the other running lines.

If a piece of equipment did fail (for example, a motor, a pump, or a conveyor), repairs were made immediately as production shifted to other lines within the factory. A shut-down piece of equipment meant the rest of the line's activity could be compromised and final volume negatively impacted, and no one wanted to risk that consequence. In the event of a shutdown, the plant managers could be found right next to the engineers and maintenance guys, on their backs with crescent wrenches, trying to beat Mother Nature's clock as tomatoes, backing up in the yard, threatened to rot in the 100-degree weather outside if not processed soon. That's why the plant managers never wore suits to work, and that's why there were many days during season when the plant manager and his supervisors never saw a bed, working through the night to ensure production ran smoothly and any repairs to bring a line back on-stream were made as quickly as possible. Pressures and temperatures ran high.

The heat, the humidity, and the noise were part of the "Disneyland"-type experience for me. I was enchanted as the equipment ran almost continuously over a two-shift per day schedule. I was spellbound by the reliability, sanitary design, safety, and maintenance of product quality and integrity provided by these machines, which were also the top priorities in design of food processing equipment.

Camden-Style Engineering

One of the best-kept secrets of CSC was the expertise of its engineers. Outside of the company, few would appreciate the significance of their intelligence and talent, but we saw it on a regular basis. Whether located at Camden headquarters (in the General Engineering department or the Engineering R&D

department[ER&D]) or located in the manufacturing plants, these brilliant professionals were the ones who designed—and in some cases fabricated—the equipment that made everything possible in manufacturing.

Food engineering is a specialized profession. Not only is a solid knowledge of fundamental engineering principles required, but equally important is an understanding of sanitary design that prevents spoilage by microorganisms in cracks and dead spots of the equipment. Cross-contamination by foreign materials is also a concern when fabricating and installing food processing equipment. The advancement of highly resistant and aggressive microorganisms make this an even more difficult challenge plaguing the meat and dairy industries. For these reasons, CSC required that a professional engineer be on the premises during the installation of all new processing equipment.

As a junior research technologist, I saw that the very foundation of CSC's 100-plus-year success, put in place by the genius of Dr. John T. Dorrance Sr., was a strong manufacturing base. All manufacturing relied on the design or modification of any needed equipment or process. We would ask the engineers to create unique, one-of-a-kind tools, machines, or systems. They had their own design and machine shops, and would often build their equipment prototypes or modify the equipment first, then contract with other fabricators to build larger or more complex versions. Building in-house kept the design process streamlined and confidential.

On large-scope projects (involving both experimental development and installation into manufacturing), engineers from both departments would be assigned. This is what happened after the pilot plant SHB tests were completed at the R&D complex in the winter of 1978. The new equipment would be used in the Sacramento paste processing plant.

Bob Winkler, head of the General Engineering department, assigned Charlie Long, a long-term employee who was the company's top tomato processing engineer, to work with the Product Technology group as the lead engineer. Ed Delate and Tom Fong (from General Engineering) and Bob Hockenberry (from ER&D) joined the team as backup support and also to facilitate the future installation in California.

We had moved into the new research facilities located in Campbell Place, the corporate headquarters on the outskirts of Camden on the Cooper River. The multi-story facility housed two floors for Product Development, and then the remaining floors housed Basic Research and ER&D. General Engineering was in the headquarters building near the GO. The Campbell Place complex also housed the new pilot plant, whose facilities were pristine and modern compared with the venerable in-town Camden plant.

Though physically located in different buildings, the product developers and I worked with the engineers on pilot designs. The engineers would clarify the requirements and costing, then mock up the idea. The prototype would be reworked to fulfill its requirements, then it would be manufactured for use in any of the various processing locations. Now we were pleasantly surprised to learn we wouldn't have to wait until the fall to test our new equipment.

February Tomato Season at the Camden Plant

New Jersey, Ohio, and even California residents recognize classic tomato season happening in the warm months of August, September, and October, so when we had tomatoes to process in the middle of February—with snow on the ground—it was a rather unique adventure for all involved.

Our president, Shaub, demonstrated his super strategic thinking ability by instructing us to plant in a warmer climate to harvest the tomatoes earlier in the year. While we had experienced some success with a modified SHB procedure at the Stockton paste plant, Shaub wanted to further develop the process specifications for the SHB procedure in Camden before committing to a full-blown production test in the fall at the Sacramento paste plant.

We planted in the Homestead, Florida, farms and by the late winter/early spring, we had mature tomatoes to work with. These tomatoes were fully-grown in Homestead, air-freighted into Philadelphia, and trucked to us in Camden. Needless to say, it was such an unusual phenomenon to have fresh tomatoes available for testing at this time of year. This two-season testing became a major part of our equipment design research efforts, and we gained an advantage over our competitors who still developed around one season. It was also the subject of high curiosity for those not assigned to the project—it seemed many people wanted to see what we were doing! So special was the attraction that Shaub asked if he could bring John T. Dorrance Jr. himself to the pilot plant to observe an experimental run.

Of course our answer was yes. When they arrived, I had the privilege of describing what we were trying to accomplish on our prototype hot break unit. Talking to the number one and number two executives in the CSC hierarchy was an incredible opportunity for me, but I was a little anxious. They were both very enthusiastic and encouraging, asking many good questions. (This was the only time that I had been on equal level with a president of a major corporation because, standing next to Dorrance, Shaub, and I were both his employees. Strangely, this is also when I learned that even presidents have bosses; they answer to the board of directors, the owners, and, of course, the customers.)

Strategic Planning 101

With new demands from two seasons of tomato production, we would have to put together a strategic plan. And Bob Subin, AKA Captain Planner, was just the person to guide me. Subin was the first strategic planner brought in by Shaub for counsel on new company direction. I remember the day I was called into his office. It started simply enough.

Hearing my soft knock on his open door, Subin raised his eyes and enthusiastically said, "Good morning, Bill. Thanks for coming over. Hope you are well. How are things in R&D?" "Great; pleased to have the opportunity to talk with you," I responded, shaking his outstretched hand. Subin directed me to a seat in front of his desk, inquiring, "What do you know about strategic planning?" I paused for a few moments before sheepishly saying, "Not much." My education was about to begin.

Subin must have witnessed a reaction to this question like mine many times since joining the company a few months previously, because he smiled and seamlessly went into a well-rehearsed soliloquy on the benefits of strategic planning to better chart the future.

Strategic planning is a process of predicting the future based on current day factors and best-guess long-range projections. Most individuals, when first introduced to the concept of strategic planning, rejected the process as being too academic, "blue sky" and not real world. One of the biggest challenges of the early practitioners of strategic planning was to convince their colleagues the process had value and could produce meaningful and actionable results. This could only be achieved, however, if everyone participated in an open and cooperative manner. Decades later, it is still true that achieving this is a lot easier said than done.

He stressed how important this process would be in the identification of new product and process developments to provide a competitive advantage in the marketplace. Archrival Heinz relied more on the innovation within the companies they acquired and created few products inside the original company; CSC's position was opposite. This was music to my ears, as I had been challenged to identify new opportunities on my own over the last several years. My small group of technologists were assigned to special projects from the various divisions, which made them vulnerable between project starts and

Prego Professional Profile

BOB SUBIN

Bob Subin was one of the early pioneers in the field of strategic planning. He had earned an MBA in accounting and finance from the University of Pennsylvania's Wharton School of Business. After graduation, he went into the army and then worked in strategic and corporate development at two large, diversified companies, Gulf + Western and IU International Corporation. These multi-national entities exposed him to a variety of personnel and operational challenges which provided him with vast experience to draw on in support of CSC's first formal strategic planning efforts.

To succeed as a strategic planning leader and facilitator, one needs to have a good understanding of human nature. Other necessary attributes include being resolute and not being easily intimidated by negative feedback and obstinacy of his fellow employees. In some cases, these people were in superior positions, so having a high level of confidence and a thick skin helped. Subin was one of those rare individuals who possessed these special characteristics. He was quick on his feet and was not easily diverted from the subject, whether seeking an answer to a critical question or putting the final platform of a strategic plan in place.

Bob Subin's talents became readily apparent to CSC's top management. Along with his strategic planning duties, he was also soon doing special assignments for Shaub, which included being an envoy to Murphy, enabling Subin to go to different departments. Murphy, the just-retired president, remained on the CSC Board of Directors and acted as an advisor and sounding board for Shaub.

In addition to Subin's technical expertise, he also had well-refined diplomatic skills which in corporate jargon meant that he could relate equally well with staff personnel or senior vice presidents and even iconic former presidents. In the public arena, he would have made a great politician. These combined abilities would carry Subin far in the corporate world, but the immediate challenges ahead would test every one of his strengths.

shut downs. To hear someone from corporate articulate a systematic planning process caught my full attention. We would finally have a plan! I knew I would enjoy learning more about strategy as well as working with Subin. Our two groups would be attached at the hip shortly thereafter when Subin was promoted to the general manager of the Grocery Strategic Business Unit (SBU) and I was promoted to the director, Product Technology group, with responsibilities as the R&D representative.

When I got up to leave that day, I noticed a stack of handwritten pages on Subin's desk and made a casual comment that he must have started work very early. Subin demurred and said, "Yes." He had been in the office since 6 a.m., but what he was working on was soliciting funds for research on a chronic disease that had made his daughter very sick. Walking out of his office, I was impressed not only by Subin's strength of vision, but by his humanity, which drew loyalty from not only me but many others.

Don't Mess with SD

At IU International, Subin had interacted closely with Dick Censitis, a fellow University of Pennsylvania graduate. Censitis was a star basketball player in the late 1950s, earning first-team All-Ivy-League and later Big Five Hall of Fame honors. The two developed a close working relationship and became good friends, a friendship that endures in retirement.

Recommended by Subin, Censitis was hired by Shaub to overhaul the financial forecasting functions at the company. CSC, especially the manufacturing division, was obsessed with numbers. At the time, their Standards Department (SD) had to be one of the best in the world. Those professionals measured and recorded everything that could be counted or timed, and dutifully reported their results to management.

The SD, later known as Industrial Engineering (IE), was staffed with engineers and analysts who were tacticians in a holy war with numbers. The enemies were inefficiency and poor yields. The analysts relied on their weapons of slide rules, Monro-Matic calculators, and the ultimate computer, the human brain. This was before the advent of the transistor chip, which allowed the digitization of logarithms to create electronic calculators and computer processors to run spreadsheets. It was a time when those with the fastest fingers and nimblest left-dominated cerebral cortexes ruled.

Within each manufacturing production office, groups of women were hunched over large Monro-Matic table top calculators punching in numbers to determine the ingredient yields and labor efficiency results from the previous shift. The clicking of the gears of the analog calculators was so loud it sounded like automatic weapons firing, but the end justified the means. These figures were then presented in the production supervisors meetings, and woe to those who did not meet the SD's target.

Many people inside the company would weigh in on new products or line extensions. We learned whose opinion mattered. When the finance guy gives an opinion on flavor, remember it's influenced only by how much things cost and you don't care about his opinion. When an engineer guy weighs in, you remember he could eat rocks and may not notice the flavor, so his opinion doesn't really matter either. However, when marketing guy or marketing research guy gives an opinion, you pay attention. They know the customer, and they know the competition and care about beating it, so you really consider their opinion. Their input helps you meet the correct balance between cost control and correct formulation to meet your consumer's needs.

But the extra-important opinions came from those in the SD. If their opinions were that your product—no matter how good it tastes—could not be brought "on-line" at a competitive cost, you won't get their approval. If you didn't get their approval, all the money, time, and effort put into its development is wasted, because the product will not go forward. For them, it came down to the numbers.

Accounting and accountability was deep in the DNA of CSC operations. So deep, one could argue, management was more fixed on the micro day-to-day production results than the macro view of the overall performance of the company as viewed by the financial community. This is not to say the company was poorly managed; quite the contrary. When an entity is working on a low profit margin, every percentage of a penny counts. CSC was excellent at operations, and this was Shaub's training ground.

One of Shaub's many gifts was to direct the company into a more professional governance of CSCs financial matters. Still, the hiring of Censitis was a bold move for him. This was a clear signal to the GO staff and the Wall Street financial community that he was not content with the way things had been done in the past, and he planned on bringing in a new order of discipline regarding strategic planning and financial accounting for the future. The proclamation echoed through the hallway of mahogany row that top positions in the company were no longer entitlements to the rarefied few who were on the top of the management pyramid. Loyalty and tenure were always cornerstones of the Campbell culture, but now these attributes no longer were an assurance of one's upward mobility.

This had the effect of raising everybody's game, and the transformation began, starting at the processing plant level.

Employees at all the plants—from the management to the line workers across the country and the world—knew our end "boss" was the customer. Regardless if the workers were in Camden, Sacramento, Napoleon, or other places around the world, they knew they were part of a team that created wholesome, nutritious, and flavorful products for their customers, and in a financially-responsible way.

I continue to think of these technology-driven manufacturing worlds as magical and the products they create as innovation exemplified—especially the special tomato paste that would become the main ingredient in the formulation of the future famous spaghetti sauce.

Four 'soup can' tanks that supply water for the soup made at the Campbell's plant are a highly visible Camden landmark until the factory is demolished in 1991. (*Courier-Post* file)

Bill Hildebolt with son Bill with Lassie,
the TV superstar dog.

Product presentation in the Product Committee Room.
Left to right Roger Schnorbus, William Hildebolt,
Chef George Berton, Jack Dodd, Steve Hough and Glenn Boyd

Chef Werner Schilling, 1977

Dave Gaehring at the Product Technology Office, 1982

Bill and Ruby Stinson Christmas Party, 1983

The Alpha and The Omega: Sandra Hildebolt and
Chef Werner Schilling at a Christmas Party, 1983

Fred Tyler, Plant Manager,
J.G .Boswell Tomato Paste Plant, 2011

Dave Gaehring, Lynn Garwood and William Hildebolt, 2011

Sandra Hildebolt, Laurel Cutler and William Hildebolt, 2016

Formulation

. . . .

The CSC has a long history of employing chefs in their product development efforts and this became one of the keys to CSC's superior quality products. Chefs worked alongside the food scientists and technologists, adding in their expertise and style.

When I started my career in product development, I did not have much use or respect for the chefs who ran their kitchens like Third World dictators. From my perspective at the time, they were arrogant, tempermental, and as a group could be classified as functional "drama queens." When they were mad, which to me seemed like a perpetual state, they threw pots, screamed at everyone (including their bosses), and threatened with meat cleavers. For these reasons, I kept my distance from them until the day Werner Schilling and I had a major misunderstanding over the dough hook.

That was my first real contact with any of the chefs and it only reinforced my anti-chef perceptions. Further compounding my prejudices, a couple of years later, I was leading a tour of visitors through the experimental kitchens and introduced one of the French chefs as the "chief cook and bottle washer" for Swanson TV dinners. Later that day in the hallway outside of his kitchen, I was informed by the offended Frenchman, "I am not a cook, and I do not wash dishes!" He then walked off in a huff, leaving me speechless. This was an important lesson for a young and inexperienced technologist like me. To be successful working with the chefs, you had to realize that they were sensitive and you had to be careful how you spoke to them. They demanded respect for their culinary professionalism, which I later learned to appreciate at a very high level.

For the next several years, I had no further interaction with any of the chefs. I avoided them and, likewise, they avoided me. After accusing one chef of stealing a dough hook and another of being a cook, I was persona non-grata among the chef cabal. But, as fate would have it, there was a major reorganization in product development. My boss, in an attempt to give me experience working with existing products (versus exclusively focused on special assignments), transferred the food service development group to me. This involved the development and product support for Campbell's Soup's line of canned and frozen products sold to the food service industry, which included restaurants and large institutions. The group was composed of several senior product development technologists and ... Chef Werner Schilling.

Given the opportunity of working on the existing product line for the first time, I was faced with a steep learning curve. I was apprehensive and realized that I was going to have to rely heavily on my new staff, including Schilling. I was more than a little wary at first, but any animosities from our previous encounter melted away like snow in an Alpine valley in springtime. As I started to work with Schilling on a daily basis, I found a very dedicated and talented individual. He

Prego Professional Profile

CHEF WERNER SCHILLING

Schilling was built for hard work and endurance. He was large boned, well-muscled, and his hefty hands were calloused from years of manual work. Schilling was born in the United States but raised in Switzerland. The influence of these early years was so deeply ingrained into his manner of speech and persona that it defined his character, like cocoa powder in a fine Swiss milk chocolate. Once the amalgam is blended together it can never be separated without losing its identity. At a very early age, Schilling began apprenticing under a master chef and later was drafted into the Swiss Army as a cook during World War II. After hostilities ceased, Schilling began working in a series of restaurants, resorts, and hotels, reaching the rank of executive chef and then being transferred to the United States. He was next hired by the CSC as an experimental chef to work on food service products.

Historically, Switzerland has always been a small Alpine country located in the midst of much larger sovereign states that were continuously at war. The Swiss, however, for the last 150 years have avoided all fighting conflicts, including the last two world wars by declaring their neutrality. This was quite a feat when you consider that their next-door neighbors are France, Italy, Germany, and Austria. Part of the reason for Switzerland's isolation was their location high in the Alps, but it was also due to their independent determination and self-sufficiency. These characteristics run deep in the Swiss population after generations of successfully standing up to neighboring dictators and hostile military forces.

Contrary to the perception that many people around the world may have, the Swiss are not pacifists. They have ferociously guarded their borders and had, and still do have, a well-trained, well-equipped, and disciplined army. They strongly believed in military deterrence and not aggression. This was exactly my experience years earlier when I first confronted Chef Schilling in his kitchen over the missing dough hook.

When I got to know him better and saw past his deterrence façade, I realized that he was not a prima donna, nor did he have the high strung, drama-prone characteristics of his French and Italian colleagues. Schilling was even-tempered and pleasant to work with, and he followed directions well. Ray Shivers remembered Schilling as the calmest of the chefs in the product development organization. But, Schilling was not immune to resorting to the dictatorial demeanor of a classically-trained European chef when his kitchen staff did not perform in a manner acceptable to him. He was a dedicated worker and he expected no less from those around him.

had a passion for developing and preparing good food, and he was well versed in almost every aspect of food preparation.

When I entered Schilling's kitchen, I was always amazed at the chefs' efficiency and work ethic. I also found it amusing to observe the chefs working amongst the kitchen staff like peacocks in the middle of a flock of chickens. With their foreign accents and aristocratic behavior, the chefs added an exotic and ostentatious flair to an otherwise sterile environment. They strutted and everyone else scurried out of their way. The helpers, technicians, and technologists were all clad in plain white while the chefs wore a uniform identifying them as the culinary professionals.

As with many traditions passed down by craftsmen, there are important functional reasons for their appearance. Take the chef's uniform for example. As Schilling explained, the white coat is made of heavy cotton with long sleeves. The white reflects the heat of the kitchen and the long sleeves protect the arms from spills of hot oil or water. The front of the coat is double-breasted, fastened with knotted cloth buttons which easily slip out of place if the coat has to be rapidly removed because of a spill. Cloth buttons also avoid the embarrassment or irritation of having a broken plastic button ending up in the béarnaise sauce. The flaps of the double-breasted front can be reversed after the top one becomes dirty.

The tall hat, known as a toque, could only be worn by a trained chef. This tradition had its origins in medieval Europe when chefs held high rank in the king's court and were permitted to wear a "crown" minus the gems. A trusted keeper of the king's food was as important to the king as all his generals and bodyguards combined. So, the chef's hat is worn as a badge of pride and as a sanitary food handling practice (i.e., keeping hair and perspiration from landing in the middle of someone's meal). Simple black shoes and finally, the gray-checkered pants help to camouflage food stains. Working with them, I came to understand that the blustering and posturing—just like wearing the chef hat and uniform—was all in the character of being a chef and they played the part with pride.

Here, in addition to their creative efforts and appearance, the culinary team took great care in keeping a clean, safe, and healthy environment for their food product formulation and testing. I remember looking inside CSC's experimental kitchens for the first time, witnessing the foreign world of the spotlessly-clean stainless steel and white porcelain. Appliances and tools gleamed in their places, ready for use. A few years off the farm and out of the academic lab, I was unaccustomed to the regality of European chefs and professional kitchens.

The CSC executives were proud of their European-trained, executive-level chefs on staff, which separated CSC from most food companies. I naïvely and somewhat arrogantly dismissed this information as so much recruiting hype and good public relations. It was not until many years later when I began to visit high-quality restaurants and touring Europe did I realize that there was a whole different world out there that was the "world of good food" prepared by professional chefs. They complemented us product development managers and technologists who, while highly trained in the technology and science of food, were provincial in our knowledge of and taste for good food. I quickly grew to expect the level of professionalism, safety, cleanliness, and quality that I learned from employing culinary professionals to produce good food for the retail shelf.

These beliefs were validated once again when Procter & Gamble (P&G), who only employed engineers in their product development department, introduced Pringles in the 1970s. P&G, one of the world's greatest retail product marketers, pulled out all the stops to promote it. They spent tremendous amounts of money on promotions to break into the well-established potato snack market.

Unquestionably, the processing technology was innovative, and later it was patented. Frito-Lay and Nabisco were caught flat-footed by the new competition, and it appeared as if there would be a major paradigm switch in this hugely-popular retail food segments. P&G had everything going for it except for one critical feature: taste. Pringles tasted like fried mashed potatoes (which they were) and the mouthfeel was even worse. Due to P&G's muscle in marketing and sales, the product had a successful launch, but later sales dropped because the product only appealed to a niche market.

This is what happens when engineers are allowed to drive new product development in the food industry. This approach may have worked well for Ivory soap or Tide washing machine detergent, but not for food that someone might actually want to eat. They needed to recognize that food prepared by a chef is going to be superior to that made by an engineer. CSC realized this early on, and incorporated professionally-trained chef talent and expertise in the formulation of every product.

Marinara

One of the many advantages of having executive chefs was that they knew what the gold standard was for cuisine, and Miller saw to it that we learned what good food was. This involved the practice of "flavor scouting." Periodically, members of the team would be sent to investigate best dishes at the best restaurants for new product ideas and to understand how they were prepared and presented, and how they tasted. It was a fun and enjoyable part of our job that often resulted in prototypes.

We had begun experimental tests on various hot break procedures in the Camden R&D pilot plant. After working with these tomatoes for two months, we had many formulations for ketchup and other tomato sauces, yet we were still working to perfect them.

The experimental hot break paste run success earlier at the Stockton plant held much promise to be the key ingredient for the ketchup, and we were looking forward to incorporating the tomato paste in the ketchup formulation plus new product concepts based on tomatoes. We had compiled a whole list of prototypes for Chef Schilling to work on, and in conversation, I added another.

"Last weekend, at a restaurant I was served a 'marinara' sauce that was thick and delicious," I told him. "I think you can create something like it." Schilling was in agreement. I shared with him my spaghetti sauce problem from my graduate school days. The marinara approach plus the experimental hot break tomato paste might just be the formula for the "non-weeping" spaghetti sauce, I hoped.

"Go to the R&D library, work through the various recipes in your Italian cookbooks, and see what you can do," I requested. The library was a vast resource with recipes in multiple languages and cuisines, and was a good place to look for base formulation. This was just the type of project Schilling excelled at, and we both were excited about the possibilities. Little did we know, the Ohio farm boy and Swiss chef were about to break the spaghetti sauce monopoly enjoyed by Ragu and Hunt's in the 1970s. The formulation of Prego had begun, and the tomato products marketplace would forever be altered.

Formulation of Tomato Products

When formulating tomato products such as tomato soup, ketchup, and V8 juice, the ratio of the sugar content to acid level must be consistent and uniform between batches. Otherwise, the flavor varies unacceptably, either being too sweet or too acidic, and the customer expects a certain flavor from the same product.

In some cases, this can be a complex calculation in that the two variables have to be simultaneously adjusted. In ketchup formulation, this is a straight-forward process of adjusting the sugar content by the amount of corn syrup added, and adjusting the acid level by the amount of vinegar (acetic acid) added.

Products like tomato soup and spaghetti sauce present more of a challenge. The sweetness of these products can be adjusted by adding or subtracting sugar, but, because there is no acid in the recipe, the tartness factor has to be controlled by the acid level in the tomato concentrate that is used. Because of this, efforts continue with tomato breeding, growing, and formulating. Like grapes used for winemaking, tomatoes vary in their sugar and acid levels depending on growing conditions, variety, water (through irrigation and rain), and maturity. The acid and sugar content of each tomato paste lot is recorded, and the lots are selected for their usage in specific products by the food technologists.

The First Hot Break Test Formulations: Campbell's Ketchup and Marinara

After the experimental hot break product from the Stockton arrived in Camden, it was given directly to Schilling. The tomato paste was special, with a beautiful red color and nice viscosity so no thickening was needed. Immediately, he formulated the paste into the Campbell's Soup ketchup recipes.

We tried diligently to replicate the sweet caramelized background flavor that lingered after the more volatile vinegar and spice notes dissipated by tweaking the sugar-acid ratios up and down by adding various amounts and forms of sugar and vinegars, caramelizing the sugar before adding it to the tomatoes, manipulating the spice blend and levels, and trying to find a balance between clove and cinnamon, but to no avail.

Stack Burn

Back in the test kitchens, nothing worked, despite the expertise of the team. One of its lead product developers was Robert Fields, who had worked on the original Campbell's Soup ketchup in the 1940s and '50s, prior to its discontinuance. Beefsteak Tomato Ketchup was produced since the company's inception through the 1950s, and the Tabasco Ketchup was manufactured from 1892-1921.[1] CSC was the leader in ketchup manufacture and sales until World War II. At that time, the War Department required Campbell's Soup to manufacture sea rations for the army and Heinz was given responsibility for manufacturing all ketchup. By the end of the war, Heinz Ketchup was the standard of the industry, and Campbell's was the soup and stew king (through Bounty Stew brand).[2] There were countless varieties of ketchups (or catsups) produced in the country at that time, but now the FDA had created standards of identity of ketchup formulation restricted to tomatoes, spices, salt, sugar, and vinegar.[3]

I had spent a summer as a quality control technician in a tomato ketchup processing plant in southwestern Ohio, and I was fairly familiar with both the formulation and process. The FDA has standards of identity of ketchup formulation restricted to tomatoes, spices, salt, sugar, and vinegar. We knew making ketchup was straightforward: chop hot tomatoes into a slurry, extract the seeds and skins, concentrate the tomato pulp in a large kettle, and add sugar, vinegar, spices, and a sweetener. Fill bottles with the resulting

Secret Formulas and Procedures

Formula and procedures for Campbell's Soup products were considered top secret proprietary information, and the documents that detailed these were held sacred. Very few people had clearance to the Procedures Room, which was controlled and monitored by the secretary to the vice president of R&D. No copy of any document was allowed to be removed from this sealed vault, nor could reproductions be stored outside of the sealed area. Dr. Dorrance created the bi-modal approach for product recipe security whereby the company divided the formulas and the procedures. To further ensure that CSC's products could not be replicated by the theft of one document, the formulas (ingredients and weights) were stored in a separate ledger from the procedures (blending instructions such as timing, stages, and temperature). In other words, if an unauthorized person gained access to a vegetable soup formula, he would have the list of specialized ingredients but not the information on how to cook them into a competitive finished product. Needless to say CSC was protective of its formulas and procedures and went to great lengths to ensure their security and confidentiality.

ketchup and then run them through a water chiller, label them, and pack them in cardboard cases.

We had the viscosity right, and other factors were spot on, but we could not duplicate the carmel-like flavor. Neither production nor formulation seemed to be the problem. It was something else. Then Fields came up with a theory: the secret of Heinz's ketchup flavor could be "stack burn."

This terminology is used when heat pasteurized or sterilized products were not sufficiently cooled down after processing and put into large stacks in the warehouse when warm. The product at the center of the stack would stay warm for relatively long periods of time, which would cause a "browning" reaction to occur in the food. In scientific terms, this is called the "Maillard Process" where the sugars and amino acids react to cause color and flavor changes. When grilling meats or making caramel candy, browning and caramelization is the desired end result, but not with most processed vegetable products. This generally reduces the overall quality of the finished product both in flavor and color, but sometimes it works to provide a unique flavor finisher.

I remembered as a graduate assistant being sent out to visit various tomato processors as part of the Ohio Department of Agriculture Extension Service. I had observed that a few of the smaller packers, who could not afford the cooling equipment, would actually "hot stack" the ketchup they made directly off the labeling line. It was a good idea to try, and with everyone breathing down our necks, we were willing to try anything! Fields and I tried to replicate the hot stack method to achieve the "stack burn," but were never able to duplicate the Heinz model.

We finally arrived at a ketchup which had a unique flavor with overtones of cinnamon and clove, using the experimental tomato paste product from Stockton plant production. First-level taste tests indicated that we had a good product, but it was not good enough to persuade Heinz lovers to switch. However, our executives pushed on to market test in select cities. Revenge is a powerful factor especially when those wanting revenge—those whose reputations were questioned in the many lawsuits—own over 50 percent of the company.

We gave it our best efforts and produced a respectable product, which launched in the summer of 1978.

8 a.m. Product Inspections

Every workday, the product development team got the opportunity to taste improvements, line extensions, and new products as the chefs and their kitchen staffs showcased their talents. At 8 a.m., the team would assemble to test the previous day's work from the kitchens, pilot plants, or special batches from manufacturing.

During the same period the new ketchup formulation was being developed, Schilling integrated the paste into his version of marinara, then showed the new experimental SHB-paste product. As usual, the chef and kitchen staff put on a show, serving a beautiful, fragrant, chunky sauce over spaghetti. It was good, really good. Given the freedom, Schilling did get creative and came up with a special spaghetti sauce that was superior to the marinara I had tasted at the restaurant, one with fresh ingredients like onions, mushrooms, whole herbs and spices (not ground or dried), parsley and garnishments, plus canned tomatoes (tomatoes were not in season) and, of course, the new tomato paste. And it did not weep!

I am continually amazed at what people can accomplish if you encourage them to be imaginative and to show you the best that they can do. At any one time, Schilling and his staff could be working on ketchup formulas, spaghetti sauce formulas, or frozen food formulas. For our special projects using the experimental SHB tomato paste, they came up with incredible enhancements like adding meat, cheese, or meatballs. Though commonplace today, four decades ago these were incredibly novel.

Over the course of eighteen months, we would taste test five or six samples of sauces and pasta at 8 a.m. two to three times a week. After multiple tastings of the same type of product, you start to identify the very smallest of nuances, as well as an ability to discern what "could be done better." With each dish prepared with pride, we were careful to offer chefs and cooks only diplomatic criticism that would continue to be supportive and offer real ways we thought the products could improve. Ultimately, the products would have to pass the Product Committee before they went to the consumer; but first, they would have to pass through preliminary market research, then home use tests, and test markets.

We provided samples of our spaghetti sauce to market research for in-house R&D taste panels, and the sauce showed some of the best results ever seen for experimental projects. Results also indicated that the consumer preferred a sweeter product along with a sweet basil background flavor. This request for sweetness was an irritation to Schilling, because he thought it departed from the more classical Italian approach he had tried to preserve, but we listened. We continued to fine-tune it, leaning on Engineering for assistance in equipment and processing precision for our main ingredient, the tomato paste.

(Endnotes)

1   Collins, *America's Favorite Food*, 23; Shea and Mathis, *Images of America*, 109.
2   Smith, *Pure Ketchup*.
3   Gaehring, *A History of Campbell's Soup*.

9

Sacramento High Drama

· ·

The quest for a superheat break process (SHB) was considered highly confidential at every level. Few people were involved in the project, and even fewer knew we were ready to test the new equipment. In the fall of 1978, we began the startup process of the secret tomato processing line. The specially-designed SHB equipment that had been installed based on the results of the pilot plant test runs from the previous winter was standing tall and stainless steel-shiny in its secret corner of the Sacramento paste plant.

Just like most Midwesterner transplants to California, the C-38 was doing exceptionally well, growing and fruiting as planned. Everyone involved in the project was enthusiastic and flush with great expectations of things to come. Everything was lined up to start the test run, or so we thought—especially because we had food engineer Charlie Long on our team.

Prego Professional Profile

CHARLIE LONG

Charlie Long was an engineer's engineer. He was one of the most respected and likable employees in the General Engineering department in corporate headquarters. In the face of adversity, he maintained a cool detachment and would defuse a tense situation with quick wit. Long's expertise was on all engineering and equipment facets of tomato paste production. He was the lead engineer responsible for supervising the installation of new and the modification of existing equipment in the tomato paste production operations. Long never advanced to the management ranks of engineering; he was too valuable as a front-line soldier getting his hands dirty and his feet wet versus sitting behind a desk in a cubicle back at the GO.

Working with Long, I began to understand true engineers. They go through rigorous academic training and spend many years on the job honing their craft. However, the ultimate success of an engineer is determined by their technical expertise and diplomacy. Those who rise to the top of their profession are the ones who have developed their diplomatic skills with multiple types of people and functions that they are dependent on to successfully accomplish their assigned project. I learned a lot from my engineering colleague, like using a smile and a joke to get better results than a frown and a request.

During the tomato season, Long was constantly on the road (primarily in California). After he arrived at the particular city, he would spend every waking hour in the processing facility, only sleeping in a motel. During the winter and spring, he supervised the installation of new equipment. When Long was not on the road, he was on call. He could be sent packing his bags on a minute's notice to solve some real or perceived crisis.

Nothing outside his work life was sacred, not even family vacations. Long stopped scheduling summer vacations after multiple times when he was forced to say goodbye to his crying children as he boarded the next flight out for work instead of spending time with them. Long was a dedicated professional and followed orders from headquarters.

One of the most enduring lessons I learned from him was the magic of polyester clothing. Both of us knew the perils of spending weeks on the road, living out of a suitcase, and working sixteen-hour days in a tomato processing operation. Chief among the other problems associated with that traveling lifestyle was keeping your clothes clean and neat. It was always a challenge to stuff enough clean clothes in your suitcase to wear for weeks on end—and if your trip was extended, you were out of luck! Long's elegant solution (if not comfortable, at least for me) was to wear polyester shirts and pants and wash them along the way. Cleaning them was so easy! At the end of the day, you put them in the sink with hot water and shampoo, let them soak, rinse them out, and hang them to dry in the shower. Next day, you had dry, clean, neat clothes with no ironing required. Genius. I never struggled with packing again.

High Drama in Hot Temperatures

From the start, the resulting paste from the SHB experimental line using the C-38 tomatoes was nowhere near the desired viscosity parameters. The viscosity was no thicker than what was produced on a parallel line running standard tomatoes and following standard procedures. This was beyond disappointing; it was a major disaster unfolding in slow motion.

Nothing we did changed the end result: Slowing the feed rate of the tomatoes into the unit, increasing the temperature, and trying to make adjustments to the extractors made no difference.

The processing equipment was enclosed and it was difficult (if not impossible) to observe what was going on inside of the vessel. Thermometer readings indicated that we were achieving the critical temperature in the exiting crushed tomatoes, but something was drastically wrong.

This was pure frustration and no one had a clue why the system was not working as designed—not the engineers, the production supervisor, Plant Quality Control Manager Steve Stewart, and worst of all, Dave Gaehring and myself. I had visions of my career ending after a week of disappointing results. This was a major setback and the only thing I could conclude was there was either a design flaw in the new equipment configuration or, even worse, my hypothesis for achieving a super-high viscosity tomato paste was not valid. My super hot break project had become my super *heart-break* project.

Time is Ticking ...

The tomato season in California is approximately seventy days long, plus there was a limited quantity of the C-38 tomatoes planted. Like a movie where the bomb's clock is set to explode, we were living in a secret world where the tomato season was full-blown, and we were in a battle with Mother Nature and Father Time. I could almost see a clock displaying the number of days: T-70 and counting down. We already invested ten days in a futile effort of the first equipment installation, so we were at T-60 with no progress to report. Each day, the anxiety quotient increased, and the pressure from corporate headquarters was compounding exponentially to produce sufficient amount of SHB paste to supply the production of ketchup for the test market and other new products.

I hustled back to our Camden pilot plant to run additional tests. We had to find out what went wrong. We were able to replicate the viscosity results achieved the previous year, but at T-40 we still had

Prego Professional Profile

STEVE STEWART

Steve Stewart grew up in Toledo, Ohio, and obtained a Bachelor of Science degree in chemistry in 1970 from the University of Toledo. Stewart attended college with the intention of becoming a medical doctor. He started as a biology major and then switched to chemistry. By the time he graduated, he realized that his grades were not good enough for medical school, and he set his sights on obtaining a Master of Science in chemistry. In the meantime, a CSC recruiter from the Napoleon plant visited the campus and offered Steve a temporary job as quality control technician. Stewart accepted the job in the anticipation that he would return to Toledo for his master's degree. He graduated in June 1970 and was married the same month. He worked the night shift during the Napoleon tomato season and did such a good job he was offered a full-time job with a promotion.

Stewart accepted the position which put him on course to become one of the leading tomato processing experts in the world. Stewart was assigned to the pesticide lab headed up by Marty Ziglar, who was known as being a tough teacher but a good mentor to his subordinates.

For the next couple years, Stewart was put in charge of Quality Control for production at the old Standard Brands V8 processing plant in Terra Haute, Indiana, which was part of the Napoleon plant operations. In October 1975, Stewart was sent to the Sacramento production operation to assist with container and microbiological issues on a temporary, two-week assignment. This led to a job offer to join the Quality Control department at the Sacramento plant, which he accepted. He started this position as chief chemist in January 1976, then was promoted two years later to quality control manager for the Sacramento plant operations.

I first met him during our Sacramento paste plant SHB experimental runs. Impressed by Stewart's technical expertise and work ethic, I offered him a position in the Product Technology group. Although I did my best to charm and convince him and his wife that this was a great career move, he politely declined in order to remain in California. When I interviewed Stewart for this book, I learned that this was in fact a turning point in his career. Afraid that he would be blackballed for any further advancement within CSC, he began looking for other employment options. In 1980, he became quality control manager for the T. H. Richards Company, but was welcomed back to CSC when he returned there in 1984. Stewart worked with Stevens at a new tomato research facility located at the Dixon paste plant.

no indication as to what was going wrong with the Sacramento production line.

I distinctly remember sitting at my desk covered in tomato pulp on a Saturday afternoon going over the process in my head and scribbling on a piece of paper when it finally dawned on me: the problem was the tomatoes were not totally submerged while they were being chopped (or broken), so the enzymes were actually being activated and thus the viscosity was *the same* as if they had not been broken. This is where my experience working with all those green beans in my graduate studies started paying dividends.

I rushed in to see if this would be true. Even though the temperature of the recirculated fluid inside was above what we needed, at the moment the tomatoes were broken, the temperature was nowhere close because of the cooler tomatoes coming from the outside. It seemed that the engineers had raised the chopping knives in the production unit above the hot slurry and were relying on steam and fluid to be pumped over the chopped tomatoes to keep them hot, but it wasn't enough to maintain our critical temperatures.

Lightning seemed to strike me when I finally made this realization. I was thrilled that this was the likely cause of our problems and embarrassed I had not figured this out earlier. Nevertheless, I immediately contacted my colleagues, Gaehring and Long, and we reviewed the design. It was obvious that what I realized was correct. Gaehring immediately understood the flaw in the system but Long was noncommittal (possibly because the design was his). Finally, another engineer, Bob Hockenbury, agreed to have the choppers removed which permitted the tomatoes to fall directly into the hot slurry.

This was a classic two-part design failure: one in design, which did not achieve the performance, and the other in oversight, by not ensuring the design was accurate before it was put into production.

In the book *Inside Steve's Brain*, the reader hears how obsessive Steve Jobs was on tracking every detail in designing a new product and process.[1] This is where I made a mistake by not staying in closer contact with the R&D engineers who were building the SHB equipment for the fall production run. They had made some modifications I was not aware of. This is no excuse, but once we completed the pilot plant test we turned our focus to formulating new products such as ketchup and spaghetti sauce using the experimental Stockton tomato paste. Our attention was on developing new products, not looking over the shoulders of the engineers.

They modeled their design on the pilot plant equipment developed during the winter tests, and the assumption was the parameters were the same only larger for the production unit. We found out later that some subtle modifications in the equipment design were made, which were not apparent until we started the production run.

Emergency Retest

It was a good news/bad news situation. The good news was this was the problem; the bad news was now we only had about T-30 days left in the season and the equipment had to be reconfigured.

The plant engineers in Sacramento were instructed to rip out the entire upper portion of the unit, which contained the chopping knives while Charlie Long redesigned the new configuration. The new replaced the old but with a setback of two or three weeks leaving us with just one week remaining (T-7) in the tomato season. If we didn't do this right, we wouldn't be able to try again for another year. I flew back to California just in time for the last loads of the special tomato variety to be delivered to the production lot. The last few harvested tomatoes were threatening to over-ripen, therefore only leaving us low quantities to create the SHB paste batch we desperately needed. Rain was forecast, impairing the possibility of collecting unharvested tomatoes, as the harvesting machines would have difficulty traveling through muddy rows.

The stakes could not have been any higher; marketing had already spent money on the ketchup label design and advertising. Custom packers were being lined up to produce the product. If we didn't get the desired tomato paste viscosity results, there would be no ketchup to test market, and there would be hell to pay. This would also be a major setback and source of aggravation to top management who had a major stake in our success or failure. We were in the second year of the Tomato Solids Task Force assignment and Shaub wanted to see results for the highly-anticipated ketchup to rival Heinz.

T-3 and Counting

On Saturday evening, the last weekend the plant was scheduled to be open—with the weather turning cold and a promise of a full moon—we started up the production line with our fingers crossed and high anxiety in the air. The bosses were demanding hourly updates. Long and I were sleepless, running on caffeine and adrenaline.

Holding our breaths, we watched as the tomatoes flowed through the modified SHB unit seamlessly. The exit temperatures were in excess of what we needed! This was encouraging, but based on previous experience this was not a reliable indicator that the desired viscosity levels would be achieved in the finished tomato paste. It was going to take hours to fill up the evaporator with the SHB pulp, and then begin the concentration process to create the paste. The anxiety weighed so heavily on me, I just wanted to be alone and not talk to anyone.

Full of nervous energy, I climbed the evaporator scaffolding and sat down. I was close to the electric motors that pumped the finished paste through the evaporator, and I knew this would be an early indicator of the viscosity of the paste. The ammeters on the motors reported the amount of energy used to pump the paste through the chillers. The higher the viscosity, the higher the power requirement. I was well aware of this fact from the experimental run made at the Stockton plant the previous year, when the plant manager almost had a panic attack when his ammeters began to max out.

It took approximately two hours for the concentrated paste to begin to exit the evaporators and enter the scrape surface chillers. I had plenty of time to wonder what the hell I had done to end up here, sitting on scaffolding, high in the air in Sacramento, on a Saturday night with the background hum of electric motors and the evaporator-induced vibrations, while staring at a glass-covered ammeter like my career depended on it. In some other life, I might have been sitting outside our home, with my lovely wife across from me at our picnic table, with the background noise of kids playing. We could stare at the moon together, instead of me staring at it by myself. One good thing was the full moon reminded me of what my

Heat Sink Temperature Challenge

The breakdown process cannot be reversed; the resulting tomato paste will have a tendency to weep. This is a challenge that is much more complicated than it would appear on paper. Breaking or chopping up tomatoes while they are immersed in hot liquid while achieving a consistent temperature above the critical point is problematic on several accounts.

First, if the tomatoes are not uniformly broken apart, larger pieces may take longer to reach the critical deactivation temperature. If this happens and the tomato pieces are slowly brought up to temperature and remain in a certain range, the enzyme is actually activated and thus pectin degradation still occurs within the flesh of the tomato chunk.

Second, in a full-scale production unit a quantity of up to a ton of tomatoes per minute could be introduced into the hot break tank, thus requiring a huge heat sink to immediately bring the "room temperature" tomatoes up to over this temperature. This requires massive circulation of the pulp and heat exchanger within the unit. This is a difficult concept to fully comprehend even if you have a food technology background, but if you are a trained engineer this is a concept as mystifying as the origins of life. This is not to disparage my engineering friends—I have as much difficulty understanding steam condensation ratios to evaporator efficiencies.

Engineers think in terms of BTUs, heat exchange rates, and fluid-flow dynamics, not enzymes and pectin structures. After some fitful starts, the engineers were able to design a prototype heat tank which gave us satisfactory results.

farmer grandfather called a "harvest" moon. I took this as a good sign that we were going to "harvest" our SHB paste tonight.

Once the SHB paste started to flow through the scrape surface chillers, their motors immediately began to draw maximum amperage. The sound of the motors groaning under the increased pressure necessary to force the paste through the chillers was music to my ears. Even before Long stepped out of the Quality Control Lab with the viscosity instrument in his hand, a smile on his face, and a thumbs-up gesture, I knew we had hit our viscosity numbers.

At 10 p.m., the paste started to come out of the chillers and the results were better than expected. We ran the production line the entire night and used every C–38 tomato that was available. We were able to run sufficient paste for the ketchup pack and have enough left over for additional experimental product development use.

And that was it. We did it.

We slid into home base just under the catcher's mitt. I let out a deep sigh of relief—I didn't realize I had been holding my breath. I called my boss, who said, "Good, now I will tell Williams. He has been bugging me all day." I heard from Miller that even with the three-hour time difference, Williams picked up, and although irritated to be called early on a Sunday morning, he remained in character and responded briefly, "About time."

More Hurdles to Come

Our united efforts in the formulation of Prego would serve us well in the wars against our "in-home" competitors and begin to win over our critics inside CSC.

(Endnote)

1   Leander Kahney, *Inside Steve's Brain* (New York: Portfolio Hardcover, 2008).

10

Proving Grounds

....

W ith the success of the paste production to create our SHB products, it was time to present the results to the Tomato Solids Task Force for inspection. The tomato showing included various prototype products, featuring ketchup and the experimental spaghetti sauce developed by Chef Schilling. Most of the attention was focused on the ketchup, which was prepared following an old Campbell recipe that was used many years ago when Campbell manufactured ketchup. Many of the individuals attending the product showing remembered the original product and were surprised on how close a match we were able to achieve. Compliments were also given to the special spaghetti sauce, but the star was the ketchup.

Directions were given to proceed to test market the ketchup in the Food Service division. The strategy was to place the product in restaurants and hope that there would be "pull-through" at the retail level. We needed to increase product awareness and build up consumer demand for retail product. The name of the product would again be "Campbell's Ketchup."

The food service sales team managed to place orders with a few restaurant chains, but after two years of uphill struggle, CSC ketchup was discontinued for a second time.

At this time, those in the product development and market research groups realized that ketchup was not going to be the vehicle to increase tomato solids usage within the CSC. The marketing research proved to be prophetic; even after the passage of thirty years Heinz retains the crown as the world's largest ketchup manufacturer.[1]

It was a humbling experience; it did however provide the momentum to gear up the tomato processing research and to implement the improved processing procedures and technology on a fast track.

More Heartbreak

Following the inspection, I was told in a side discussion by the senior vice president of marketing that, in no uncertain terms, "The sauce was good, but forget about developing a spaghetti sauce. First of all, it would have to be packed in glass jars which would break, and that would not be allowed in the canned food processing plant. Secondly, you'll need deep marketing pockets and we can never afford to go up against such an entrenched product line as Ragu. Just stop the sauce, and make ketchup."

Looking back, I do not fault the executive who told me to shelve the spaghetti sauce project. He was correct when he said Ragu and Hunt's were spending a ton of money in advertising and had dominant positions. And there were numerous other jarred spaghetti sauce manufacturers who were regional players. It was also true that Campbell's Soup had a poor track record when it came to new product introductions outside of its core product portfolio. Plus, the relatively recent failure of Red Kettle Soups (a freeze-dried instant soup targeted to compete against Lipton's dehydrated products), which was withdrawn from the market, was a wound still open. When I compared the sauce idea to the success of the ready-to-serve Chunky Soup line (which was introduced to the market a couple of years earlier), I could see that this executive was not entirely wrong in his assessment.

However, at the time, I was crestfallen. I approached Miller for instructions on what we should do with the experimental sauce with outstanding results in taste tests. He shrugged his shoulders, laughed, and directed me to proceed with the work but to do it underground. I was not to involve anyone in marketing but could work with the market research group, and I would have my own budget to fund more research. He said any new idea or innovation is going to have its critics and distracters within the organization. If you're going to pioneer a new idea you need tenacity and a tough skin. He was right. I knew what we had to do. We went covert.

Skunkworks

Most of Product Development's efforts were occupied finding a custom packer for the ketchup, fine-tuning the recipe, and continuing the development of the SHB tomato paste procedures. We continued to perfect the taste and appearance of the product through consumer testing. Here is the intriguing part: we had a group of passionate believers in R&D and market research, but we had to fly under the radar when it came to the top marketing management and management in general. The hope was that we would continue to get such compelling numbers, that someone within the GO would recognize the product's potential and we could launch. We were so close.

Market Research and Re-Search

Meanwhile, in his continuing efforts to solidify product strategy and improve product offerings, Shaub directed the hiring of two additional outside professionals, Charlie Lehman and Paul Massaraccio. These men were to head up a corporate marketing effort on new products, which made for a difficult situation because existing marketing groups for both divisions were also working on new products within their own product categories. There was major overlap and resource allocation problems regarding support from product development and marketing research.

Lehman and Massaraccio had no product portfolio and from day one were in a constant scramble to identify potential new product opportunities to champion. They had brought several ideas with them from their previous marketing positions at other large food companies, but most of these ideas required the use of either artificial ingredients or changes in processing procedures, which were not compatible with CSC's operating philosophy.

Both men came to my office many times to discuss projects they were contemplating and to become familiar with the work that was being done within my group. The tomato-based products that were part of the Task Force assignment were confidential, and I refrained from discussing the spaghetti sauce. Consumer taste testings continued with numerous product reformulations and the experimental SHB sauce was beating the competition hands-down in taste tests, and I thought it would be a winning combination to have them support it, but I held back not knowing if I could trust them. They saw their careers on the verge of extinction, with no product concepts to pursue.

For nearly a year, the sauce project was conducted in secrecy, and I knew it was time to get marketing re-engaged. I made the decision to share the sauce concept and results with Lehman and Massaraccio. The consumer testing results were so compellingly positive (We were beating the leading brand, Ragu, three to one in blind taste tests.) that we were encouraged to continue our clandestine cooperation. For them it was like Christmas and the Fourth of July at the same time. They were beyond enthusiastic, immediately seeing the potential, and made it their number one priority. With the support of my boss (and a very determined product development and research marketing team), work on the spaghetti sauce product also become one of our top priorities.

Slow Start

The next piece to prepare was advertising support. We needed concept work on developing a name and packaging recommendations. CSC's longtime agency, Needham, Harper & Steers (NH&S) was called in to help. True to its Franco-American experiences, they came up with the idea that the product should be packed in a tin can and named "Campbell's Very Own Spaghetti Sauce." Old habits die hard even for creative hard-charging ad agency executives, it seemed, but none of us at CSC liked the idea.

The brand concept test report came back with zero consumer enthusiasm and the prospects for going forward were as flat as an empty can crushed by a steamroller. To give our new sauce the advertising firepower it was going to need for a successful launch, we would need to bring in some advertising heavyweights.

Leber Katz Partners

Charlie Lehman and Paul Massaraccio, our marketing executives, did two things that altered their careers and the launch of our spaghetti sauce forever. The first was agreeing to champion the product. The second was inviting Leber Katz Partners (LKP) to pitch for developing the creative positioning on Campbell's Soup's brand new category of spaghetti sauce.

Lehman had hired LKP, a New York City-based ad agency, in his previous position at another major food company. He invited the principals Stanley Katz and Laurel Cutler to Camden for a product showing. Known to be an aggressive ad agency, LKP was eager to break the duopoly that advertising agencies NH&S and Batten, Barton, Durstine & Osborn (BBDO) had at Campbell's Soup Company.

Stanley Katz and Laurel Cutler understood market share and what activity was necessary to win it. Co-founder Katz was an icon in the agency world. He was recognized as one of the top three founders of ad agencies, along with David Ogilvy and Bill Bernbach. Cutler was hired by Katz from McCann-Erickson (where she was a senior advertising executive) to be his co-chairman and to create a market planning and research group.

Cutler and Katz made a formidable team during the pitch process, and they were not afraid to get their hands dirty. The pair did not delegate the tedious task of learning all the details of their assignment to underlings. They spoke to numerous individuals connected to the product to learn everything they could. They visited the research kitchens and the product development offices. This was quite unusual; it was most often more junior employees from our existing ad agencies who visited to do the legwork for new product ad campaigns.

Katz and Cutler continued to dedicate their undivided attention and poured all their resources into the creative process. LKP beat out Campbell's Soup's other two advertising agencies to win the spaghetti sauce contract.

The Genius of Laurel Cutler and the Birth of Prego

Working around the clock was not uncommon for Cutler and her team, who often worked evenings and weekends with her clients. Several weeks into the CSC project, she was still in bed late on a Sunday morning. She was exhausted and fighting the effects of a lingering cold. She had stayed up late the night before for yet another

Prego Professional Profile

LAUREL CUTLER

Laurel entered Wellesley College at age fifteen, as the youngest student to ever attend the college, just as hostilities began to break out in World War II. She graduated at nineteen and applied to law school. Her belief was that if she was accepted to Yale Law School, her father would be pleased and proud, but his reaction was just the opposite. Even though he was a lawyer, he informed her he did not believe women should be lawyers and he would not financially support her law school education. Her brother, too, did not support Cutler continuing her education. She went to work instead.

Her first job was to judge contest submissions of jingles written by lay people. From there, she went to work as a clerk with the ad agency specializing in the entertainment business, where she rapidly advanced to the next level because of her shorthand skills. She was requested to submit copy, writing ads, to be promoted to the next level. Cutler informed her supervisor that she was not interested in advancement because she wanted to get married and have children. When the supervisor informed her that if she did not submit copy and get promoted, she would be terminated from her position. She did, and her advertising career took off.

Joining McCann-Erickson, she became senior vice president, creative director, and a director of the company for eight years before joining LKP. "She joined LKP in 1972 to establish the Marketing Planning function, dedicated to building the brands that preempt the future," according to her biography on the Advertising Hall of Fame website. "The department developed systematic assumptions about the consumer marketplace five years out. Laurel Cutler was named the first woman to receive 'Man of the Year' in the Advertising Hall of Fame for her work on Prego Spaghetti Sauce.[1]

client dinner in a downtown Manhattan restaurant. Although tired, she could not sleep anymore; her mind was racing thinking about the week ahead. She had to get ready for a Chrysler Board of Directors' meeting and a private session with President Lee Iacocca later in the week. Also, there were numerous client status meetings scheduled with her partners at LKP. She did not have the energy to give much thought to the pending problems that always arose at these meetings. It was better to work on another project.

She knew precisely what she was going to do with her nervous energy. She was going to scan an Italian dictionary. With a box of tissues, she set out to identify Italian words or phrases that would have potential as brand names for her new spaghetti sauce client.

When Cutler finally got out of bed that day, she had scanned the entire Italian dictionary. She had found several words that seemed to fit, but one word stood out as her favorite, and that was the Italian colloquial term "Prego." Prego has multiple meanings depending on how it's used. Most commonly, it is a familiar term for greeting friends in person or answering the phone, but also "Thank you" and "You're welcome."

Cutler presented the list and her specific recommendation of Prego to CSC's marketing group. Though the name was not immediately popular with me, it received favorable ratings based on consumer testing, and we moved forward on it. There was, however, a problem in that Seagram's owned the rights to "Prego," but CSC was able to approach the company, negotiate, and purchase these rights. "Prego Spaghetti Sauce" was born.

Homestyle Positioning

The hands-on work by Cutler and her account reps continued. They held multiple meetings and interviews with Schilling, me, and the technology team assigned to the project. When the LKP advertising account reps were developing the creative content for this new product launch, they visited the R&D labs to interview the product developers, especially Schilling, who repeated the now-famous phrase, "It's in there" numerous times in response to the account reps' questions.

When the artwork for advertising was sent to Product Development for review several months later, the positioning statement of "Homemade taste. It's in there" created a third segment in the spaghetti sauce category. (Later, we refined the tagline to be "It's in there.")

The intel surfacing from Schilling's home use test and other market research showed the differentiator of this product was its chunky style, similar to homemade Italian sauces. My team and I knew from our focus groups that the competition for Prego was the homemakers who followed traditional recipes. This was a tremendous revelation. Though Ragu and Hunt's had established spaghetti sauce products, Prego was not in their *exact* product category and therefore, Ragu and Hunt's were not considered our biggest competitor anymore.

Prego would have to be positioned against traditional cooking in the homes. In another bit of creative artistry, Cutler coined the term "homestyle." This would both attract the attention of the consumers wanting a product just as they had made at their house (but more conveniently), and differentiate it from Ragu or Hunt's. Cutler understood that this product represented a new product category. "Homestyle" would become a prime descriptor of the sauce, featured prominently on the label and in broadcast and print ads.

Political Aplomb of Herb Baum

Herb Baum, CSC's account executive at the advertising firm of NH&S, was brought in-house as the new associate director of marketing in the Canned Foods Division. After a year of covert efforts, Prego was moved into an overt program with renewed corporate

Prego Professional Profile

HERBERT BAUM

Herbert Baum's professional crucible was a slick Chicago ad agency and public relations firm, which honed his political and administrative skills. Most of his CSC executive contemporaries were "homegrown," coming up through the company manufacturing ranks or advancing from an entry-level position in marketing or finance. Baum's resume more closely resembled that of Bev Murphy, who also was hired into CSC after a successful career in consumer research.

Baum was born in Chicago to a "neighborhood" lawyer and his homemaker wife. Baum's high school years were uneventful and he described himself as a "nerd," but he found his element when he moved south to Drake University. There, he became president of his fraternity Alpha Epsilon Pi, was elected a member of the Student Senate, and even had time left over to don the Drake bulldog mascot costume to join the cheerleaders for football and basketball games. No one would ever guess that the young man running up and down the sidelines dressed as a bulldog would become one of the leading corporate CEOs and board member of the twenty-first century. Yet, he graduated Drake University in 1958 with a B.S. in Business Administration (majoring in finance and philosophy), and did just that.

Baum's career began as an agent for a public relations agency located in Chicago. Full of charm, Baum accepted a job to accompany movie stars around the city as they attended opening nights, visited nightclubs, and were interviewed on TV shows. He was then hired by a small advertising agency, Dole Dane Bernbach, which was a stepping stone to the much larger, internationally-known agency NH&S.

During Baum's tenure at NH&S, he worked on the marketing

efforts for V8, Franco-American canned pasta products and Campbell's Pork and Beans. He worked with Jack Dodd and Don Gorke in CSC's marketing department. Bill Williams admired Herb's work and went directly to Paul Harper, one of the principles of the ad agency, to convince Herb to come to work in the marketing department at CSC's Camden, New Jersey, headquarters. Baum initially refused, but relented when Harper indicated to Herb that if things did not work out on the East Coast he would be guaranteed his job back. Luckily, he never had to pursue that.

Baum's tenure as a brand manager at a major ad agency served him well in that he had developed and polished his leadership and diplomatic skills to a fine edge. He also had the added advantage of knowing most of the key marketing people and executives within the CSC hierarchy, which smoothed his transition to the brightly-lit and highly-charged environment of the GO.

support, thanks to the diplomacy of Baum. Massaraccio had championed the product through the labyrinth of getting approvals through the GO hierarchy. When marketing aces Lehman and Massaraccio moved on (Lehman left the company and Massaraccio was promoted to other projects), Baum became the marketing lead to take Prego to test market. The hurdle Baum had to clear was none other than the person who had recruited him to CSC, Bill Williams.

Baum was willing to fight the battle against Williams to launch a new product in a category that CSC had no previous experience with. In a short time, he was noticed by Shaub, who took him under his wing and gave him special projects. This did not mean Baum got a free ride; Shaub still retained his industrial engineering roots and demanded assurances that any investment, whether it be equipment or marketing, would make a targeted internal rate of return. While they were working on the advertising concepts, Charlie Long and I had to finalize a few sourcing and production details, like scaling production at Dixon.

(Endnote)

1   "Advertising/Marketing Trailblazer: Laurel Cutler," *Advertising Hall of Fame*, March 10, 2017, advertisinghall.org/members/member_bio.php?memid=2746.

11

Dixon Greenhorns

. . . .

I n 1977, Campbell's Soup had purchased the T. H. Richards Canning Company located in Dixon, California. For many years, CSC had been its largest customer, and though most of its operations were established for Campbell's Soup, modifications had to be made for the new SHB process. In the fall of 1979, the Dixon paste plant in California was retrofitted with the new SHB equipment to bring the process in full production.

Gaehring and I travelled westward again to run processing variable tests to perfect the SHB paste procedure. In Dixon, we would use the same tomato variety we used at Sacramento—the C-38 midwestern high solids, high-viscosity tomato. It seemed straightforward after all the heartache we had endured; we thought we had overcome all possible problems. We knew what the plan was, and we naively thought we were seasoned tomato processing experts. We were soon proved wrong.

Dixon Plant Manager Fred Tyler sized up us newcomers with the knowing smile and demeanor of a Wild West sheriff. With the sun silhouetting his massive shoulders, you could imagine the music from *High Plains Drifter* playing in the background. All that was missing from the caricature was a ten-gallon hat and six shooters on his hips.

Tyler had received the directive from the GO and understood our intention, but he was still the plant manager, and what he said, went. He gave us permission to use one of the lines but did so with a warning: "You can jack up temperatures for SHB to knock out PME, but if you do, you can't pump paste through rotators at 46 percent solids. You must lower the total solid level to 32 percent before it can be pumped to fill drums for shipping." Even at the lower solids level, the paste thickness maxed out the pump motors and their irritation with us continued.

By the end of the first week, Tyler's attitude concerning the "greenhorns" (as he referred to us) he was forced to endure changed from covert disdain to benign tolerance. This probably had more to do with his attending a plant managers' meeting and receiving marching orders from the VP of Production than it did with any show of competence on our part.

Spending so much time in the plant, certain routines would be established. One of these was to go out for a quick dinner between the first and second shifts. This was always an entertaining adventure since Tyler knew all the local watering holes and eating establishments. On one occasion, we were standing around a bar waiting to be seated, watching couples dance to a country and western band. When two girls started to dance with a single guy, Tyler tipped his long neck beer bottle in my direction and said, "Watch this. I'm gonna cut those two fillies away from that dude just like a cutting course at a rodeo."

And that is exactly what he did; he cut in front of the bewildered chap with a smooth Texas two-step move that delighted the female dancers and left their former partner shadow-dancing off the dance floor with Woody Allen-style facial expressions and hand gestures of resignation. The "King of the Dance Floor" morphed to dancing dunce in the time it took Tyler to click his heels. There was no protest, just quiet surrender. Tyler was just too imposing to even consider any other alternative.

This story shows how Tyler managed his production plant. This was Tyler's world, and you were welcome in it as long as you knew his rules of engagement. If there was a problem, whether it is with equipment or personnel, he stepped in the middle of the issue and stayed there until a resolution was worked out. He didn't believe in delegation or standing on the sideline watching while others did the work.

Production had volume quotas, yields, and laborer targets to meet, and any disruptions to production were met with reluctance and sometimes not-very-well-concealed resistance. The product researchers' goals were to develop new products and processes which required careful, sometimes repetitive work, making changes to form discoveries. Research means that one searches and then researches some more. This drove the production staff crazy, because they were used to more linear, assembly-line processes. And they would rebel. The plant was their home, and the researchers were the intruders.

For example, when we requested processing parameters be changed to run various tests on final product quality, the production staff would all nod their heads in agreement. We spent extensive sixteen-hour days of running multiple statistically-replicable tests with *supposedly* different variables, but we didn't have the viscosity and numbers we were expecting and didn't know what was going on. We checked every step, and soon discovered that Tyler had secretly co-opted our directions to the supervisor (in this case to increase the temperature of the heat sink). No changes had been made, except

with the labeling, to trick us into thinking that this batch was produced at the higher temperature.

Our tests were actually one continuous production run, which
did not produce differences needed for our decision making on
production variables. It was as if we hadn't done anything different,
in effect wasting time, energy, money, and most sacredly, tomatoes.
Tyler and several members of his team laughed about it afterwards
because to them their priority was daily production not entertaining
researchers—they didn't care if we accomplished what we had set
out to do. This was the game that was played many times between
R&D and production people in all the plants. My learning was to
start understanding people's stresses and agendas, and work with
them to accomplish my own.

I could work with what I was exposed to, but I couldn't impact
what I didn't know was going on. More dubious tricks were happening right under my nose. Tyler had sized my co-worker up perfectly as a shy, straight-laced guy, who didn't have much experience
with the girls. The Dixon plant was filled with good-looking blonde
California and brunette Hispanic female employees. Gaehring was a
church-going boy who never drank or cussed; he avoided trouble. If
Gaehring ventured to part of the manufacturing floor or to an area
Tyler didn't want him to go into, Tyler would send girls to start flirt-
ing with him. Embarrassed, Gaehring would leave early or move to
another area. Unbeknownst to me, when Gaehring would check the
test temperature and flows, Tyler would send over girls to distract
him in hopes of him not thoroughly getting the readings—another
way to sabotage our tests. I was there when this was happening,
but on other side of the city-sized plant, and Tyler never sicced any
females on me. Had I known what was going on, I would have tried
to intervene.

Eventually, their efforts stopped and our processes were ironed
out. By the end of the tomato season, what could have turned out
to be a reenactment of the shootout at O.K. Corral turned into a

peaceable parting with mutual respect. Tyler realized that Gaehring and I did, in truth, understand tomato processing. The "greenhorns" recognized Tyler as a knowledgeable and efficient plant manager. Best of all, the SHB processed had advanced and we had produced the paste we needed.

Finally, a Breather

Following a long day inside the plant monitoring a production run, I ventured out to the unloading area where the trucks delivering the tomatoes were weighed and then unloaded. It was an early mid-September evening, and the sun had just slipped past the vast western horizon, so there was a dry, coolness to the air and the yellow glow of the halogen overhead lights created dark shadows outlining the trucks and the overhead fluming equipment, which transported the tomatoes into the processing plant. Walking outside, I always felt a magical sensation leaving the tropic-like environment of the processing plant running at full capacity with steam belching from the evaporators while in the background a constant din of racing pump and conveyor motors.

In the plant, your senses are overwhelmed by the 360-degree sights, sounds, and smells of constant motion and activities. One's safety and in some cases, survival, depends on being mentally and physically alert; there are hot pipes, electric wires, and running machinery at every turn, and this was just on the ground floor. If an evaporator, condenser, or an extractor had to be inspected, that meant climbing catwalks and squeezing into areas that were even more hot and noisy.

This is where I had spent most of my day going from the hot break tanks to the extractors and then on to the evaporators checking on the progress of our precious pack. The higher you climbed in the factory, the hotter it got, and the evaporators were on the top floor. The only relief was to step outside on the outer scaffolding surrounding the evaporators. Inside the evaporators the tomato pulp rolled and boiled in volcano-like eruptions causing the whole structure to pulsate and the floor to vibrate under your feet. Steam hissed overhead, as it escaped from the condensers into the dry desert-like air.

After the steam had given up its latent heat of fusion it was transformed from a gas to an invisible liquid vapor. When the conditions were just right and you were on the outer catwalk, a gentle breeze would blow the condensing steam in your direction, and you would be surrounded in a cloud-like mist of tiny water droplets that moistened your face and then instantly evaporated, creating a cooling and refreshing feeling of calmness. This was a rare but pleasant experience in what was otherwise a hot and dirty business.

By the time I reached the ground floor, it was late afternoon going on evening. I nodded to my colleague, Gaehring, who was in a deep conversation with a foreman regarding temperatures of the hot break units, and gestured to indicate that I was headed to the rear of the plant to go outdoors. Passing through the exit door to the receiving yard was an immediate transformation into another realm. This was especially true during the evening; gone were the diesel trucks and tractors moving tandem truckloads of tomatoes over the scales into lines leading to the dump station. In its place were orderly rows of tandem gondolas, overflowing with tomatoes majestically waiting their turn to join the river of tomatoes going into the paste plant.

On the opposite side of the large expanse of tarmac were the empty units to be picked up early the next morning to make their way back to the tomato fields to start the journey all over again. The reason for going outside was that I was going to check on the quality and quantity of the special tomato variety that remained in the holding area. This is partially true; the real reason, however, was I needed a break from all the controlled chaos of being inside the factory for twelve straight hours and I wanted a few moments of serenity walking among the parked gondolas and observing the tomatoes as they exited the flume on a roller conveyor on the way into the processing facility.

Standing on the walkway just above the dump station as the tomatoes were being "washed" from the swimming-pool-sized fiberglass gondola parked parallel to the flume, I could feel a gentle shifting breeze against the back of my neck. I stood still listening to the only sound being made—the rush of water flowing into the gondola to gently sweep the tomatoes into the waiting stream to transport the tomatoes to the factory. There was a mingling of scents as the wind shifted and drifted across the open lot; in one breath there would be the sweet aroma of cooked tomatoes coming from the direction of the evaporators and in the next instant there would be the sour odor of rotting tomatoes on the ground at the base of the flume that the day cleanup crew had missed. This was a mesmerizing experience; standing on this platform for fifteen minutes, I would see as many tomatoes as were processed during an entire day in my former job as a quality control technician while an undergraduate student.

The years that I've been absent from the tomato growing and processing industry had brought major developments and shifts in the dynamics of how tomatoes were raised, harvested, transported, and ultimately processed. During my two college years working as a quality control technician in the production of tomato juice, whole packed tomatoes, and ketchup, all the tomatoes were hand-picked and delivered to the factory in thirty-three-pound wooden hampers similar to what can be seen in farmers' markets displaying peaches, apples, and other produce. Sometimes I would almost become hypnotized watching the tomatoes cascade into the muddy soup of the catchment flume and then be elevated by conveyor rollers to the secondary flume which swept the tomatoes into the processing plant to be washed, inspected, sent through the hot break unit, and extracted, and the resulting juice pumped into the evaporator to be reduced to paste.

The best way to inspect the tomatoes before they entered the plant was from this vantage point. The tomatoes were elevated out of the flume by a conveyor that consisted of parallel horizontal stainless steel cylinders, approximately three inches in diameter. The cylinders were set one inch apart to allow the water and other debris to be separated from the tomatoes. Overhead spray nozzles showered the tomatoes with fresh water to remove surface residues and any clinging leaves or other undesirable matter. The action of the upward moving rolling cylinders rotated the tomatoes several full turns before being deposited in the next flume. This helped to make sure that all sides of the tomato were rinsed with clean water. In this manner the tomatoes could be closely observed for color, size, and state of quality. I would usually stand in this position for fifteen to twenty minutes to ensure that I saw a representative sampling of the tomatoes being processed. This is where, out of the corner of my eye, I saw an individual emerging from the shadows of the parked gondolas and started to walk toward me and the dump station.

Prego Professional Profile

THE GROWER

The gentleman was small framed but distinguished looking even though he was wearing coveralls and work boots. As he approached me in silence on the platform and under the halo of the overhead light, I could immediately identify that he was not an employee of CSC. The giveaway was that his boots and coveralls were stained a dull chlorophyll green to his mid thighs, a telltale sign that this individual had come straight from working in a tomato field.

As he moved a few steps closer, I could see the deeply-tanned face and the dirt under his cracked, rough fingernails.

This was an individual who had been working outdoors for most of his life. His confident walk and posture conveyed that he was most likely one of the contract growers that supplied CSC with tomatoes; his slender frame and delicate hands revealed his Japanese ancestry. After a few more steps, he gave a wide smile and said, "I have not seen you around here before, so you must be one of those R&D guys from back east I have been hearing about." I was immediately taken aback. How could he have so quickly identified me?

Our presence within the factory was supposed to be a secret. Only a few people within the company knew that we were in California. The mystery of his identity was soon solved when my new best friend pointed to the tomatoes going up and over the conveyor belt and said that they were his and he had just picked them this afternoon. He went on to say that he was a long-term contract grower for the Davis Paste plant, but this was the first time that he had grown this special Ohio C-38 variety. At this point, I felt there was no value in maintaining a charade that I was just some technician from the production operation, so I said, yes, I was from corporate headquarters and proceeded to ask him questions on the growing characteristics of the special cultivar that we had provided. We had some concerns, because the cultivar selected, due to its high viscosity characteristics, was developed for Midwestern growing environments, and this was the first time this tomato strain was being grown on the West Coast under full-scale production conditions.

He indicated that the tomato plants grew well, produced good yields, and the majority of the fruit matured all at one time—which was a critical factor when mechanically harvesting tomatoes. The mechanical harvester is a one-pass operation. As it cuts the plant from the ground, it shakes the plant over a series of shakers which dislodges the tomatoes from the vine onto a conveyor which transports them to a gondola trailer. A majority of the tomatoes are not ripe within about a ten-day time frame, huge yield losses occur because the immature green tomatoes have to be discarded in the field by workers riding on the harvester. This was incredibly valuable grower feedback.

The conversation turned to our backgrounds, and as I shared that I had grown up on a farm and had advanced degrees in food science, the grower's eyes brightened, and he stood a little bit more erect. He, too, had an advanced degree, a master's in chemical engineering. This at first seemed a little curious to me, that a grower would have training in chemistry and engineering, but then that should not have been a surprise because my grandfather and father were farmers who had gone to college. He had either anticipated my thoughts or experienced this reaction many times previously, and went on to tell one of the more captivating stories that I've ever heard.

He reached up with his left hand and cocked his sun-bleached, sweat-stained cap, revealing a full head of jet black hair with only a few silver rays. "I got my education thanks to the U.S. government," he began, as his smile faded. "Have you ever heard of the Japanese internment camps during World War II?" he asked with his eyes squarely focused on me. I was momentarily taken aback and confused because at first a Japanese internment camp brought to mind a prisoner of war camp in which many allied soldiers endured torture during the Pacific campaign. The visuals in my mind were supplied by those I had seen on the newsreels many years ago. No history book or history class that I had taken ever mentioned Japanese internment camps in the United States. My puzzlement must have been readily apparent as he quickly added, "You are too young to probably know about this business, and growing up in the Midwest, even your parents probably did not realize what was happening to Japanese-American citizens who were living on either the West or East coast."

His story continued. Immediately after Pearl Harbor on December 7, 1941, President Franklin D. Roosevelt declared war on Japan and then issued an executive order which bypassed the Constitutional rights of all U.S. citizens; it decreed all Japanese-American residents—120,000 in all—would be forced to leave their homes, farms, jobs, businesses, and schools and live in camps patrolled by armed guards.

In the view of our government, these were desperate times requiring desperate measures. He related that his parents, brothers, and sisters were all gathered up and only allowed to take clothing and other simple processions with them when they were transported to the internment areas. Since he had recently graduated from high school and showed good aptitude, it was determined that he would be sent on to college at the University of Colorado. This was far enough into the interior that he would not be a threat to national security. After four years, he earned his bachelor's degree in Chemical Engineering, but the war still lingered on and so the government, not knowing what else to do, encouraged the recent graduate to continue on to graduate school. He did this, earning a master's degree in Chemical Engineering the following year. The war had ended but the anti-Japanese sentiment had not, so now no job prospects were available to him.

He had grown up in Sacramento and returned to California to be with the rest of his family, who had been released. His family roots were in agriculture, so when he returned to California he started leasing land to grow tomatoes and other produce. After many years of hard work and struggle, he was able to start purchasing land.

When he had finished his story, I was in a state of total amazement. Not only was I not aware that this travesty had occurred during the last world war, but I was also ignorant of the amazing fortitude that individuals can demonstrate under great adversity. The other truly astonishing thing I remember about this serendipitous meeting was the grace of the grower: no acrimony or latent resentment. As he was finishing this story he smiled as he did with our first greeting and said, "Looking back on this experience, it is probably the best thing that could have happened to me. I got a great education that I could never have dreamed of achieving." Then he added soberly, "But I do feel sorry for my parents' silent suffering." Then, it struck a chord when long-suppressed memories surfaced of my grandfather telling me how German-Americans were viewed with suspicion during World War I. My tomato-growing friend's pain became real and no longer abstract.

I had lost track of the time, and I knew I needed to get back inside the plant. Dave was already most likely thinking that I'd fallen into the flume or was taking a nap on the dock. We shook hands, said our goodbyes, and parted company. I never saw the venerable grower again, but I did find out later from Fred Tyler, the Dixon plant manager, that my companion on the catwalk was one of the largest and most successful tomato growers in the area.

Later when I was telling Gaehring of my conversation, I embarrassingly noticed he was wearing a red Campbell Institute for Research and Technology (CIR&T) baseball cap exactly like the one on top of my head. "Of course," I thought to myself, "That was how my catwalk friend knew I was from corporate. In the future, I hope we prove to be better product developers than undercover operatives in California."

Leadership En Route

We were continually striving to improve our product development methods and our interactions with the plant personnel. I was fortunate to learn from two of the top executives in the company during this time. I traveled with Lew Springer and Milt Zimmerman on various company trips and attended numerous tomato

Prego Professional Profile

LEW SPRINGER

Lew Springer was a charismatic and a high-energy leader whose career was forged on the concrete floors of the soup factory as he advanced his career from supervisor to plant manager to the president of the Frozen Food Division and later head of all production operations. Springer had many followers and admirers as he left his mark in his various positions. There were a few detractors but they were in the minority. Springer's inner circle were individuals much like himself, who had production backgrounds, and had proven themselves leaders with the skill set and dedication to achieve the results that they were directed to produce.

He wore pinstriped suits and sat in a leather executive chair surrounded by mahogany paneling, but that was as far his executive demeanor extended. He could yell, scream, jump up and down, and make outlandish statements in the manner of Vince Lombardi going after a referee making a bad call against the Green Bay Packers. What was so unique about Springer (versus other high-level managers and executives) was that he could pull off this act without losing his temper or insulting or humiliating the individual or group being admonished. Springer's performances could at times be mesmerizing and only afterward did the person admonished realize that he was not going to be banned from the kingdom and fed only bread and water for the rest of his career.

Springer's reputation was sometimes larger than reality and this was especially true of his exploits when he found himself in management positions removed from Campbell's Soup's GO. He was legendary as a motivator and in his ability to animatedly communicate his message. Springer was probably tougher on his own personnel because he took such ostentatious pride in leading what he considered to be the best food manufacturing group in the business. This man was convinced that, "The smartest guys are not in the General Office; they are in production," and the production employees loved him for that.

processing meetings on the West Coast. I met Zimmerman after he had moved over from the VP of Human Resources to head up the Canned Food Production Operations which included the Dixon plant, and he reported to Springer. I grew to like Springer and gained a good appreciation of his dedication and hard work.

Springer Leadership

There were numerous stories about Lew Springer and his exploits, but one in particular always stood out in my mind as the quintessential Springerism, told to me by a fellow product development colleague. When Springer was the plant manager of the Toronto soup factory, he headed up the management team that was trying to reach a new contract with the various unions within the manufacturing operation. After several days of meetings, which were going nowhere, Springer sat down at the table opposite the union leaders, he looked them square in the eye, pulled a cigar from his suit pocket and as he was lighting it, he said, "Gentlemen, when this cigar is finished, our meeting is over. If we have not come to a mutually-agreeable contract at that time, then we will pull whatever offer we have on the table." He did this while blowing smoke in their direction as he sat back in his seat and smiled. As the story goes, the contract was signed before Springer had taken his last puff.

Over the last thirty years, I have told this story countless times and, on occasion when I was going into a contentious meeting, I would fleetingly consider using the same "cigar" tactic. I never did resort to this ploy, first of all because I figured I would get dizzy smoking a cigar and second smoking has been banned in most conference rooms for many, many years.

It came as a great surprise when I was interviewing Lew Springer that he had no idea what I was talking about when I relayed this story to him. Apparently, this urban legend was circulated throughout corporate headquarters with no basis of truth other than the fact that he smoked cigars and was a highly animated, charismatic character, an example of the mythology that can build up around great leaders. And after enough time, these stories can become truths in people's minds.

The first ten years of my career, I did not know Springer well. I had of course heard of him by reputation as related above, but, since I was working primarily on the Canned Food division projects and Springer was one of the top managers of the Frozen Food division, our paths rarely crossed. This, however, changed when Springer was promoted to head up all operations. At that point, I began to work with him and his people on various projects ranging from poultry processing to the work that we were doing in California with tomatoes.

One day, while attending a production status meeting in the place of my boss, I observed Lew Springer fielding questions regarding ingredient yields reports from the soup plants. Product usages were very closely monitored by both the Industrial Engineers (IE) group for yields and the Technical Administration (TA) department for quality. TA later changed its name to Quality Control. IEs were praising the plants for having such great yields while the Quality Control (QC) reps were criticizing that any reported yield over 80 percent, depending on the material, was most likely bogus.

As usual in these types of meetings, the exchanges between the protagonists went from routine reporting to heated discussion with tempers rising with each volley. In the middle of this debate, Lew looks and then points at me saying, "It's Product Development's fault. You guys write your formulas and procedures in a manner that makes us in production have to cheat to make our numbers!" At first, I was incredulous; I thought I was safely on the sidelines, trying not to get sucked into the perpetual argument between manufacturing and technical administration regarding yields. But now Springer had cleverly switched the spotlight from him to me, and all eyes were focused in my direction with a few heads nodding in sympathy with his declaration.

A couple of his lieutenants chimed in with, "Yeah, that's right; you guys make us into criminals because you write formulas impossible to follow!" Even the QC guys looked at me and smiled with the implied message, "You are on your own, buddy!" Walking back to my office after the meeting I reflected on what at the time I considered an outlandish ambush. But, the more I thought about it, I could see there was some truth in what Springer had said. Our formulas and procedures were complicated and this did create problems in a large manufacturing operation. The challenge is, of course, to develop formulas and procedures that ensure the quality of the products being produced while at the same time not overly complicating the process and forcing shortcuts to be taken during production. It was powerful lesson for me.

Communication is an important element in leadership, one where Springer and I clashed. He spoke of production in terms of black and white while I, from a technical standpoint, responded in shades of gray. The reason for my "gray" answers was simple: when processing a fresh product, such as tomatoes, there are so many biological and operational variables which have to be considered, that a simple answer was not possible. We came from different perspectives, and when trying to communicate, we simply drove each other crazy.

With our reporting structure as it was, interfacing was unavoidable, but we found refuge in a translator Milt Zimmerman. He was

Prego Professional Profile

MILT ZIMMERMAN

Homegrown executive talent is the best way to cultivate trust and ensure that corporate culture is self-sustaining. Managers like Zimmerman were made, not born, especially if they were born right before the Great Depression. As a teenager, he was a star athlete in high school lettering in four sports (later he would be inducted into New Jersey's Rancocas Valley Region High School Sports Hall of Fame), but knew he had to contribute to his family's financial situation by finding employment as soon as possible. In 1940, at age nineteen, Zimmerman approached the first wooden step of CSC's recruiting platform. He was one of a multitude of people who had lined up along Second Street in Camden in hopes of being tapped on the shoulder. That was a signal to go inside the employment office to fill out a job application. (Charlie Gaehring had gone through the same process twenty-two years earlier and at this moment was in charge of tomato processing at the CSC facility.) Zimmerman did not want to disappoint his mother, who had been working at CSC since 1928 (and on a journey that would last for forty-two years).

Then came the touch that changed the young athlete's life forever and launched the career of one of the longest-tenured executives in CSC's history. Zimmerman was directed to the employment office and once inside was handed an application. He was given a temporary position in the personnel office then later he was permanently placed in the SD and assigned to do labor studies.

Zimmerman adapted quickly to his new position in the SD. He was a quick study, good with numbers, and had keen observation skills. His work ethic was unimpeachable, and he quickly became a top performer within the future IE department.

Zimmerman's career path seemed secure until early one Sunday morning his world, along with that of the nation, was turned upside down. The date was December 7, 1941, when the Japanese bombed Pearl Harbor. Along with many of his colleagues, he enlisted in the military. He chose the U.S. Army Air Corps and was sent to flight training school in Pensacola, Florida. He earned his wings and graduated as a second lieutenant. Zimmerman was such a standout as a student that he was assigned to be an instructor in advanced single-engine flight training at the Army's airbase in Laredo, Texas.

After the war, Zimmerman returned to CSC, rejoined the SD, and was later promoted to corporate director of this group. Zimmerman excelled at his work and, in recognition of his leadership potential, Campbell management nominated him for a prestigious Solon Fellows fellowship at MIT. The aviator was accepted, moved to Boston, and spent a year of full-time intensive coursework earning a Master of Science in Industrial Management in 1960. This is an impressive honor for anyone but even more so for someone without a college degree.

a cool-headed, forward-thinking manager, the living example of a true professional. During my interactions with Springer, Zimmerman would smile and benignly watch the two of us debate. He never took sides even though he reported to Springer. Zimmerman was the prototypical CSC manager who rose out of the hourly workforce, and one to be emulated.

Away from the factory environment, Springer and Zimmerman were great traveling partners for me as we spent significant time together on airplanes, in cars, and in long planning sessions. They were constant sources of entertaining stories from both outside and inside the company.

One of my favorites from Zimmerman was in his early days of management. He was surprised to be assigned the recent Princeton graduate and son of Dr. Dorrance—John T. Dorrance Jr.—as his assistant. The future chief executive officer of CSC, John Jr. (or Jack, as they called him) was a tall and lanky youth who had the refined social skills and graces that the best private Main Line Philadelphia education and upbringing could provide.

Zimmerman found Dorrance to be modest, humble, and unassuming, which was astonishing to him, as he was a member of one of the richest and most powerful families in America. Dorrance would take direction and training from him, the son of a lady who worked as a supervisor on the production floor at the Camden soup plant. Almost sixty years later, Zimmerman still shook his head in amazement about the time while they were working together, Dorrance asked if he could be excused to go to a meeting. Permission was given and later Zimmerman found that "the meeting" was actually a company board of directors meeting and that his young assistant was actually a board member. You never know whom you're really interacting with, so the lessons for me were to treat everyone with respect, and regardless of your role, act with humility.

Next Steps

With support from management, including Zimmerman and Springer, we passed all the preliminary product reviews and defined our formulation. We were ready for the perilous home use tests.

12

External Wars

. . . .

Ragu and Hunt's were in an outright marketing and advertising battle. Each invested millions of dollars in its own market-ing programs to "out-thicken" and "out-spice" the other. It was more of a marketing contest than an effort to produce a good quality food product. To deliver on the promise of product claims such as "thick and zesty," both companies added starch thickeners to their sauces, resulting in products that were off-red in color. They then added herb and spice extracts (not whole herbs or spices) to deliver on "zesty," which created the metallic taste and muted any semblance of tomato taste. Our food technologists thought it was insane from a product quality standpoint to continue to play that flavor ping-pong; but, to the marketers and ad agencies for the two warring sides, it was a brilliant move to capture market share. CSC stayed its course on no artificial additives or thickeners, but had to be sure marketing efforts caught the consumers' attention with smaller budgets. We had to be sure that our product was superior in taste, color, and mouthfeel, and the best way we knew to evaluate that was through home use tests.

Home Use Test

"This product is garrrbage, pure garrrbage!" One of the more boisterous homemakers who was chosen to participate in the consumer taste tests in the late fall of 1980 drug out the "r" sound in the word like the guttural roar of a lioness in a perfect North Jersey accent. Dark hair and an attitude to match, she represented the epitome of the make-from-scratch consumer the product development team would need to convert to meet projected sales numbers of the SHB paste spaghetti sauce.

Garnering information from the focus groups of potential consumers played a major part of the launch of any new product. After months, sometimes years of creation dedicated to plant breeding and growth, ingredient processing, and recipe formulation, the product would be brought in front of consumers to gather their opinions, which would sometimes dictate future formula changes or optimizations.

CSC regularly utilized many types of market and consumer research, often in parallel. Marketing Research went into full gear conducting continuous optimizing taste testing, focus groups, and home use placements. Home use testing often involved sending a product sample to a homemaker with a questionnaire, asking her to fill it out after using the product and sending it back. Sometimes, the home use testing would be followed by a focus group, where the opinions would be gathered in person under the watchful eye of the focus group moderator.

For the SHB spaghetti sauce, the process was no different. The highly-anticipated day chosen for the focus group following a home use test had been one of those steel-blue days with the temperature in the mid-forties and the sun hidden by clouds and a hazy mist. We were heading north to where there was a high concentration of Italians, worth the hour-up and hour-back drive on the New Jersey Turnpike. Schilling's cloudy outlook matched the heavy sky as we walked into the focus group that evening. He was apprehensive as to the feedback he was to receive from a panel of twelve women who had tried his product in a home use test. Though he had been perfecting it for the last twelve months, he didn't know if he would be headed back to his kitchen for more refinements or receive confirmation to move forward to start scaling up for market testing.

Schilling had even more reason for his anxiety; this was the first time in all his years as a research chef that he would be attending a focus group. He had apprenticed as a teenager under a series of master chefs, served as a cook in the Swiss Army, and worked as an executive chef in restaurants and hotels in Europe and the United States. He had withstood their various forms of scrutiny but he had no experience that would prepare him for face-to-face feedback from customers.

Even though there would be a one-way mirror between him and the panelists, Schilling feared for the worst. When he was working as a restaurant executive chef he mainly stayed in the kitchen allowing the waiters and the maître d' to communicate with the diners. Chef Schilling never had to interface with customers while he was at CSC and little did he know he was about to meet some of the harshest food critics concerning spaghetti sauce outside of Italy.

The panel of twelve women was selected because they prepared their own spaghetti sauce. Every woman sitting around the discussion table had an Italian surname, and a New York City-sized attitude as to what constituted good food. No wallflowers among these ladies, they were Italian proud and not shy about sharing their opinion. Each woman was given the test product and asked to prepare it in their homes. Then, they were asked to serve it to their families. If they agreed to show up for the focus group discussion about the experience, they would be compensated monetarily for their time and efforts.

The inside of the viewers room was framed with black painted walls containing three rows of folding chairs facing the one-way mirror. The only light in the room was that which shone through the mirror from the fully lit interview space. Our room was also fitted with speakers. Not only could we observe the participants but we could follow every word of their discussions.

A professional moderator facilitated discussions and asked pertinent questions without trying to influence or prejudice (either positively or negatively) the responses of the focus group participants. If focus group moderators try to control the group too tightly, they will not get informative and candid responses; if they allow too much freedom, a Tower of Babel results; if you overly direct questions, then the client becomes upset.

This is a much more difficult job then you would first anticipate, like a ringmaster in a twelve-ring circus trying to keep order when all twelve individuals try to express their opinion all at the same time and also trying to prevent the "lead cow" syndrome from occurring. That is when an overly dominant individual expresses their opinion so strongly that it sways the other participants either negatively or positively. It takes a combination of charm, tactfulness, and the quick-thinking ability of an air traffic controller to keep the group focused and on task.

By this time in my career, I had attended many focus groups, and usually walked away with an unsettled feeling. My experience was that you rarely received overwhelmingly positive results, but more like negative direction in various shades of gray. This was a necessary step in developing and improving a consumer product, but you needed a strong sense of humility and a thick skin to survive the process, as was the case that night.

When Schilling sat in his seat in the front row less than a foot from the one-way mirror, I could see by the reflected light of the interview room as the ladies started to take their seats, the stress in his face and his fingers folding into an ever-tightening fist. Chef Schilling had the stoic personality of most northern Europeans; he did not talk much but when he did, everyone listened. He was slow to anger, but when he did get angry, it was best to clear out. Harry Truman gave good advice when he said, "If you cannot stand the heat, get out of the kitchen." Having worked closely with Schilling for several years and knowing his temperament, I sat down next to him, anticipating there may be some heat tonight. If there were an all-out product lynching, I wanted to be at Schilling's side. My instincts proved on point. Before even half of the ladies had made their comments, it was evident that this was going to be another rough night in the dark room behind the looking glass.

Garrrbage

When the focus group participant laid out her insulting, "It's just pure garrrbage," instantly Schilling was out of his chair swearing in his native language, his nose only inches from the glass. He seemed ready to pounce on the thin membrane of glass that separated the two rooms. Schilling was as strong as a weightlifter. It would have taken only a flick of his forearm or a swift head butt to shatter the four-by-eight-foot mirrored glass into a thousand shards of rubble. The Swiss are passionate about their crafts, food, and watches. The Swiss are also known for their discipline, and being Army-trained, he had great respect for his superiors. With one touch to his forearm, I was able to coax him back to his seat.

The discussions continued on the same negative theme. The session ended with no further dramatics on either side of the mirror, though I perceived a few nervous glances toward the mirror, and wondered if they heard Schilling's outburst. As they cleaned up and we prepared to leave, Schilling and I sat in bewilderment

at receiving such negative feedback. Until this time, all the consumer and taste tests were positive, and even glowing, against the
commercial competition. What had we calculated so wrongly?
This should have been the indication, right then and there, that
we had ventured into an unchartered product category. We had
dared to enter the holy ground of homemade spaghetti sauce and
broken the sacraments of the kitchen and offended generations of
old recipes. The ladies were insulted we would try to compete with
their grandmothers' recipes with something presented in glass.
We had committed sacrilege and were infidels in the eyes of these
high priestesses.

The Long Ride Home

I slid into the driver's seat of the car and groaned when my legs
touched the cold seat, and my hands grabbed the frigid steering
wheel. The temperature had dropped below freezing while we
were in the focus group. Our moods had sunk as well, because of
the criticisms of our new product prototype. I was trying to be as
upbeat as possible to reassure Schilling things would be fine, and
this was a learning experience and not a setback. From past experience, I knew Schilling was sensitive to criticism and could go into
a funk, especially if he considered the criticism unjust. I attempted
to engage him in a discussion as we drove from the parking lot and
pulled onto the New Jersey Turnpike.

With the heater blower set on maximum, Schilling responded in
polite short sentences, but he had spent a full day of work back at
the R&D department and was by now exhausted. All he wanted to
do was lay his head back, close his eyes, and forget what had trans-
pired in the little chamber of horrors. Just before nodding off he
apologized for the third time for losing his temper and standing,
and hoped he had not caused a problem. I reassured him I was close
to doing the same thing, and there was no damage caused. Plus, he

should look on the bright side of things—we would have a good laugh in his kitchen with the staff in the morning.

The crystal clear night air made for excellent driving conditions, and with light traffic ahead I tried to make myself relax, clear my mind, and focus on the road. This proved to be an impossible task. For the last several weeks, the tension of the multiple tasks I was trying to manage both domestically and internationally was starting to build, and tonight's negative reviews were only going to add additional stress on my already overflowing schedule.

The marketing and ad agency people were going to demand that the issues raised in the focus group be addressed immediately, which would mean weeks of reformulation work in preparation for another round of consumer tests. Management was already skittish about launching a new product in a new product category, so any news on product quality problems would be a convenient excuse to withdraw support to proceed to test market.

These were concerns but not the biggest reason for my building angst. Since the formation of the Product Technology group, more projects had been assigned with reporting responsibility to the newly-formed beverage and grocery strategic business units (SBU). With more projects, more people were brought on board with MBAs, advancing our business operations. This was an exciting time and I welcomed the increased responsibility and advancement within the product development department, but the constant meetings and travel was starting to wear me thin. I was spending more and more time away from home, which meant that my wife was doing much more than her share in raising our two small boys, and I missed them.

According to the organization chart for R&D, I only had one boss and that was Miller, but in actuality I was accountable to multiple bosses (the SBU directors, numerous MBA-trained marketing managers, and ultimately Shaub). Keeping one boss pleased was challenging enough, but balancing the egos and priorities of hard-charging executives was a skill set that this farmer-turned-product-developer was struggling to perfect.

Plus, Shaub had his sights set on another project. Encouraged by the success of the Tomato Solids Task Force, Shaub desired to improve the efficiency of CSC's poultry processing operations. Shaub instructed Miller to set up a special poultry processing research group within the Product Development department. Not only was CSC one of the top tomato processors in the world, it was also a world leader in raising and processing poultry. Since Swanson Foods was acquired by CSC in the 1950s, increasing priority was placed on poultry processing as well as frozen food processing. CSC became one of the leading frozen food manufacturers and subsequently had grown into a major presence in the poultry industry. Their top-selling product was frozen fried chicken for TV dinners and bulk pack. Shaub's plan was to be the dominant player in poultry, just as the company was in tomato processing.

In recognition of Miller's superb management talent and tenable expertise, he was promoted to VP of Product Development for both the Canned and Frozen Food divisions. He had the unenviable task of keeping the presidents of both divisions happy along with overseeing special assignments from Shaub. Miller approached me with the directive to set up a poultry processing development research group, but he demurred, indicating he thought the Product Technology group already had too many projects and were too busy to take on any additional assignments especially as big as this project was anticipated to become. I relished challenges (especially ones with high visibility) so I aggressively lobbied Miller for the assignment. My argument was the work on the Tomato Solids Task Force was gearing down (now that most of the experimental work had been completed on the SHB process) and the sauce project was in its final stages of development. Miller reluctantly relented; he assigned the project to the Product Technology group and arranged a meeting with Shaub to receive our marching orders.

The first directive was for me to make a visit to the Sumter, South Carolina, and Fayetteville, Arkansas, poultry operations and report back with my recommendations. There, I toured the chicken hatcheries, feed mills, grower houses, and the processing plants. Both operations were impressive examples of true vertical integration. Dr. John T. Dorrance Sr. would have been proud. But there were efficiencies to be realized, and I was tasked to lead that charge. I was looking forward to continued work in poultry processing but knew I had to finish work on the sauce.

Now the chickens were proverbially coming home to roost on *my* shoulders as I sped down the dark ribbon of highway. It was a disconcerting feeling to be both tense and exhausted all at the same time. I reflexively pushed hard on the steering wheel so my back, shoulders, and head would be flattened against the back of the seat in an effort to relieve the tension in my arms and neck. This was a technique that I successfully used many times in long trips back to Ohio with my family, but nothing was working on this starlit night. Ideas and thoughts were exploding inside my mind like popcorn in a microwave bag. The unpleasantries of the focus group faded as I began to realize that the scope of poultry project was way beyond anything I had worked on previously. Not only was I starting from a knowledge and experience base of zero, but the really scary issue was the realization that the crux of the problem about to be tackled was not a process or an equipment design issue but one of biochemistry.

The full immensity of the project I had agreed to take on—actually champion—was starting to sink in at the primal level. Feeling overwhelmed, I allowed myself to slip into a funk even though I had tried to prevent Schilling from doing the same thing only thirty minutes previously. Serenaded by the monotonous drone of the car tires on pavement, I was holding my own private pity party. "Why do I always do this to myself? Sign up for 'mission impossibles' or worst yet, create them for myself and end up with perpetual grief!"

This was not the first time I had felt this lament, nor would it be my last. For those of us who are highly ambitious, being chosen for big assignments is highly motivating, and the fear of failure, of loss of "face," is worse than a demotion or loss in pay. The mindset is, "If I fail at this, I may never get another big project." Star athletes feel something similar; they feel if they don't perform, they won't start the next game. Quite simply, we must keep striving or we'll never get to do it again.

Fortunately, the exit ramp was only a few miles ahead. When I reached over to gently wake Schilling to ask for directions to his house, I realized that I was not alone in this enterprise and was surrounded by an excellent team starting with the gentleman sitting next to me. "Garbage, my ass! Tomorrow promises to be a great new day!" I said, pounding on the steering wheel as Schilling opened the door of the car, got out, and waved goodbye.

Back in the Kitchen

The information that we gathered from the focus group was incorporated into successive kitchen batches as they started the repetitive process of reformulating the spaghetti sauce. Additional consumer tests were conducted and again the results indicated that the product needed to be sweeter and less acidic. It became a joke in the kitchen that every time the results came back with request to make the product sweeter, Schilling would grumble that he was no longer making an Italian sauce, but a dessert sauce.

CSC's policy was to use no artificial ingredients, which meant finding natural sources of antioxidants, colorings, flavorings, etc. This was a product researcher's and developer's paradise. It opened up all kinds of process and product development opportunities and challenges. With a corporate philosophy of "all natural," there were no easy fixes for a product that was off-color or off-taste, like adding a coloring or boosting the taste with an artificial flavoring. The artificial ingredient producers, who had excellent quality and safe product offerings, just hated Campbell's Soup. They tried hard, but could never get a toe, let alone a foot, in the door to sell to any of the chefs. They would go the natural route, no matter how long it took, or how expensive it was—but we still had to be conscious of the costs.

The Cost Study: The Odyssey Continues

More than two years after Harold Shaub created the Tomato Solids Task Force (and launching my odyssey into "everything tomato"), we had finally arrived at the critical decision point known as the cost study. We had survived two years of "endless summers," eleventh-hour heroics to produce the SHB tomato paste at the Sacramento paste plant, being instructed by a senior executive not to work on spaghetti sauce, the failure of the ketchup test market, being told our product was "garbage" by a critical focus group, and too many formulations to count. Marketing finally had given their approval of the product formulation and was deeply involved with the ad agency in creating the label design and developing ad copy. We were eager to present the product to the Product Committee for the Market Test approval. All was in place except for one last hurdle—and it was a big one—known as the "cost study." Now was the time to bring in the industrial engineers.

Newly created, the Industrial Engineering (IE) department took the former SD responsibilities to a whole new level of quality and cost awareness. The IE department was responsible for conducting an in-depth cost study, as we did with all products and processes, of every cost point in the manufacturing of the proposed new product or product extension. Simultaneously our allies and our foes, the analysts who costed out our processes for approval could also help defeat a new product if the numbers exceeded their cost barriers. Argument after argument ensued between the Product Development team and IE to keep quality high and costs low.

They flow-charted every phase of the unit operations to produce the final product that would be on the grocery shelf, starting with the special tomatoes to the investment to be made in the paste plant upgrades, the installation of new blending tanks, the glass filling and labeling line plus the formula and procedures. On top of these process and production expense reviews, the marketing and ad agency expenses had to be included. All during this in-depth review, they never shared information; they just asked question after question. This dreaded cost study was a bane to all product developers; it was the boneyard of numerous new product developers' ambitions. Some would describe the process as "having a root canal while being questioned by a tax accountant."

More high anxiety. Passing Prego's cost study was the last box we had to check before being approved to present to the Product Committee.

Having gone thru this process many times previously, I was well aware that no compromises would be made in analyzing the internal rate of return and margin goals of the company. If the numbers didn't fit, Prego was a "no-go." It was as simple as that. I also was aware that we had submitted a premium formula to achieve our consumer acceptance scores, putting further pressure on the profitability of the product. We were apprehensive that we weren't going to make the numbers.

It seemed like an eternity, but it probably was only a couple weeks of anxiously awaiting the results. Finally, I heard a knock on my partition as Ziggy, my contact in IE, walked over to my desk saying casually, "Hey, Bill, you got a moment? Good news, we finished the Prego analysis and it looks like it's a 'go.'" I let out the breath I didn't realize I was holding.

The traffic light went from red to yellow to green. Next stop was the Product Committee.

Prego in the Shark Tank

I watched the CEO and the other major executives take positions around the presentation table and prepared for the tension-filled affair. Unlike my two younger brothers, I was not a natural born salesman, being far too introspective. Since my pumpkin pie experience, though, I had gained confidence. I learned that the key to a successful presentation was to capture the imagination of the senior executives, sharing with them the product vision.

Most of the product showings at the Product Committee were routine and perfunctory, but scratch one millimeter below the surface and the ambience was that of a prize fight. Each participant protected and projected the interests of their respective departments. If an executive balked at a new product introduction because it would take dollars from his capital expenditure budget, even the best ideas could be rejected. It was a delicate dance of verbal and body language.

More than one naïve individual had his career sidetracked by inadvertently venturing into the minefield by making a comment when one or two of the executives were in a protective mode. This lack of political judgment was most hazardous during product cost and quality decisions. Passions ran deep. Depending on the issues being presented, sometimes strange alliances were formed between proponents previously on opposite sides of the argument. It took an adept awareness and sensitivity by the presenters, who were mostly the product developers, to know where the mines were buried. Experienced helped but it was best to have a strong mentor in the R&D department, as I did in Ralph Miller, and I was confident in our product.

The product showing began. The executives tasted it and nodded. I went through the standard routine of outlining a brief background on the product, the SHB paste process and the consumer test results. Herb Baum next presented the projected sales figures and costs, and when it came to the money, that's when the real drama started.

A Big Garage

When the authorization was finally given at the Product Committee meeting, Shaub pointed his finger and actually backed Baum into a corner, calmly saying, "Herb, you better hope that this test market goes well, or otherwise you're going to need a large garage because this is where all the leftover product is going to go." Baum with his back to the wall meekly smiled and commented that he thought the test market would do well. Once this melodrama had acted out, Shaub smiled and approved test markets to be conducted in Youngstown, Ohio, and Green Bay, Wisconsin. Youngstown was chosen because it was a highly developed spaghetti sauce market with a large Italian population. As a counter balance, Green Bay was a low developed spaghetti sauce market with a low ethnic Italian presence. As they adjourned the Product Committee meeting, I whispered to Baum that I had a large garage and Baum was welcome to use it to store any surplus product. Baum, the consummate diplomat smiled, nodded his head, and thanked everyone for their efforts.

Financial Duel

Behind the scenes, another internal duel was threatening that no one on the Product Development team was aware of—one that would have influenced culinary history had the outcome been different. Bill Williams, president of the Canned Foods division, envisioned the next step of his long-term career with CSC as company president, covertly campaigning to replace Shaub when he stepped down. In this type of corporate organization, the "higher" you go, the fewer positions there are, and the competition for the top spot was fierce. With internal promotion a long tradition within CSC, every long-term employee in a leadership role likely viewed the company presidency as a possibility. In turn, each of those division heads was being considered for that role, and faced severe scrutiny and intense pressure to manage his budget and make his production numbers. When it came time to make the pledge of corporate support, Shaub saw the potential of

Prego and knew a substantial allocation of funds would be necessary to produce and launch it.

Baum Drops a Bomb

Shaub had vested interest in Baum's success; he had given Baum the special assignment of marketing Prego. But Baum had proposed a radical investment strategy: if your target was 20 percent of the market, you needed to spend 20 percent of the market value. This suggested marketing budget epitomized deficit spending and was counter to CSC's traditional marketing approach. In the middle of the financial calendar, Shaub told Williams to take $40 million out of his regular operating budget and put it toward upgrading production equipment in Napoleon and marketing campaigns for Prego.

Bill Williams was livid. How could this junior associate, whom he personally recruited, pose this? Williams had admired Baum's work. He had created a new position for Baum. And now, he was the source of this audacious request of $40 million. This is how he was repaid for giving Baum this incredible career opportunity?

He held fast to his budget. Investing in hard assets, like the upgrade at the Napoleon plant, was understandable. If you bought a new piece of equipment there was potential for reuse, but once you spent money on marketing, it was gone. He could not see the logic in moving money away from existing operations of known revenue producers for an unproven product in his huge division. Williams was responsible for 80 percent of the company's revenue, and had little interest in a startup. Meeting his numbers with $40 million less would be a challenge, and Williams did not want to comply.

The financial duel was on: Williams versus Shaub-backed Baum.

History had shown there would be no product success without major exposure to build market awareness and demand. That work needed to be started immediately in advance of market tests. Baum demanded more support and would not back off on his marketing program. Baum courageously approached Shaub in a critical conversation asking for more support. The product showed glowing consumer reports, and no one besides Williams questioned the product. In Baum's view, it just came down to numbers.

Decisions had to be made. Shaub was in the middle.

In a chess-like move, Shaub sent Baum to CSC's VP of Finance, Dick Censitis, to work it out with Williams. Censitis countered with the offer that he would approve the project if Baum would reduce the spending to half of the original request. Baum said no and received the silent treatment from Shaub for six weeks. Shaub then finally relented and gave him the go-ahead with the original plan of $40 million. Shaub could have mandated this allocation, but instead chose diplomacy. Censitis and Williams came to agreement between the product forecasts and projections, and the money was allocated for Prego.

The financial duel was over and the spaghetti sauce production was approved; however, the high-tension situation continued, with Williams displeased at the outcome. The spaghetti sauce production and launch escaped derailment because of the funding issue. Had the financial duel ended another way, the spaghetti sauce would have been delayed or permanently shelved in Product Development. Funding requests for marketing and production became a little bit easier, but never without a fight.

I learned two lessons from this about leadership versus management. First, Shaub could have wielded his authority and "forced" Williams to change his budget. He displayed leadership instead, encouraging a discussion through which Williams made his decision. Thus, the relationship between the Shaub and Williams was preserved. Diplomacy is a requirement for dealing with others you depend on. The second lesson I learned is the value of having like-minded people speaking the "language" (in this case numbers) during cross-functional negotiations. Sometimes you need to escalate the issue to someone who speaks multiple "languages" to find a solution.

Make It Sweeter!

Meanwhile, with the approval of the Product Committee, Prego continued to be prepared for the test markets. Why were so many iterations on the formulation necessary? It boils down to overcoming the emotional connection most people have with food. Eating is a multi-sensory and emotional personal experience. Change the appearance, texture, flavor, or color of a food product and it will most likely be rejected by loyalists to the original. Therefore, changes had to be subtle and gradual in nature.

After many iterations, the desired sugar-acid ratio was achieved and it became the gold standard going forward. Based on the success of Prego in the marketplace, this was the proper direction, but at the time, Schilling and everyone else on the Prego development team seriously questioned the wisdom of making a sweeter product. This was a classic example where doing extensive consumer research and product testing was about to pay large dividends. We were ready to go to test market.

The Two-City Test Market

Herb Baum headed back to his office after the Product Committee approval, anxious to begin the arduous task of putting together a plan to launch two test markets. He had been put through the ringer with Shaub, now he had to execute against it. He had to deal with a new ad agency, a new product concept in a new product category packaged in a glass container instead of a tin can. This was going to be a triple paradigm shift for the company, and it was do-or-die for him. If his marketing plan was not implemented or implemented well, the product would not jump off the shelf the way it needed to do. A slower adoption would have given Ragu time to catch up and likely crush the young competitor.

Baum instinctively repeated a successful lesson from CSC's history. From the outside, the parallels between Baum's plan for launching Prego and Dorrance's plan for launching the condensed soup products were clear. History does repeat itself, what works and doesn't work, and people are people.

The target of advertising was both the consumer and the competitor. The real competitor for both condensed soups and Prego was not other products but the housewives. John T. Dorrance Sr. realized that the competitor and the consumer were the same. He focused his advertising on the convenience, low cost, and nutrition of condensed soup in magazines catering to women such as *The Saturday Evening Post* and *American Magazine*. In another stroke of brilliance, Dorrance included the price of a can of soup in the advertising copy, establishing a standard retail price of $0.10 (versus an arbitrary one set by the retailers). A customer could go into any store and know what the price would be. No retailer was willing to withstand the wrath of a customer confronted by a higher shelf price than what was advertised.

In Dorrance's time, housewives were making the purchase decisions across the board for all socio-economic classes, and the same was true six decades later in Baum's time. Baum would aggressively advertise directly to Prego's consumer/competitor, the housewife. Campbell's Soup had created a jarred prepared spaghetti sauce that was of acceptable quality to those who made their own sauce. This created a new segment and expanded the entire category. He knew that sales would not solely come from Ragu and Hunt's buyers, but also the housewives who previously made their own spaghetti sauce without a comparable quality product until they tried Prego.

Baum knew from his ad agency experience working on the CSC product lines that to introduce a brand-new product with no name recognition that "heavy upfront" (pre-launch and launch) marketing with aggressive advertising and couponing would be needed to get consumers to purchase the product. His intention was to spend 60 percent of budget in the first launch, creating consumer demand from the marketing and enticing people to try it.

Like Dorrance offering in-store soup samples, Baum was confident once people tried the Prego product, they would repurchase it and tell their friends. With the help of LKP, Baum would focus advertising on the "homestyle" all-natural chunkiness and convenience of Prego, encouraging a purchase with the money-saving coupons.

Baum's launch plan, while costly, was necessary to fight the entrenched incumbents of Ragu and Hunt's and to capture the attention of the housewives making their own sauces. Their trial and conversion to Prego users would require carefully executed tactics; this would be important in the test markets but critical in the national distribution after the test markets were the success Baum expected them to be.

Next, Baum had to address the impending distribution of Prego. For the condensed soups, Dorrance's plan was to make sure that Campbell's Soup was made available on the shelves of both large retailers like A&P (The Great Atlantic and Pacific Tea Company) all the way down to small mom-and-pop grocery stores. He also ensured the retail price of a can of soup was the same to the customer regardless of regional location or whether the retailer ordered a single case or a whole truckload at a time. This would be important for Prego as well; Baum identified his major grocery store chain contracts as well as smaller grocers and planned Prego's staggered launch to various markets within Campbell's Soup's distribution. Prego was almost ready to launch.

Prego Professional Profile

DR. BILL STINSON

A swish of leaves, cracking of branches, and a dull thud echoed through the orchard. "There he goes again!" sang out a teenage boy, high in a neighboring apple tree. "Paratrooper Bill has hit the deck again! It's the second time this afternoon. He'll risk life and limb to be the top apple picker," continued the young farm laborer laughing so hard that he almost toppled from his tree branch, too. Even as a teenager growing up in northeastern Ohio, Bill Stinson was determined to achieve his goals. Whether it was delivering papers in a blinding snowstorm or stretching to pick the farthest apple, Stinson never backed down from a challenge, and, when he fell out of the tree, he always climbed back up and picked more apples than anyone else.

Stinson loved working outside, even hand-hoeing corn in the summertime at thirty cents per hour. He learned early on the meaning of "a long row to hoe" as he weeded cornrows in ninety-degree temperatures. Growing up, Stinson wanted to be a farmer, specifically a dairy farmer. He idolized his uncle, who owned and operated a successful nearby dairy. Stinson thought that this was the career for him, despite his living in town with his parents, who were both non-farm professionals. His mother was a nurse and his father a highly-respected superintendent of schools in Stark County. (Later, the W. S. Stinson Elementary School in Canal Fulton would be named after him.)

Stinson headed to OSU, enjoying membership in the Alpha Gamma Rho fraternity, and scoring the privilege of playing tuba with the marching band every Saturday at the football game. When Stinson enrolled, he had no intention of studying food processing. His goal was to be on the other side of the food chain—being a dairy farmer and producing milk. However, when he took an introductory agriculture survey course, he realized that large amounts of capital would be necessary to start a dairy cow operation and he had no hope of raising money to purchase land, equipment, and the livestock.

During a faculty presentation, Dr. Gould had a profound impact on Stinson (like all of his students), who immediately switched his major to horticulture. Stinson graduated with his B.S. degree in June 1961 when the country was in the middle of a standoff between East and West Berlin. Because he was in the advanced ROTC program, he was immediately inducted into the army and commissioned as a second lieutenant. After he completed his tour of duty in the Quartermaster Corps, he returned to Columbus and met Gould about the possibility of attending graduate school. Gould had served in the Quartermaster Corps himself, and welcomed him back with open arms.

Stinson was offered a fellowship and assigned to Dr. Jean Geisman. Stinson's graduate studies were focused on strontium 90, a heavy radioactive isotope produced during an atomic bomb explosion, a highly-toxic contaminant to plant and animal life. With literally thousands of nuclear armed missiles facing each other in the East and the West at the height of the tensions between the United States and Russia, there were major concerns about hazards of fallout and food safety. Working alongside his advisor, Stinson did both his master's and PhD research on this subject. Dr. Geisman was an excellent mentor to Stinson and provided invaluable support in the statistical interpretation of his data.

In 1966, Gould introduced General Foods to Stinson, and the young PhD was hired to work in the JELL-O Division product development group located in White Plains, New York. Later, Stinson was assigned to work on developing a shelf-stable popcorn chip; Bill's team successfully developed a prototype but the test market results were disappointing.

After four years, Stinson left General Foods to join the Frank

Tea and Spice Company as their head of R&D and Quality Control. This was an exciting time for Stinson; a lot of venture capital dollars had been invested into this company, and it had an atmosphere of a startup. However, the economic downturn of the early 1970s, coupled with President Nixon's ninety-day wage–price freeze in 1971 created a major head wind for this Cincinnati-based condiment supplier. Over the next several years as prospects dimmed, Frank Tea and Spice Company was bought out by Durkee Foods and Stinson was forced to review his options. Fortunately, the CSC was looking for a product development manager, because Shaub felt that new ideas and people with different perspectives would help improve the creativity and innovation of the company's research and development activities.

Continuing Responsibilities

While Baum was fighting the financial battle, we were getting production details in order and handling some international projects as well. I relied on Bill Stinson as manager to handle the remaining product development details. (The relationship with Stinson went way back to my undergraduate days at OSU, with my looking up to him as a graduate student. We had a lot in common, starting with being Ohio farm boys.) With Prego in good hands, I could go focus on other projects such as diced tomato sourcing, poultry processing, protein texturization, and the juice work in progress within my group.

Bill Stinson's next contribution was overseeing the retrofits at the Napoleon plant.

13

Napoleon Plant Retrofits

. . . .

I n preparation for the two-city test market, a Prego production line was installed at the Napoleon, Ohio, V8 processing building in early 1982. The Napoleon plant was chosen as the ideal location to produce the product because the V8 facility was a separate building from the main soup operations and vacant during the "off-tomato season." The plant, originally designed for vegetable juice blending, filling, and labeling, was soon to be challenged to produce a thick spaghetti sauce packed in a glass jar.

Predictions of the Napoleon Staff

Having lunch in the plant manager's dining room would sometimes resemble a tag-team wrestling match. When attending these affairs, it was sometimes difficult to distinguish the combatants because, depending on the day, it could be Production versus Quality Control, Quality Control versus Purchasing, Engineering versus Accounting, or everyone being upset with everyone else, including the plant manager. Visitors from corporate were advised to stay neutral, especially if they were from R&D. If you sided with one group, you ended up being the enemy of the others. If you tried to stay neutral as a conscientious objector, you usually ended up in the middle of this proverbial food fight. After one or two experiences of this kind, most R&D visitors would beg off invitations to the plant manager's dining room by saying that they were too busy running tests or had to go to the warehouse to check on product that was being shipped back to the GO. Refusing to attend also had its downsides, in that one could be labeled an "elitist from the East" and in turn would not receive cooperation while visiting the plant. It was difficult to know the best course of action.

When the time came to run the first full-scale production test of Prego at the Napoleon plant, I volunteered to go. When I arrived, I was glad to be invited to lunch in the plant manager's dining room. "What a difference this trip was than when I toured it as a star-struck undergraduate," I thought. I was sure that the plant manager and his staff would be excited and pleased that Napoleon was chosen to run this important first pack and especially appreciative of the extra production volume that this product would represent. I also thought this would be an excellent time to share the results of the recent consumer test and market projections for Prego with the Napoleon leadership team.

Unfortunately, these proved to be incorrect assumptions. The superintendent of production was upset at yet another disruption. The Quality Control manager, Hank Springer, was grousing that the formula and procedures documents did not seem to be in proper order, and the head engineer was angry at corporate engineering because the project authorization only provided enough funds to shoehorn the sauce-making equipment into the V8 line. Everyone expressed doubt that the existing blending and filling equipment could handle a thick and delicate product like spaghetti sauce.

The plant manager seemed oblivious to all these expressed concerns; he was on a high horse because one of the local state representatives had voted on a tax issue contrary to a CSC directive. Consequently, he was getting heat from corporate. The first thing out of his mouth as he was buttering a saltine cracker to eat with his bowl of tomato soup was, "Well, what I always say is, either you are for us or you are against us! There is no middle ground." The whole time he was making this declaration, he was staring directly at me.

Fortunately, it was hunting season and someone out of his line of sight said, "I shot two of the biggest Canada geese over the weekend that I ever have seen. Boy, are they fat this year." Like a ballerina doing a pirouette, the plant manager changed the subject and the "High Noon" showdown moved into a sideshow. No one was interested in what I had to say. They were not buying anything that anyone from corporate had to sell. They had already heard too many promises of "the next great thing," and very few had ever lived up to the hype. These were combat veterans of the soup wars and always viewed anyone from headquarters with cautious suspicion.

Startup Crew, Part I

"Hello, my name is Ross Kelley and I am the supervisor who will be helping you with your Prego startup special batch," said a smiling young man vigorously shaking my hand as we walked into the hallway from the dining room. I was feeling rather spent after lunch, but Kelley was energized. Dressed all in white, he cradled his blue hard hat in his left arm indicating that he was from the Manufacturing department. After the argumentative environment of the dining room, this was definitely a welcomed relief; here was someone who was obviously excited about the prospects of starting up a brand-new product line. Kelley was "Midwest

friendly" and approximately the same age as me, with the quali-
ties of enthusiasm and positive determination of many of the production floor-level people. But there was something special about
Kelley—he seemed much more polished and knowledgeable than
his contemporaries.

Kelley had a distinct advantage over his fellow manufacturing
employees in that he had scientific training, specifically in food
technology, and he had a true understanding and appreciation for
the technical aspects of food manufacturing. This allowed him to
communicate on an equal footing with the chemists from Quality
Control and the food technologists from R&D, thus creating within
himself a quiet confidence as well as the respect of his team.

Kelley also developed a stubborn streak of self-independence
which would mature into finely-tuned leadership skills later in his
life. He had stints in human resources and financial planning but
volunteered to be the area manager of the Prego production startup
line. His staff of maintenance professionals, cooks, machine operators, supervisors, and quality control individuals had also volunteered to be on the prestigious Prego startup production team. They
were motivated by the excitement of a new challenge and wanted
to do something else besides make soup. Equally important was the
opportunity for overtime pay and future advancement.

As he escorted me to the Prego production line, Kelley explained
that they had been busy retrofitting the blending kettles, the filling
machine, and the labeling equipment. Quality Control Manager
Hank Springer had voiced his concerns in the dining room that the
V8 blending and pumping equipment would be too harsh, but what
really bothered Kelley was the filling and labeling equipment. These
were old units, originally built for tough tin cans, not glass. No one,
from Engineering to Manufacturing, had any experience with glass
jars. Everyone was anxious, which would have helped explain the
tension in the plant manager's dining room. They had been working

Prego Professional Profile

ROSS KELLEY

Ross Kelley was no stranger to getting dirty and confronting challenges. Growing up in the 1960s in Lima, Ohio, meant that most teenage boys worked odd jobs like delivering papers, baling hay in the summer, or bagging groceries to earn spending money and to save for college. It wasn't much different for Kelley except that his fondest job (for which he received no pay) was to gather road kill to feed an eclectic collection of raptors and other injured birds under the care of a family friend. He went on to do volunteer work with the local large animal veterinarian and determined that this was the profession he would pursue. In a cruel twist of fate, Kelley's father passed away his senior year in high school. The younger Mr. Kelley felt obligated to help his mother and younger brother after the loss of the major breadwinner for the family. Therefore, he enrolled in the nearby Lima regional branch campus of OSU instead of the main campus in Columbus. This allowed him to live at home and supplement the family's income working part-time jobs ranging from construction to sales at Montgomery Ward. He also continued to do volunteer work for his veterinarian mentor.

He began taking the prerequisite courses to apply to veterinary college. In the 1970s, the vet school was actually more difficult to get into than the medical school. His good grades and a sterling reference from the local veterinarian were not enough to meet the very restrictive guidelines for admission to OSU's College of Veterinary Medicine. He kept the rejection letter as a reminder of what could have been, but more importantly, as an anchor that helped him remain humble and hungry.

As providence sometimes provides, when one door closes, another door opens. In Kelley's case, two doors opened. The first was his marriage to his longtime girlfriend Nancy, and the second was his introduction to Wilbur A. Gould, head of Food Technology in the Horticulture Department of the Agricultural College at OSU. Nancy was a talented stenographer and typist and soon found a job as an administrative secretary to the dean of the College of Engineering. This helped relieve the financial stress of attending university and Kelley was allowed to focus all his energies on his new passion, food technology.

All his coursework for veterinary medicine transferred seamlessly, and under the watchful eye of Gould, he began building the foundation for what would become a highly successful career in the food industry—all of which would be spent with CSC in operations and executive management. Kelley's first experience, however, with CSC was not a good one.

When Kelley earned his Bachelor of Science in Food Technology, he transferred to the Poultry Science department and began working on a Master of Science degree. His studies were interrupted when Hank Springer, the quality control manager of the Napoleon, Ohio, CSC factory, offered him a position in the Quality Control department. Kelley determined that this was a position he could not pass up, and he dropped out of grad school. However, by the time that he was to begin his employment, a corporate-wide personnel cutback had eliminated his job. This was in 1975 in the middle of the economic crisis with interest rates reaching 20 percent and major cutbacks in employment being made across the country. Hired and fired without even working a day and no place to go, Kelley and his wife moved back to Lima where he found work as a janitor at an oil refinery.

After a couple of months, a position as an entry-level production supervisor opened up in the canned soup filling line. Kelley readily accepted the offer even though the pay was less than that of his janitorial position. Kelley started working at the Napoleon soup factory in 1975 in the central filling and labeling section.

for weeks on the retrofit, but no one knew exactly how the first run would play out.

Pepto-Bismol

As predicted by the Napoleon staff, the first production run was a total and complete failure. The V8 blending kettles could not handle the thick consistency of the sauce without mushing up all the garnish of diced tomatoes. The centrifuge pumps used to transfer the sauce to the filling line, which were perfect for thin products, couldn't handle the thicker sauce. They acted more like Waring blenders, and by the time the sauce was filled into the jars, the product looked like homogenized Pepto-Bismol with green flakes of parsley and basil. I was upset, the plant management was furious, and many who had sat in judgement around the lunch table shook their heads with "I told you so" expressions.

I had no option but to fly back to the corporate offices, my tail between my legs, to inform Engineering that they had to totally redo the production line if we had any hope of producing an acceptable product for the test market. Back at the GO, they were less than receptive but nonetheless workable solutions surfaced. I had a very strong team, and there were many whom I could always count on. One of these, whom I relied on daily, sat next to me in our department's open "bull pen": my invaluable secretary, Lynn Garwood.

Startup Crew, Part II

After the proper equipment was installed and modified, the Prego team was informed that the Napoleon plant was ready for the test pack. Marty Ziglar, senior product technologist, was chosen to oversee the startup. Ziglar, my OSU fraternity brother, was well-respected at the plant level.

Ziglar had another major distinction going for him. He started

Prego Professional

LYNN GARWOOD

She looked up from her IBM Select-O-Matic typewriter and smiled. Lynn Garwood may have been smiling, but she was not happy. The warning signs were there: a forced grin, stiff body posture, and a narrowing of her eyes. These were dead give-aways that she was not pleased with something or somebody. She had not yet reached the level where her face would start to flush, her eyes would narrow, and her hands would make rapid gestures, all signifying an intense anger alert.

Garwood was not a local Camden woman, but she was born and raised in North Jersey, which qualified her as a "Jersey Girl." She had an open and vibrant personality to match. There was nothing subtle about anything she did. Most of the time, she was very pleasant and fun loving. What made her indispensable to the department was her positive, can-do spirit and the skill set to handle the most challenging secretarial and administrative functions. In those rare times when she was not happy, the entire group descended into a black hole of dysfunction. A primary function of my role as the leader of the Product Technology team was to do everything in my power to keep Garwood happy. With this priority in mind, I returned her smile and said as calmly as possible, "What's up?"

The job description for Garwood listed typing, filing, answering the telephone, and scheduling meetings as the primary responsibilities. No mention, however, was made of her most important one: being a wrangler on a long cattle drive. Hers was a never-ending challenge to keeping the herd of research technologists and scientists in the outer office moving in the same direction and not stampeding off a cliff. She had to schedule their meetings, type up their reports, book their trips, and provide counsel when necessary. Experience being a "den mother" and having an advanced degree in human behavioral psychology were not required for her job but would definitely have helped in the performance of her wide-ranging duties.

Garwood looked up again from her typing. This time the smile was gone and she replied, "This phone will not stop ringing! It is maddening. Dave wants this formula and procedure note to Technical Administration (TA) by noontime on the V8 modifications approved by the Product Committee. It is six pages with carbon paper, and, every time that phone rings, I make a mistake and then I have to erase it from six pages with Wite-Out. As you know, formula and procedures cannot be Xeroxed and all six pages have to be identified by page number [a required security precaution]. On top of that, Ray's going to the Napoleon plant tomorrow and he needs a special batch request for the Prego test run."

"Yeah, there's no compromise with those TA guys," I said, hoping to calm her down, as I left the area to give her space. Later when I returned, she gave me a genuine smile and updated me, "TA has the V8 formula and procedure note. I'm just finishing Ray's special batch request, and John is on the phone." As was typical, in just a few minutes, she had everything under control, which was why she was so highly regarded in the department.

his career in quality control at the Napoleon plant and, most importantly, could not be intimidated. Marty "Bear" Ziglar was a big man, but he spoke softly and, when he did speak, everyone listened closely. He did not abide by foolishness in his work, and everyone knew it. Ross Kelley, working closely with him said, "Marty was a master of the 'pregnant pause.' He had eyes like lasers. It was like if you didn't agree with him, he would stare at you with those eyes, which instilled fear that you would be vaporized." If someone were foolish enough to bark back at Ziglar, he would threaten to go back to the GO and let them sort the problem out. This was his ultimate weapon—and a very effective one—which he only used as a last resort. He had solidified his place in leadership at Napoleon. These characteristics made him one of the top startup artists in all of Product Development.

Prego's startup crew also included technologists Dave Gaehring and Ray Shivers—whom Garwood referenced—who would rotate assignments. During the tomato seasons, Gaehring concentrated on the SHB production for all products, but other times he was assigned to Prego and V8. Shivers did the early development work on the production of Prego and Campbell's Ketchup; as ketchup was removed from the market, he worked almost exclusively on Prego. He spent a year and a half working at the Napoleon plant, only returning home every third weekend. He was also in night school during this period, which created a major difficulty in juggling his schedule. He spent so much time in northern Ohio that management granted him an apartment there. Shivers and Gaehring were perfect examples of the sacrifices people made for Prego's success in the two-city test market launch.

Second Line

When Prego was introduced into the selected test markets of Youngstown and Green Bay, the results exceeded even the always-optimistic Marketing department and advertising agency's expectations. This was great news for the executives in the GO, however the increased demand caused a headache for production. The higher volume was significantly beyond what the makeshift blending and filling line was capable of producing. Bill Williams' answer was shoehorning in a second line.

Like any executive incentivized to watch his budget, Williams was not going to let go of his $40 million easily. Although he had agreed to spend part of his budget on readying the production facilities in Napoleon for the test market, he encouraged the engineers and managers to upgrade as cost-effectively as possible. Months later, in the summer of 1982, the Napoleon plant began the second Prego production retrofit for the national introduction. Going "the cheap route" by appending existing juice lines instead of building new ones caused major problems which turned out to be more costly in the end.

Ross Kelley had volunteered to supervise the national launch of the Prego product at the plant. They needed inventory. Lots of inventory, which meant opening up a second line at the Napoleon plant to meet projections on one of the most promising new products CSC had released in decades.

Getting Dirty

Kelley had learned from his early years working on the soup labeling section of the production line that hard work, intelligence, and dedication to the job were a few of the traits that go into making a successful production supervisor. With no previous thought of manufacturing as a career, he soon found himself working eight-hour shifts that extended into routinely ten-hour-plus days under continuous noise, heat, and chaotic conditions. He quickly grasped his duties and excelled. It was his responsibility, along with his other supervisor colleagues, to oversee the filling of over 1 million cans of soup per day. He also learned that the differentiating factor between candidates wanting to become a plant manager, or any other operations leader at CSC, was a willingness to get hands dirty and feet wet, learning every aspect of the manufacturing process.

Working his way up to the role of production manager, Kelley saw that any ambitions for future advancement rested solely on his ability to successfully move Prego into full production. Having some success on the juice line retrofits, he assembled a first-rate team of workers from the main soup plant and focused all his energies on training these individuals as to their respective accountabilities. Next, he marshaled all the resources he could gather to achieve his objectives of an efficiently-run operation producing the highest-quality product possible.

Despite meticulous planning, the first couple of weeks were disasters piled on top of disasters. The maintenance and machine operators tried to work miracles to get the old canning equipment to handle the glass jars. Their Herculean efforts included but were not limited to: synchronizing the production lines, manipulating the bulky equipment not designed to handle breakable glass, and retooling the can lines because the jars were a different size.

Even with substantial hard work and commitment, problem after problem surfaced. It was an engineering nightmare. There seemed to be broken glass at every juncture and contact point where glass touched steel or another jar where it could shatter or crack, then hot spaghetti sauce would be spilling onto everything, causing shut downs after only a couple minutes of running.

When the engineers successfully modified pumping equipment to fill the glass jars (using decreased pressure) and "capping" equipment to put the lid on, the jars were conveyed to the labeling equipment. No one anticipated the major mechanical problems near the labeling machines.

When filled jars of spaghetti sauce backed up at the labeling machine, the area resembled a macabre scene from a B-grade Hollywood movie. The backed up jars were under such tremendous pressure that, when the glass would break, it would actually explode, spewing hot sauce, lava like, over the operators, equipment, and floor. Personnel in the area ran the risk of being scalded and cut by broken shards of glass simultaneously. When this happened, everything had to be shut down and cleaned up before making modifications and starting over. Setback after setback and twelve-hour-plus days did not diminish Kelley's enthusiasm and sense of excitement.

One of Kelley's primary jobs was running interference between the plant staff and upper management (such as Lew Springer, VP of Production), who were forever hounding him for better, faster, and more production despite limited time and resources. He built loyalty from the line with each probing call from management, typically coursing like this:

"Yes, Lew, we're making progress," he would equivocate through a frown and clinched teeth, regardless of the actual disaster that was coursing on the floor in front of him at the time. "I don't know the case count. I haven't had time to go to the warehouse. We've really been busy on the floor; I'll do a count at the end of the shift."

Kelley's enthusiastic spirit was shared by all the team members who were as dedicated and professional in their respective areas of expertise as was Kelley. Their collective work ethic made it possible to achieve impossible tasks in launching Prego. For the next couple weeks, slow but steady progress was made. With adjustments made in blending, filling, sealing, labeling, and packing—nearly every phase of production—the line issues were solved.

We could finally launch Prego.

Many times, the behind-the-scenes heroes are not celebrated; they have no public relations professionals promoting their accomplishments. Often, they would be too embarrassed to be singled out and would deflect attention to their teammates.

It is these committed workers who inherently knew the importance of being part of a team effort and who contributed mightily to the accomplishment of this project. They are deeply appreciated and their importance cannot be overstated.

Make no mistake: without this team's dedication, Prego would not have been brought to the test markets or its national rollout, realizing its tremendous impact on millions of consumers.

14

The Consumer's Blessing

· ·

"It's taken off like a rocket!"

After its first year, Prego captured a market share of 28 percent, which exceeded Baum's gamble in securing his marketing budget by 8 percent. In the financial duel between Williams and Baum, Prego customers showed Baum as the winner, and he and I breathed a collective sigh of relief that no garage space was needed to store extra product inventory. As I said, it had taken off like a rocket, and landed in customer pantries or on the grocery shelves.

National Introduction

In the second year of the test market, management authorized the national product introduction, beginning with the East Coast rollout. This three-year launch plan included production enhancements to create sufficient production capacity for national distribution. Once considered a major obstacle, the plant changes now happened readily. The production people had seen the latest consumer results and were proud of their contribution to Campbell's Soup's success. Additionally, they had overcome their fear of filling glass jars, based on the success of the Napoleon plant production experience. They were now happy to make the capital expenditures and process changes in manufacturing.

By 1984, three years after its introduction, Prego was a huge success on the national level. Through thorough market research, direct-to-consumer taste testing, and assertive advertising campaigns, the Prego team was able to successfully introduce the product and win over even the most discriminating customers, including homemakers who made their own sauce. The market expanded with the creation of a homestyle segment and the increased demand for healthy, low-fat foods, such as pasta (people were more concerned about fat than carbohydrates in those days). Several other trends were emerging. Gone were the "three-square" meals a day at home; they were replaced by "grazing," microwaved foods, and restaurant dining. Having more women in the workforce encouraged more men to grocery shop and cook, and everyone was looking for convenience. CSC was at the forefront with its convenience products such as Swanson TV Dinners, Chunky Soups, and, of course, Prego. These factors collectively boosted Prego's market appeal and resulting sales.

The Earthquake

A major shift had taken place in the tomato sauce marketplace with the introduction to Prego, akin to the introduction of CDs and the MP3 players to the portable cassette and tape player market. Sony had dominated the market in the 1980s with their Walkman product line, despite heated competition from Toshiba, Aiwa, and Panasonic. Each year, the company released an updated product built on their foundational technology—once the best in the world—and refused to change. The compact disc and MP3 players were launched in the early 1990s with updated, superior technology in lighter weight, higher capacity, and less expensive products. They represented a whole new product category that Sony never saw coming. Just a few years after holding the market leader position, the cassette format of the Walkman was completely phased out. Sony was forced to stop resting on its laurels, and instead evaluate its product portfolio and release more innovate products.

Similarly, the two national spaghetti sauce players, Ragu and Hunt's, were caught flat-footed (along with the smaller regional manufacturers) when they took their first look at Prego. Not only had a superior product come out of left field from stodgy old CSC, but it was a totally different class of homestyle product. The worst news was their realization that this product was based on new, high-viscosity tomato paste and processing technology that would take them years to replicate. Prego was superior in flavor, appearance, and thickness, so it immediately began taking market share away from the competition.

In desperation, Ragu dumped major marketing dollars into television and print advertising, as well as coupon promotions. This was, at best, a stop-gap strategy from the marketing side. The company continued to lose market share to Prego among the consumer base that preferred a homestyle, thicker spaghetti sauce.

Finally, a Sense of Accomplishment

The promise made in my graduate student days was fulfilled.

Fourteen years had passed before Prego's national launch in 1981. The culmination of agricultural innovation, culinary artistry, engineering marvels, marketing magic, and talented individual contribution was the thicker, non-weeping spaghetti sauce I vowed to make.

And, as the market attested, I was not the only one envisioning a thick, non-runny spaghetti sauce. The product garnered sales over $100 million its first year, becoming an instant success by CSC's standards. Very few products—an estimated ten within the ten years prior to Prego's development—reached that amount of sales at launch.

In the very same office that I had sweated out so many meetings, phone calls, report writing, and formulation rewrites, I read every consumer communication coming in regarding Prego. It was the responsibility of all product development supervisors to review the correspondence and be kept aware of the consumers' responses to the product to be able to respond to them. Some considered it "penance"; you could be pulverized with negativity or bolstered with effusive praise. With Prego, the steady flow included few complaints and many compliments.

One unforgettable letter convinced me that we had finally accomplished what the Product Development team had set out to do with Prego. A lady, with an Italian-sounding surname living in the Northeast, wrote that she'd been cooking her husband's mother's spaghetti sauce recipe for the last twenty years. She explained that she had tried Prego for the first time because she had received a coupon in the mail. After her unsuspecting husband had finished eating his Prego supper, he looked up from the table and said, "Honey, this is the best spaghetti sauce you have ever made!" She then wrote, "You know what I told him?" "Thanks!" At the end of her note, she said that because of this new product, she was never laboring over her mother-in-law's spaghetti sauce again.

I had to smile. What a fitting end to a long journey, I thought. "Prego: Thank You, and You're Welcome."

Epilogue

· ·

A fter our successful launch of Prego and my term in International, I left CSC in 1984 to accept the position of vice president of R&D at R. J. Reynolds Tobacco Company. The team continued to work on Prego as it developed into one of the flagship products in CSC's portfolio.

R. Gordon McGovern had been elected president and chief executive officer of CSC near the close of 1980. His friendly management style was reflective of his marketing background and a refreshing change to the Shaub era. CSC had benefited over the years with leaders alternating between production and marketing. Murphy's legacy included great strides in marketing and company expansion; Shaub was a detailed operations and numbers man. McGovern had a big picture perspective with good marketing and consumer instincts.

The food and beverage industry took note. Multiple publications recognized CSC as an innovative leader in new product and process development. Before McGovern finished his full year as president, he was on the cover of *Process Prepared Foods'* September 1981 issue, naming CSC the "Processor of the Year." *Food Engineering* magazine ranked the company number one in new product introductions with sixty-nine; General Foods Corporation placed in a distant number two #2 with fifty-five. *Process Prepared Foods* headlined its October 1981 issue with "Campbell's Strong R&D Commitment Leads to Product Innovations."

In 1987, eighteen years after being founded by CSC, Champion Valley Farms was sold to H. J. Heinz Company. Its product portfolio included some of our early projects like Recipe Can Dinners, Recipe Treats, and Dinner Rounds.

Herb Baum handed over direct accountability for Prego to Jack Horn as a managing director, and Horn's first priority was putting the right people in place to leverage the Prego brand name with line extensions and introductions into other product categories.

Prego had its first major setback with "Prego Plus with Meat" line extension, which was Prego "plus" meat. In theory, this was an attractive proposition with few formulation and production changes. However, when they were launched, the new products were not successfully executed. "Prego Plus with Meat" was not a very attractive product in taste or appearance. The market responded with low sales and bad reviews; this had the potential of jeopardizing the image of the flagship "Prego Homestyle" product line. Ragu had approximately 50 percent of the market share while Prego weighed in at 25 percent. Pressure was on by top management to increase this share percentage from both sides.

Ragu went on a line extension rampage after Prego's national introduction. In the words of a former Prego marketing executive, Ragu flooded the market with "junk" line extensions as direct competition against Prego. They were quickly releasing products in the marketplace, in the hope that they would slow down Prego's inroads. Instead, the consumer was confused with multiple types and styles, creating a wall of sauces with no obvious distinction between them. Meanwhile, Hunt's seemed to drop totally out of the competition.

Campbell's Soup Strikes Back

Jack Horn had three immediate problems on his hands: the first was a failed line extension in the form of Prego Plus; the second, a compromised Prego Homestyle brand; and third, even more daunting than the other two, was a cluttered product category because of all the competition now in the category.

In the Strategic Business Unit (SBU) reorganization, Jim Dorsch was named marketing director in the Grocery SBU under Horn. Dorsch had been at Vlasic for seven years. He worked his way up to the head of the Marketing department, catching the eyes of Herb Baum and Jack Horn, who promoted him. Dorsch's instructions from Baum were deceptively simple: "Raise the bar of the SBU to Vlasic marketing standards." Vlasic was a "best practices" marketing leader which had propelled them to the head of the retail pickle segment.

At Vlasic, Dorsch and Kathleen MacDonnell (Prego's then brand manager) had worked closely with the BehaviorScan company and a behavioral psychologist/consultant named Howard Moscowitz, PhD. Moscowitz had helped Vlasic to achieve the status as a Top Ten *Advertising Age* advertiser, guiding product innovation through taste profiling. Seeing his potential contribution to Prego, Dorsch brought in Moskowitz to help with spaghetti sauce prototypes in 1986.

Moscowitz had developed a consumer optimization protocol which aided in screening more than 100 prototypes and giving development directions for those that made the cut. He did multiple variable studies, fine-tuning the line extension ideas with very sophisticated marketing research. Seeing his potential contribution to Prego, Moscowitz was brought in to help with spaghetti sauce prototypes in 1986.

Moscowitz had developed a consumer optimization protocol which aided in screening product prototypes and giving product development directions. He did multiple variable studies, fine-tuning the line extension ideas with sophisticated sensory testing.

Monica Wood from Marketing Research was asked to lead an

optimization program on Prego. Wood was teamed up with MacDonnell and Al Ahren from Product Development and their collaborative efforts resulted in consumer tests indicating that Prego was the preferred product for flavor, but the real insight came from the advertising analysis done by Wood in that it was not actually its flavor but rather its thickness superiority that drove consumer appeal. Wood analyzed the results in detail and made recommendations, which were passed on to the ad agency to start developing a new advertising campaign based on thickness.

A series of ads were later created with close-up pictures of Prego versus "the leading brand," with each being poured into sieves that had been suspended over pasta. There was little denying the thickness comparison, as very little of their sauce adhered to the pasta. This campaign had a positive boost on sales and market share. Product development was then directed towards "chunky style" spaghetti sauces. The two-pronged advertising effort showcasing the consumer taste preference of Prego two to one over Ragu and the thicker sauce jumpstarted sales and captured additional market share in the spaghetti sauce category. The Prego brand was saved, and the product continues to be sold on grocery store shelves around the world thanks to the excellent work done by the team of Wood, MacDonnell and Ahren.

Afterword

There you have it, the creation story behind the beloved jar of Prego on grocery store shelves around the world. True to our promise in the Introduction, this tale has contained:

- Revenge—After its reputation was damaged by Heinz in multiple lawsuits and complaints to the FTC, CSC pushed back by developing its own ketchup and other new products to build up its brand standing and capture precious ketchup market share from Heinz. Campbell's Ketchup competed with Heinz for two years, achieving some success by breaking the monopoly Heinz had in the food service industry.

- Passion—Many members of the CSC family showed their dedication to Prego from executive championing, tomato breeding, formulation, processing, market research, and marketing. Through long days and sleepless nights, the Prego team refused to give up when the going was tough, trying any means necessary to make the "impossible" possible.
- Sex—Steamy processing plant romances aside, biological reproduction was the beginning point of the Prego formula. The tomato plant cultivars bred by the top scientists of the CIR&T grew tomatoes able to withstand mechanical harvesting and offering the precise sugar-acid ratio for the sauce.
- Intrigue—Despite direction from some senior executives to stifle product development, the Prego team had support from its direct management to continue work, thereby "going underground." The top-secret project was not only secret from the company's direct competitors (Heinz, Hunt's, and Ragu), and other supply-chain entities that continued to do business with those competitors but also the rest of CSC.
- Politics—With internal promotions the norm for CSC, vying for top positions was commonplace. Each product introduction or presentation was an opportunity to showcase your value and make your place in leadership. How well you managed your budget was another key driver in promotability, and a $40 million budget impact almost derailed the spaghetti sauce project.
- Disappointment and Self-Doubt—The judgments of internal company critics and the external market testers left us questioning our product's viability at every step. We were constantly wondering if it would pass taste tests, overcome processing issues, secure corporate approval and funding, and be marketed to its full potential.

- High Drama—With production numbers to be met, equipment challenges, hot product explosions, tomato season and sourcing obstacles, market deadlines, infighting, and outside competition raging, there was no shortage of high drama.
- Happiness and Accomplishment—Our hard work and discipline finally paid off. Sometimes you don't know when it will, so you have to be tenacious! It took half a decade to formulate and launch Prego, but it was worth it.

The Prego product led the pack in disruptions in several areas within the food processing industry: the tomato breeding program, the refinement of procedures for the production of the special tomato paste, the formulation of the sauce, the production changes that occurred during manufacturing, and the national marketing of the sauce. Prego is the only major brand in the Campbell's portfolio that was internally-developed besides condensed soup. (Chunky Soups are actually a line extension of the condensed soup line.)

Further paradigm shifts happened with Prego's introduction; Ragu and Hunt's were knocked sideways when Campbell's Soup created a new category at the retail shelf level known as "homestyle." Housewives no longer spent hours in their kitchens recreating their mother-in-laws' spaghetti sauce recipes.

All the suppliers of tomato paste had to scramble to upgrade their hot break processing capabilities to meet the demands for high-viscosity paste by spaghetti sauce manufacturers. Plus, they now had to source high-viscosity tomato cultivars. Along with that, seed companies reviewed their seed inventory and started developing high-solids cultivars.

Prego was one of many in a line of notable contributions to the food processing industry that CSC has made. Prego continues to be a strong brand in the Campbell's portfolio, and the company has continued its long tradition of innovation and industry impact.

The Prego Professionals

· ·

S ometimes in one's career, a rare combination of people, projects, and possibilities come together. While creating Prego, I
was very fortunate to have the privilege of being a member the
Product Technology group. Looking back, this team of young men
and women was a collection of current and future all-stars and by far
my favorite corporate group.

This book, *It's in There,* is the story of those professionals who
contributed to the creation of Prego. Many of these were the
people behind the scenes who actually did the physical work in the
corporate monolith known as CSC. As Ray Shivers said, "Everyone's career improved who worked on Prego." It was the other
way around as well; everyone who worked on Prego improved the
product, and its success today rests on the talents of those now
managing it.

Many years have passed, and the professionals profiled in the
book have continued making important contributions:

- **Herb Baum** rose to the president of the U.S. division. He
  left after being offered the chairmanship and CEO position
  for Quaker State. Over his career, Baum has served on over
  twenty Boards of Directors (for both corporate and charitable foundations). Retiring as CEO, Baum continued his
  directorships and turned his prodigious talents to more
  spiritual pursuits. At the age of 77, he was bar mitzvahed at
  the Jerusalem Wall by a New York City rabbi friend.

- **Laurel Cutler** worked with LKP through its transition into Foote, Cone & Belding Communications, Inc. She became executive vice president and global director of Marketing Planning, and also vice chairman of FCB/LKP. Now retired, she is still serving on many Boards of Directors and Advisory Boards. Cutler is focused on her family, as well as opera, theatre, movies, and books.
- **Dave Gaehring** led the product development effort on Extra Chunky, which delivered against consumer expectation. He then joined Kelley as part of an initiative to improve communications and efficiencies across the entire company. Now retired, he travels on mission trips and volunteers with his church.
- **Lynn Garwood** became the executive secretary to Dr. James Kirk, vice president of CIR&T. She retired from CSC and several years later, her husband Paul Garwood retired from his position in the Packaging Research Group. They now live in Delaware.
- **Ross Kelley** joined Lew Springer at the GO in the Total Quality Management program working personally with Dr. W. Edwards Deming and the Philadelphia Area Council for Excellence. Promoted to product manager, he became the first plant production person appointed to the GO Leadership team, which was followed by plant manager assignments in the thermal and poultry divisions. He is now a consultant and management advisor from his home in the Adirondack State Park in New York.
- **Don Maley** worked on the chew biscuit project and the Dinner Rounds development with Champion Valley Farms. He was reassigned to other product development projects and he was promoted through the CSC ranks. He is retired and lives in North Carolina.
- **Ray Shivers** continued to work on Prego's line extensions,

specifically Extra Chunky. Shivers left CSC in 2001 after being offered a generous early retirement package.

- **Allen Stevens** became the vice president of Agriculture and Research, leading the move of all tomato research to California. He left the company to work with Seminis, retiring in 1999. Stevens was on the faculty at UC Davis, as professor and geneticist.

- **Steve Stewart** served thirty-six years at CSC, becoming director of Tomato Processing. In 2006, he started his consulting firm called Tomato 101 where he acts as technical advisor on tomato ingredients, tomato products, and innovative manufacturing technology. He occasionally consults with Fred Tyler.

- **Bill Stinson** "retired" only to continue to pursue his passion of being a "farmer" on his wife's ancestral homestead, where he tended fruit trees and occasionally fell off the ladder while pruning. He's now fully retired and living in Hershey, Pennsylvania.

- **Bob Subin** became president of International Specialty Foods unit, which was being expanded to include Argentina. He retired and now lives in Naples, Florida.

- **Fred Tyler** continued to work for the T. H. Richards Plant, then left to become VP of Tomato Operations for J. T. Boswell. His dream is to design and build one more tomato processing plant and may realize that dream with CSC colleague, Steve Stewart.

- **Alexander M. "Bill" Williams** was promoted in 1982 to president of the International division.

- **Marty Ziglar** spent his entire career with CSC and now lives in the Outer Banks of North Carolina. He spends his time building boats with his son.

In Memoriam

A few of those featured in this book are now deceased, and they are listed here with respect and gratitude:

- **"Onion Mary" Comanda** continued to work for CSC her entire career. We are uncertain of the exact date she passed away, as her formal obituary was not available online.
- **Arnold (Bud) Denton** continued to work for CSC for more than three decades. He made time for charitable pursuits with educational and professional causes. He passed away in 2016.[1]
- **John T. Dorrance Jr.** rose to chairman and served on the Board through 1984. After, he continued board service at multiple organizations including the Philadelphia Museum of Art, the Philadelphia Maritime Museum, and World Wildlife Fund. He died from a heart attack in 1989.[2]
- **Charlie Gaehring** worked for CSC through the length of his career, fifty-four years, continued to guide his children and grandchildren, many of whom worked with CSC. He passed away in 1973.[3]
- **Wilbur A. Gould** continued to teach at OSU until 1985. He remained the face of the school for many years, and held memberships in Guard Society of the Food Industry, and the Institute of Food Technology. He died in 2005.[4]
- **Ralph Miller** was promoted through the ranks to become VP of Product Development and would forever be remembered

by Hildebolt as a mentor who would fall on his sword to
maintain the quality and integrity of the original products.
The rest of the world would remember him for Spaghetti-
Os and Chunky Soup. Facing heart conditions, he retired in
1991 and died in 2001.[5]

- **W. B. "Bev" Murphy** maintained a position on CSC's
Board of Directors after his presidency. Active with MIT,
he was a member of the visiting committees for multiple
departments including the Department of Nutrition and
Food Science, and the School of Industrial Management.
He was awarded the Henry Laurence Gantt Memorial
Medal for "distinguished achievement in management as a
service to the community." He died in 1994.[6]

- **Werner Schilling** was promoted from research chef to
master chef, working with CSC the rest of his career. He
passed away in 2004.[7]

- **Harold Shaub** retired after thirty-eight years with the
company. He served on numerous boards including Exxon
Corporation, New Jersey Bell Telephone, and the Federal
Reserve Bank in Philadelphia. He died in 1998.[8]

- **Lew Springer** was given company-wide responsibility for
developing and implementing a Total Quality Management program based on the teachings of Dr. W. Edwards
Deming. Springer was promoted to the top operations position as senior vice president of Manufacturing. He moved
to Palm Harbor, Florida, where he lived for twenty-six years
before he passed away in 2015.[9]

- **Milton Zimmerman** rose to the ranks of VP of Operations, amassing forty-six years with the company. He was
a member of the Society of Sloan Fellows, and a founding
father of Cherry Hill Little League. He died in 2012.[10]

(Endnotes)

1   "Arnold Denton Obituary," *The Philadelphia Inquirer*, June 26, 2017, http://www.philly. com/philly/news/new_jersey/20160921_Arnold_E__Denton__91__vice_president_ at_Campbell_Soup.html.

2   "John T. Dorrance Jr. Dies at 70; Was Chairman of Campbell Soup," *New York Times*, June 26, 2017, http://www.nytimes.com/1989/04/10/obituaries/john-t-dorrance-jr-dies-at-70-was-chairman-of-campbell-soup.html.

3   Gaehring, *A History of Campbell's Soup*.

4   "Wilbur A. Gould," *Legacy*, June 22, 2017, http://www.legacy.com/obituaries/dispatch/ obituary.aspx?n=wilbur-a-gould&pid=3526489.

5   "Ralph A. Miller, Research Chemist," *Washington Post*, June 22, 2017, https://www. washingtonpost.com/archive/local/2001/06./16/deaths/13547ac7-3e54-47ce -b4f0-0951ab62d7d7/?utm_term=.449b38c8814d.

6   "William Beverly Murphy," *Wikipedia*, June 26, 2017, https://en.wikipedia.org/wiki/ William_Beverly_Murphy.

7   "Werner O. Schilling Obituary," *CourierPostOnline*, June 15, 2017, http://www.legacy.com/ obituaries/courierpostonline/obituary.aspx?n=werner-o-schilling&pid=131053834.

8   "Harold Shaub, 83, a Former Campbell Executive," *NY Times*, May 22, 2017, www.nytimes. com/1998/12/16/nyregion/harold-shaub-83-a-former-campbell-executive.html.

9   "Lewis William Springer," *CourierPostOnline*, July 28, 2017, http://www.legacy.com/ obituaries/courierpostonline/obituary.aspx?pid=177174166.

10   "Milton Zimmerman Obituary," *CourierPostOnline*, June 7, 2017, http://www.legacy. com/obituaries/courierpostonline/obituary.aspx?pid=159721873.

ACKNOWLEDGEMENTS

Bill would like to give special thanks to the following individuals:

Sandra Hildebolt, my wife for over 50 years, who has provided unwavering support and encouragement throughout my career and life; and most notably her "weepy" spaghetti sauce which launched the whole Prego odyssey.

William H. Hildebolt, my son, for his encouragement and support for undertaking the documentation of the development of Prego and also for his excellent editing skills.

Charles F. Hildebolt, my uncle, for his academic and scientific discipline in reviewing and editing multiple drafts of the book.

James A. Hildebolt, my brother, as the Hildebolt family cheerleader for prodding me to tell the true story of Prego to counter the false claims being made on social media.

Harold Threatt, my former colleague, and current good friend and hiking partner for his encouragement and support. An engineer by training Harold excels at editing details everyone else seems to miss.

Bonnie Daneker, my cowriter, who helped encourage me to overcome the inertia of five years of work on Prego's narrative with her professional book writing experience in organizing and structuring the book in a much more readable form.

Contributors who were directly involved in being interviewed and/or shared written material and pictures: Herb Baum, Laurel Cutler, Jim Dorsch, Ed Delate, Dave Gaehring, Lynn Garwood, Ross Kelley, Ray Shivers, Allen Stevens, Steve Stewart, Bill Stinson, Bob Subin, Fred Tyler, and Marty Ziglar.

Bonnie would like to express gratitude to:

My husband, George Daneker, whose quips of "Prego-ing" about book pregnancy, "50 Shades of Red," and other cleverness brought laughter to my many late nights composing and editing. You help me squeeze every drop of joy out of life.

Bill Hildebolt, my cowriter, who shared wisdom and showed patience during every interaction, especially while I was learning about PME and tomato breeding. Your dedication to this project and your industry colleagues is inspiring.

Betsy Rhame-Minor, for adding reliable editing expertise and being a pleasure to work with. Jan Deswik and Frank Dolik, for reference assistance — It's nice to have extra, talented hands helping out.

We would like to also thank:

Our early reviewers who added insight to structure and storyline: Melissa Rosati, Karin Stawarky, Mike Shaw, Debby Stone, Gary Bernstein, Mark Myette, Mary Lou Foley, and Miriam Salpeter. Your comments made this a more cohesive effort.

Supportive entities within OSU:

The College of Food, Agricultural and Environmental Sciences, specifically Andy Gurd, Chris Delisio, and Kelly Elisar

The Alumni Association, specifically Jim Smith

The College of Arts & Sciences, specifically Rick Harrison, Dean Jan Box-Steffensmeier, Chair Robyn Warhol and the English Department.

We are proud to be part of Buckeye Nation and look forward to contributing proceeds towards scholarships for The Ohio State University students.

ABOUT THE AUTHORS

William M. (Bill) Hildebolt

A product developer to his core, William M. (Bill) Hildebolt has dedicated the majority of his career pursuing innovation. Currently, he is CEO and Owner of Nature's Select Premium Turf Services, Inc., a biologically-based lawn care business. Nature's Select provides products based on the agricultural practices instituted on his family farm, as well as composting research at OSU with advice from Dr. Harry Hoytink, a retired plant pathology professor.

Prior to starting Nature's Select in 1994, Hildebolt spent six years as vice president of R&D for R. J. Reynolds Tobacco Company. In the nearly fifteen years prior to that, Hildebolt worked with CSC, where he was involved in the development and improvement of numerous domestic and international product lines. Hildebolt holds over twenty patents in food processing and food products.

Hildebolt has earned a BS, a MS, and a PhD in Food Technology from OSU. His other publications include *The Professional Entrepreneur*, a book on the characteristics needed to become a professional entrepreneur in the green industry. All proceeds from this book go to green industry college scholarships.

A native of Eaton, Ohio, Hildebolt is President of Hildebolt Farms Inc., President of WMH Farms, LLLP, and a principal of AgriEnergy of Ohio, all based in Eaton. He is married to Sandra and has two sons, William H. and Joseph R., with two grandchildren, Hannah and Hazen.

Though he resides in Winston-Salem, North Carolina, he still spends several months each year on his southwestern Ohio farm, where he retains ownership and supervises the management. To reach Bill Hildebolt, inMessage him at https://www.linkedin.com/in/william-hildebolt-242633b/or an email at billh@naturesselect.com.

Bonnie B. Daneker

Bonnie B. Daneker is Founder and Principal of WasteLine Sustainability Communications, launching fall of 2017. WasteLine will offer content and program management services to assist clients in promoting sustainability efforts. Formerly, she was CEO of Write Advisors, providing composition, production and distribution services to clients working to fulfilling their dreams to publish nonfiction material in the genres of business, biography, and health and wellness. A significant portion of her businesses support authors of scientific and medical topics.

She has earned a BA in Journalism from OSU and an MBA in Strategic Planning and Entrepreneurship from The Goizueta Business School at Emory University. Additionally, Daneker has completed the Sustainability Associate Certification from the International Society of Sustainability Professionals. When she isn't writing, Daneker can be found volunteering or exploring nature, especially by hiking, flying, cooking, and traveling. She is married to George and has three stepsons. They reside outside Atlanta, Georgia. To reach Bonnie Daneker, inMessage her in https://www.linkedin.com/in/bonniedaneker/.

BOOK CLUB QUESTIONS

1. Why was this book appealing to you? Why did you want to read it?
2. Discuss the book's structure, the authors' use of language, and the conventions used (Sidebars, Profiles, and Epilogue). Which conventions did you prefer and why?
3. How did you respond to the author's "voice?" Does the narrator convey his story with comedy, self-pity, or something else?
4. Throughout the book, the narrator talks about the lessons that he was taught, both directly and indirectly. What was the greatest lesson that the narrator learned?
5. Were there any instances in which you felt the narrator was not being truthful? How did you react to these sections?
6. What is the narrator's most admirable quality? Is this someone you would want to know or have known?
7. Who of the Prego Professional Profiles would you have liked to have met?
8. What have you learned about agriculture or food production that was surprising?
9. Was there any area on which would have liked to have more information?
10. What did you like or dislike about the book that hasn't been discussed already?

BIBLIOGRAPHY

"Advertising/Marketing Trailblazer: Laurel Cutler." *Advertising Hall of Fame.* Mar. 10, 2017. advertisinghall.org/members/member_bio.php?memid=2746.

"All Aboard! Railroads and New Jersey." *Rutgers University Libraries.* July 6, 2017. https://www.libraries.rutgers.edu/rul/exhibits/nj_railroads/.

"Arnold Denton Obituary." *The Philadelphia Inquirer.* June 26, 2017. http://www.philly.com/philly/news/new_jersey/20160921_Arnold_E__Denton__91__vice_president_at_Campbell_Soup.html.

"August Anheuser Busch, Sr." *Wikipedia.* July 6, 2017. https://en.wikipedia.org/wiki/August_Anheuser_Busch_Sr.

Baer, Christopher T. "A General Chronology of the Pennsylvania Railroad Company Its Predecessors and Successors and Its Historical Context." *Penn Railroad Records.* July 6, 2017. http://www.prrths.com/newprr_files/Hagley/PRR1828.pdf.

Bellis, Mary. "Mmm Mmm [*sic*] Good: The History of Campbell's Soup. The Work of Joseph Campbell, John Dorrance, and Grace Wiederseim Drayton." *Thought Co.* June 26, 2017. https://www.thoughtco.com/trademarks-and-history-of-campbells-soup-1991753.

"Campbell News Roundup." *Campbell Soup Company Internal Communication* (Camden, NJ), May 15, 1961.

"Campbell Reassigns Executives." *New York Times.* June 9, 2017. http://www.nytimes.com/1993/06/26/business/campbell-reassigns-executives.html.

"Campbell Soup Company." *Advertising Age.* May 22, 2017. http://adage.com/article/adage-encyclopedia/campbell-soup/98376/.

"Campbell Soup Company." *Wikipedia.* June 26, 2017. https://en.wikipedia.org/wiki/Campbell_Soup_Company.

"Campbell's Active Retiree." *Harvest* (Camden, NJ), July/Aug. 1965.

"Campbell's Goes Marbles." *CampaignLive.* May 31, 2017. http://www.campaignlive.com/article/history-advertising-no-163-campbells-marbles/1384734#Czo1ye880iGdGpyu.99.

"Charles Secondat, Baron de Montesquieu." *America's Survival Guide.* July 6, 2017. www.americassurvivalguide.com/montesquieu.php.

Chen, Aric. *Campbell's Kids: A Souper Century.* New York: Harry J. Abrams, Inc., 2004.

Coatney, Kathy. "The Machine That Revolutionized a Harvest." *Ag Alert.* June 22, 2017. www.agalert.com/story/?id=554.

"Coby Lorenzen Jr., Biological and Agricultural Engineering: Davis." *Calisphere.* June 7, 2017. http://texts.cdlib.org/view?docId=hb987008v1;NAAN=13030&doc.view=frames&chunk.id=div00041&toc.depth=1&toc.id=&brand=calisphere.

Collins, Douglas. *America's Favorite Food.* New York: Harry N. Abrams Inc., 1994.

Cooper, John Milton, Jr. *Woodrow Wilson.* New York: Alfred A. Knopf, 2009.

Cruess, W.V. *Commercial Fruit and Vegetable Products.* New York: McGraw-Hill Book Company, Inc., 1958.

De Rosier, Norman W., PhD. *The Technology of Food Preservation.* Westport: AVI Publishing Company, Inc., 1963.

Dooley Family. *Dooley Family Archives History of Treble County.* Cleveland: H. Z. Williams & Bro., 1881.

"Dr. Allen Stevens Retires from Seminis." *SeedQuest.* June 9, 2017. https://www.seedquest. com/News/releases/usa/Seminis/n2218.htm.

Esposito Shea, Martha, and Mike Mathis. *Images of America Campbell Soup Company.* Charleston: Arcadia Publishing, 2002.

Federal Trade Commission. "Complaint in the matter of Campbel Coup Company, et al. [*sic*]." June 2017. http://rms3647.typepad.com/files/campbelsoupftc.pdf.

Filmer, Ann. "How the Mechanical Harvester Prompted the Food Movement." *UC Davis Department of Plant Sciences.* June 8, 2017. https://news.plantsciences.ucdavis. edu/2015/07/24/how-the-mechanical-tomato-harvester-prompted-the-food-movement/.

Gaehring, Dave. *A History of Campbell's Soup.* Camden: Dave Gaehring, 2011.

Gould, W. A. "Introduction to Food Technology 421–Class Notes." *The Ohio State University* (Columbus, OH), 1966.

Gould, Wilbur A., PhD. *A Passion for Sharing and Caring.* Doylestown: CTI Publications, Inc., 2000.

"Harold Shaub, 83, a Former Campbell Executive." *New York Times.* May 22, 2017. www. nytimes.com/1998/12/16/nyregion/harold-shaub-83-a-former-campbell-executive.html.

"History of advertising: No 163: Campbell's marbles." *US Campaign.* May 31, 2017. http://www.campaignlive.com/article/history-advertising-no-163-campbells-marbles /1384734#ExPLucZBv5ZrOweq.99.

"John T. Dorrance Jr. Dies at 70; Was Chairman of Campbell Soup." *New York Times.* June 26, 2017. http://www.nytimes.com/1989/04/10/obituaries/john-t-dorrance-jr-dies-at-70-was-chairman-of-campbell-soup.html.

Kahney, Leander. *Inside Steve's Brain.* New York: Portfolio Hardcover, 2008.

Lamb, Frank C. *Tomato Products Bulletin 27-L,* 5th ed. (Westport, CT), Jan. 1977.

"Lewis William Springer." *CourierPostOnline.* July 28, 2017. http://www.legacy.com/obituaries/courierpostonline/obituary.aspx?pid=177174166.

McDonough, John, and Karen Egolf. *The Advertising Age Encyclopedia of Advertising.* New York: Routledge/Taylor& Francis Group, 2015.

"Memoir Discussion Questions." *ReadingGroupGuides.com.* June 15, 2017. http://www. readinggroupguides.com/memoir-discussion-questions.

"Milton Zimmerman Obituary." *CourierPostOnline.* June 7, 2017. http://www.legacy.com/ obituaries/courierpostonline/obituary.aspx?pid=159721873.

"Norman Borlaug." *Wikipedia.* May 31, 2017. https://en.wikipedia.org/wiki/ Norman_Borlaug.

"Ohio's State Beverage–Tomato Juice." *Ohio History.* May 24, 2017. http://www.ohiohistorycentral.org/w/Ohio%27s_State_Beverage_-_Tomato_Juice.

"Ralph A. Miller, Research Chemist." *Washington Post.* https://www.washingtonpost.com/archive/local/2001/06./16/deaths/13547ac7-3e54-47ce-b4f0-0951ab62d7d7/?utm_term=.449b38c8814d.

"Remembering Tomato Man Jack Hanna." *South Carolina Courier.* June 8, 2017. https://southcarolina1670.wordpress.com/2009/09/22/remembering-tomato-man-jack-hanna/.

"Robert Gibbon Johnson History." *Tomato and Health.* May 22, 2017. http://www.tomatoandhealth.com/index.php/en/article/story/robert_gibbon_johnson.

Scott, Linda M. "Shooting Marbles: Another Look at the Landmark Campbell Soup Deceptive Advertising Case." *Advertising& Society Review* 12, no. 4 (2012). Accessed June 24, 2017. https://muse.jhu.edu/article/468053.

Sidorick, Daniel. *Condensed Capitalism: Campbell Soup and the Pursuit of Cheap Production in the 20th Century.* Ithaca: ILR Press, 2009.

Sims, Mary B. *The History of Commercial Canning and New Jersey.* Trenton: New Jersey Agricultural Society, 1951.

Smith, Andrew T. *Souper Tomatoes: The Story of America's Favorite Food.* Rutgers: Rutgers University Press, 2000.

Smith, Andrew T. *Pure Ketchup: A History of America's National Condiment.* Washington, D.C.: Smithsonian Institution, 2001.

Smith, K. Annabelle. "Why the Tomato was Feared in Europe for More than 200 Years." *Smithsonian.* May 24, 2017. http://www.smithsonianmag.com/arts-culture/why-the-tomato-was-feared-in-Europe-for-more-than-200-years-863735/.

Stanton, Lucia. "Tomato: An Article Courtesy of the Thomas Jefferson Encyclopedia." *Thomas Jefferson Foundation, Inc.* May 31, 2011. www.monticello.org/site/house-and-gardens/tomato.

Stewart, Steve. "Steve Stewart." *LinkedIn.* June 9, 2017. https://www.linkedin.com/in/steve-stewart-450b3120/.

"Tomato." *Wikipedia.* June 22, 2017. https://en.wikipedia.org/wiki/Tomato.

"Value of $2,000,000 in 1920. Inflation Calculator for Today's Dollars." Saving.org. July 6, 2017. http://www.saving.org/inflation/inflation.php?amount=2,000,000&year=1920.

Webb, Raymon E., and W. M. Bruce. "Redesigning the Tomato for Mechanized Production." *NALDC.* June 14, 2017. https://naldc.nal.usda.gov/download/IND43895151/PDF.

"Werner O. Schilling Obituary." *CourierPostOnline.* June 15, 2017. http://www.legacy.com/obituaries/courierpostonline/obituary.aspx?n=werner-o-schilling&pid=131053834.

"Why Did Campbell Soup Start There [*sic*] Company?" Answers.com. June 26, 2017. http://www.answers.com/topic/campbell-soup-company.

"Wilbur A. Gould." *Legacy.* June 22, 2017. http://www.legacy.com/obituaries/dispatch/obituary.aspx?n=wilbur-a-gould&pid=3526489.

"The Wilbur A. Gould Food Industries Center." *The Ohio State University.* June 7, 2017. https://foodindustries.osu.edu/.

"William Beverly Murphy." *Wikipedia.* June 26, 2017. https://en.wikipedia.org/wiki/William_Beverly_Murphy.

INDEX

Published by Ice House Books

Copyright © 2019 Ice House Books

Written and edited by Kayla Clibborn
Illustrated and designed by Sophie Willcox

Ice House Books is an imprint of Half Moon Bay Limited
The Ice House, 124 Walcot Street, Bath, BA1 5BG
www.icehousebooks.co.uk

ISBN 978-1-912867-43-1

Printed in China

SO YOU WANT TO HEAL YOUR
HANGOVER

Written by Kayla Clibborn ⭐ Illustrated by Sophie Willcox

ICE HOUSE BOOKS

STRETCH YOURSELF BEFORE YOU WRECK YOURSELF

There's no denying the power of the foetal position when you're nursing the aftermath of two-for-one after-work cocktails. But if you can find the courage to roll from the couch to the yoga mat, you'll be amazed at what it can do for your hungover soul.

FOR THE HANGOVER JITTERS

When a hangover makes you revert to the emotional intelligence of an infant, tumble into child's pose to stimulate the nervous system and find your inner (adult) calm.

FOR WHEN IT'S ALL A BIT MUCH

Feel like you want to crawl into a hole and die? Corpse pose is a good alternative. Lie down, take a few deep breaths and let this chilled-out pose relieve any morning-after anxiety.

FOR THE BELLY BLOATS

Regret topping off that bucket of beer with a 4am kebab? Hold a lying spinal twist on both sides to *ahem* stimulate your digestive system.

FOR THE SLEEP-OF-THE-DEAD STIFFNESS

Feel like you've slept face-down on concrete? Actually slept face-down on concrete? Crawl into a few cat/cow stretches to boost your circulation and get that creaky body moving again.

WALK IT OFF

Remember endorphins? They make you feel happy and joyful and are generally pretty absent on a gloomy hungover Sunday. An excellent endorphin generator is, of course, exercise! Now, we are absolutely not suggesting you attempt a half-marathon or a hard-core weights class. That would not only be terribly cruel, but also far too harsh on your struggling body. Keep it simple and try one of these gentle exercises to bring you back to life.

Try a short, light weights session. Emphasis on LIGHT.

Slip into your comfiest shoes, grab your water and take a short walk in the fresh air.

Hop up off the couch and gently stretch out those lazy limbs.

TAKE IT EASY, PAL

Before you go jumping on the treadmill, remember alcohol dehydrates you – meaning you probably haven't got a lot of spare water to sweat out. Rest first and keep hydrated before, during and after attempting any personal bests.

WATERED DOWN

Apart from washing you clean of last night's sins, water can do wonders for your hungover hell. If you are beach- or pool-blessed, dive in and emerge reborn like the mermaid you are. Cold outside? Take a quick dip anyway to shock the hangover dust bunnies right out of your head. No beach or pool nearby? Hop in the shower or bath and crank up that cold tap.

SAFETY FIRST

If you're still feeling a bit tipsy from the night before, swimming is not a good idea. In this case, steer clear of the beach and pool — a cold bath or shower will do the trick.

COLD WATER CAN HELP TO ...

Shock your system into giving you a much-needed energy boost.

Give you the adrenaline rush you need to make it through the day.

Relieve the muscle soreness from your passed-out sleep.

Get the blood pumping to all your organs. Hello, liver!

GET
SPIRITUAL

LET'S ROCK

Before you reach for the bacon, try curing the rocks in your head with a few rocks beside your bed. At the very least, crystals are prettier to look at than cold pizza.

ROSE QUARTZ:
THE WARM FUZZIES

Calms negative emotions and promotes self-love to cure the hangover sads.

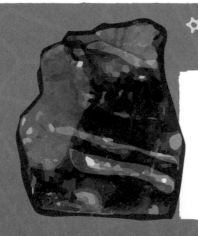

SHUNGITE:
THE DETOXIFIER

Stacks of natural antioxidants help to detoxify your wine-ravaged body.

FLUORITE:
THE SPIRITUAL VACUUM CLEANER

Clears away the dust bunnies from your cloudy, foggy head.

MOONSTONE:
THE ROCK

Balances out that bundle of feelings when things get a little too emosh.

UNDER PRESSURE

Unique hangovers call for unique remedies — like acupressure! Don't worry, you don't have to stick any needles in your face (that's acupuncture). Acupressure involves using the fingers to apply pressure to certain points on the body, helping to relieve muscle tension, increase circulation and kick those hangover symptoms to the curb.

FOR YOUR DODGY BELLY

Use your thumb to apply pressure between the two tendons on the inside of your wrist, a few centimetres below the base of your hand. Holding this for a few minutes can help to relieve nausea.

FOR YOUR WORRIED MIND

Place your thumb between your eyebrows. Apply gentle pressure in a circular motion for around five minutes. This can help to reduce stress and anxiety.

FOR YOUR POUNDING HEAD

Take your thumb and index finger and apply pressure to the space between the thumb and index finger of your opposite hand. A few minutes on each hand can help relieve headaches.

JUST THE ESSENTIALS

Ready to take a big whiff? Essential oils have long been used to soothe and relax the body — and hungover bodies are no exception. Add a few drops to your temples or wrists, or use an oil diffuser to carry the scent over the couch and to your nostrils.

LAVENDER:
THE CHILL PILL

Add a few drops to your pillow to help you relax and enhance your afternoon Netflix nap.

ROSEMARY:
THE DE-FUZZER
The scent of rosemary oil can help improve mental clarity and clear that beer-induced brain fog.

PEPPERMINT:
THE BELLY BFF
Inhaling the scent of peppermint oil can help settle your sambuca-sensitive stomach.

FRANKINCENSE:
THE FIXER
Massage a few drops onto your temples to relieve a raging wine headache.

GOOD VIBES ONLY

As if your pounding head isn't punishment enough, hangovers are often laced with the gloomy clouds of guilt and regret. Embarrassing dance moves, questionable hook-ups, pavement tumbles: boozy nights are full of cringeworthy, wish-I-hadn't-done-that moments. Learning how to calm your mind and process those negative feelings can make your morning after much more bearable.

MEDITATION 101

Find a comfortable, quiet place to sit or lie down.

Close your eyes and breathe normally.

Focus on your breath, taking note of the rise and fall of your chest as you inhale and exhale.

When a thought enters your mind, acknowledge it and let it pass on. It's like people watching at your local café; you notice each person as they walk past, but once they pass you, they're out of sight, out of mind.

If your mind starts to wander, gently bring your focus back to your breath.

CLEANSE THAT SH✕T

A LITTLE FRUITY

While pizza and jalapeño poppers are unquestionably delicious, greasy foods can actually make your hangover worse. Your body is already scrambling to digest all that alcohol, so it will store any greasy fats for later, leaving you feeling hungover for longer. Thankfully, there are many glorious foods that have all the healthy hangover-curing magic you need.

Packed with antioxidants to detox your system.

Full of fructose to give your body the energy to process all that booze in your blood.

A tasty way to get some much-needed water. Hello, hydration!

Pumps up your potassium levels to replenish those electrolytes.

Full of efficient little enzymes to ease-up your digestion

SO JUICY

A great way to absorb some of those hangover-fighting nutrients is to whack 'em in a blender for a refreshing burst of juicy goodness. Try one of these blended beverages next time Friday night drinks get out of hand.

TROPIC THUNDER

INGREDIENTS:
300 ml (10.1 fl oz) coconut water
300 g (10.6 oz) fresh pineapple
Handful of fresh mint
Handful of ice

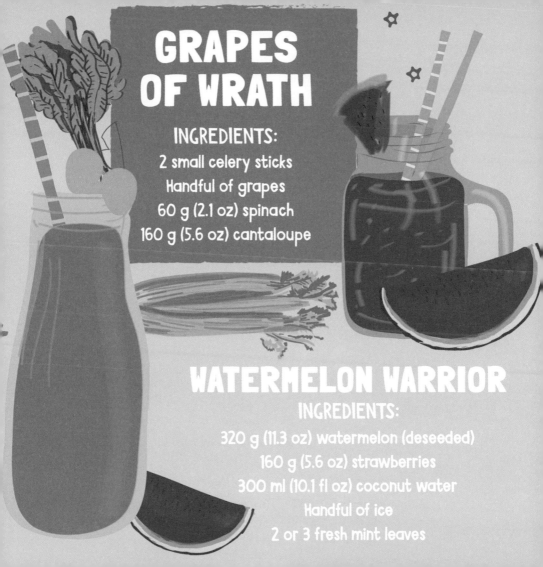

GRAPES OF WRATH

INGREDIENTS:

2 small celery sticks
Handful of grapes
60 g (2.1 oz) spinach
160 g (5.6 oz) cantaloupe

WATERMELON WARRIOR

INGREDIENTS:

320 g (11.3 oz) watermelon (deseeded)
160 g (5.6 oz) strawberries
300 ml (10.1 fl oz) coconut water
Handful of ice
2 or 3 fresh mint leaves

SMOOTH OPERATOR

Looking for something a little more substantial than juice? If you've got the energy to chuck a few extra ingredients in the blender, try one of these hangover-busting smoothies instead.

THE BERRY BEST
INGREDIENTS:
100 g (3.5 oz) blueberries
100 g (3.5 oz) strawberries
100 g (3.5 oz) raspberries
½ of 1 banana
1 tbsp chia seeds
250 ml (8.5 fl oz) coconut water

A FRUIT PUNCH

INGREDIENTS:

150 ml (5 fl oz) coconut water
320 g (11.3 oz) watermelon (deseeded)
160 g (5.6 oz) pineapple
160 g (5.6 oz) mango

GREEN MACHINE

INGREDIENTS:

1 small banana
100 g (3.5 oz) mixed berries
1 handful spinach
½ small avocado
250 ml (8.5 fl oz) coconut water

ICE-ICE BABY

A particularly big night on the sauce calls for something a little gentler on the stomach. If you're having trouble keeping things down, con a sympathetic housemate into making you a few of these frozen treats.

THE ENERGISER

INGREDIENTS:

1 large mango, peeled and chopped
125 ml (4.2 fl oz) coconut water
Juice of 1 lime
100 g (3.5 oz) strawberries, chopped

MAKES:

approx. 6 ice lollies
(depending on the size
of your moulds)

METHOD:

1. Add the mango, coconut water and lime juice to a blender. Blend until smooth.
2. Add the chopped strawberries to the mixture. Do not blend.
3. Divide the mixture evenly into an ice lolly mould.
4. Insert one ice lolly stick into each mould. Your mould set should come with its own sticks, but if not, you can use plain, food-safe craft sticks.
5. Freeze for 4-5 hours or until set.

Ice lolly moulds are widely available at gift shops and supermarkets.

Obviously, ice lollies will take a few hours to freeze. If you've got a big night ahead, consider making these before your night out so they're ready and waiting for the morning after. Thanks, past-self!

THE REFRESHER

INGREDIENTS:
150 ml (5.1 fl oz) coconut water
2 or 3 fresh mint leaves
Juice of 1 lime
450 g (15.9 oz) watermelon,
deseeded and chopped

MAKES:
approx. 5 ice lollies

METHOD
1. Add coconut water, mint, lime juice
   and 400 g of watermelon to a blender.
   Blend until smooth.
2. Add the remaining chopped watermelon to
   the mixture. Do not blend.
3. Divide the mixture evenly into ice lolly moulds.
4. Insert one ice lolly stick into each mould.
5. Freeze for 4–5 hours or until set.

THE SOOTHER

INGREDIENTS:
160 g (5.6 oz) pineapple, chopped
160 g (5.6 oz) cantaloupe, chopped
½ of 1 banana, chopped
250 ml (8.5 fl oz) coconut water

MAKES:
approx. 8 ice lollies

METHOD
1. Add all ingredients to a blender. Blend until smooth.
2. Divide the mixture evenly into an ice lolly mould.
3. Insert one ice lolly stick into each mould.
4. Freeze for 4–5 hours or until set.

THAT GUY NEEDS THERAPY

FROM MINDLESS TO MINDFUL

Put down your phone, climb out of that Wikipedia hole and swap the mindless scrolling for a spot of colouring instead. Don't worry — there'll be no mandalas or intricate floral scenes here. Just a few of your fellow hungover comrades to remind you you're not alone. Before you start, you can feast your blurry eyes on the benefits of mindful colouring below.

IT CAN HELP TO ...

Reduce anxiety

Promote calm feelings

Induce a mindful or meditative state

Relax the brain

UNFOLD AND UNWIND

Contrary to craft-hater beliefs, origami can be a great way to calm your mind. Focusing on each folding step can induce a meditative state, helping to combat those anxious hungover feelings. Try folding these origami diamonds to make yourself feel sparkly and new again.

1.

2.

3.

4.

5.

6.

7.

8.

flap   pocket

9.
pull

pull

10.

DRAW SOMETHING

Feeling a little tangled up inside? Put those feelings onto paper with this relaxing art therapy exercise. You don't have to get out of bed – in fact, you don't even have to sit up. Roll over, grab a pen and de-tangle those morning-after jitters.

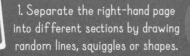

1. Separate the right-hand page into different sections by drawing random lines, squiggles or shapes.

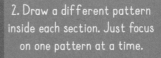

2. Draw a different pattern inside each section. Just focus on one pattern at a time.

HANGOVER
DOs AND DON'Ts

Apart from the initial mistake of thinking you could handle *that* many margaritas, there are many common errors you can make in your fragile, hungover state. Knowing some basic dos and don'ts can ensure you don't make a bad hangover worse.

DO

Drink water.
<u>Lots of it.</u>

Avoid social media. You don't need to see your annoyingly active mate bragging about their Sunday morning hike.

Eat or drink something at least a little bit nutritious.

Watch tried-and-tested comedies. *Forgetting Sarah Marshall* cracks you up every time? Perfect. Whack it on.

Be kind to yourself. It's okay that you're hungover. You're not the first and you won't be the last.

Nap, wake, nap, repeat. Your body needs that sweet, sweet shut-eye.

DON'T
CLUBBER
Eat super greasy foods. The 'lining your stomach' trick only works *before* you start drinking.
Drink more. It just delays the inevitable – your hangover will still come. Sorry, pal.
Oh sh*t.
Dwell on the sins of the night before. Let that sh*t go.
Stay inside all day. At the very least, crack a window or crawl out to the garden for a few minutes.

YOU'RE NOT ALONE

Hungover people don't often get much sympathy because their pain is self-inflicted. While this may be true, it doesn't change the fact that hangovers are the absolute worst. When the guilt is high and the regrets are piling up, take comfort in the fact that many drunkards before you have gotten a little too confident at karaoke or fallen over in the club.

While on a cruise, Gerard Butler drank 17 Long Island iced teas and 17 beers in one night, before hanging off the side of the boat screaming, "Abandon ship!"

Jennifer Lawrence once got so drunk at the Oscars she threw up on Madonna's front porch, right in front of Miley Cyrus.

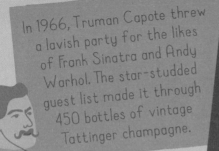

In 1966, Truman Capote threw a lavish party for the likes of Frank Sinatra and Andy Warhol. The star-studded guest list made it through 450 bottles of vintage Tattinger champagne.

In the 15th century B.C., Ancient Egyptian inhabitants of the Nile River Valley would throw a yearly 'Festival of the Drunkenness', where they drank until they collapsed in the name of a bloodthirsty warrior goddess named Sekhmet.

In 1694, a British Royal Naval officer named Admiral Edward Russell threw a week-long party that used a garden fountain as a punch bowl. The punch contained over 900 litres of brandy and more than 400 litres of wine.

I'M NEVER DRINKING AGAIN

Is this forever? Am I going to die? Can I ever show my face at the pub again? No, no and yes. Stretch out your limbs, drink your smoothie, have a little nap and then stick your favourite funny show on the telly. Today might feel horrible, but tomorrow is a new day.

"I feel bad for people who don't drink.
When they wake up in the morning, that's
as good as they're going to feel all day."

– Frank Sinatra